In Default

Latin American Perspectives Series

Ronald H. Chilcote, Series Editor

Haiti in the World Economy: Class, Race, and Underdevelopment Since 1700, Alex Dupuy

† *The Battle for Guatemala: Rebels, Death Squads, and U.S. Power,* Susanne Jonas

Repression and Resistance: The Struggle for Democracy in Central America, Edelberto Torres Rivas

† *Radical Thought in Central America,* Sheldon B. Liss

† *Marxism, Socialism, and Democracy in Latin America,* Richard L. Harris

† *Cuba in Transition: Crisis and Transformation,* edited by Sandor Halebsky, John M. Kirk, Carollee Bengelsdorf, Richard L. Harris, Jean Stubbs, and Andrew Zimbalist

† *The Cuban Revolution into the 1990s: Cuban Perspectives,* edited by Centro de Estudios Sobre América

† *The Latin American Left: From the Fall of Allende to Perestroika,* edited by Barry Carr and Steve Ellner

In Default: Peasants, the Debt Crisis, and the Agricultural Challenge in Mexico, Marilyn Gates

† Available in hardcover and paperback.

In Default

Peasants, the Debt Crisis, and the Agricultural Challenge in Mexico

Marilyn Gates

Westview Press
Boulder • San Francisco • Oxford

Latin American Perspectives Series, Number 12

Published in 1993 in the United States of America by Westview Press, Inc., 5500 Central Avenue, Boulder, Colorado 80301-2877, and in the United Kingdom by Westview Press, 36 Lonsdale Road, Summertown, Oxford OX2 7EW

Library of Congress Cataloging-in-Publication Data
Gates, Marilyn.
    In default : peasants, the debt crisis, and the agricultural
challenge in Mexico / Marilyn Gates.
        p.   cm. — (Latin American perspectives series ; 12)
    Includes bibliographical references and index.
    ISBN 0-8133-8455-9
    1. Peasantry—Mexico.   2. Agriculture and state—Mexico.
3. Debts, External—Mexico.   4. Peasantry—Mexico—Campeche (State)
5. Agriculture and state—Mexico—Campeche (State)   I. Title.
II. Series: Latin American perspectives series ; no. 12.
HD1531.M6G38   1993
338.1'87264—dc20   92-44178
                                                                            CIP

Printed and bound in the United States of America

10   9   8   7   6   5   4   3   2   1

Contents

Tables and Figures

Figures

Acknowledgments

This book is the product of twenty-five years of field work in Mexico, and thus much is owed to the many individuals and institutions who have helped me along the way. First, one has to be able to get to the field. For this, I am greatly indebted to the Social Sciences and Humanities Research Council of Canada, which funded a number of field seasons from 1969–1972 (a doctoral fellowship) to 1989–1990 (a sabbatical research grant). Simon Fraser University's flexible leave policy has also been invaluable in optimizing research conditions—getting around in the Mexican humid tropics is a much less daunting proposition in the winter dry season. SFU's Dean of Arts, Dr. Robert C. Brown, has been particularly supportive in this respect.

Learning what to do and what not to do once in the field is another matter. Here, I am eternally grateful to the engineers of la Comisión del Grijalva in Cárdenas, Tabasco, and the campesinos of Poblado C-28 in Plan Chontalpa, who taught me—a naive graduate student in the late 1960s—appropriately vernacular Spanish and when to throw the research methods textbook out the window and, most important, gave me invaluable insights into the workings of the Mexican "system." In particular, I owe much to Ing. Carlos Molina Rodríguez, who showed me, by example, that the most effective field method is to be oneself.

In Campeche, my debts are myriad. Numerous engineers of the Secretaría de Recursos Hidráulicos and the Secretaría de Agricultura y Recursos Hidráulicos have provided unquestioning assistance in the course of my investigations, especially friends such as Ing. Fernando Escalante Canto and Ing. Sergio Gutierrez Repetto. More than a friend, an inspiration, has been Ing. Joaquín Repetto Ocampo, who has never stopped trying to do something to make life better for Campeche campesinos. Dr. William J. Folan, Director of the Centro de Investigaciones Históricas y Sociales of the Universidad Autónoma de Campeche has been an outstanding colleague. His enthusiasm and energy in excavating key Maya sites and in promoting the Calakmul Biosphere Reserve have done much to stimulate interest in research in Campeche, and he has been more than generous in including us in his plans.

xii   *Acknowledgments*

Most of all, I am indebted to the campesinos of Campeche for always making me welcome and sharing many hours of conversation and good fellowship, even under conditions in which it was hard to see cause for humor, such as after Hurricane Gilbert. In return, they have asked me to tell their story as they told it to me, with tears and laughter, cynicism and optimism, critical insights and concrete suggestions for ways out of the crises. Here it is.

In the production of the book, I have been greatly encouraged by the editor of this series, Dr. Ronald H. Chilcote, and Westview's senior editor Barbara Ellington. Barbara Metzger performed her usual miracles in copy editing: The remaining abuses of American English are my fault (after twenty-five years in North America, I still think in "English English"). At Simon Fraser University, I am grateful to the Instructional Media Center, Anita Mahoney, and Carol Martyn for assistance with figures and tables, as well as to the many graduate and undergraduate students who, in my courses, have heard more about Mexican peasants than they ever wanted to know. Colleagues in SFU's Department of Sociology and Anthropology and in the Department of Latin American Studies have restored flagging enthusiasm on many occasions, as have mentors and friends Dr. Alfred H. Siemens and Dr. Philip L. Wagner.

Without my husband, geologist Dr. Gary Gates, it is highly unlikely that this book would have materialized. Collaborator, critic, chauffeur, "chaperon," field medic, and friend, he was there and is looking forward to the next twenty-five years of field work.

Marilyn Gates

1
Introduction

Which crisis? The government's crisis? . . . If you mean our crisis, here in agriculture, that's nothing new. We have been living with crisis in the countryside since the conquest. (I-1, *ejidatario*, Pomuch, March 1990)[1]

Life is more or less the same here. You put more water in the soup, eat more tortillas, and forget about beans. The government owes us a better life, that's the social contract, but they never keep their promises. It's all a game, based on lies and deceptions. (I-2, *ejidatario*, Pomuch, December 1989)

The Mexican debt crisis has attracted considerable interest since its onset in 1982. Much has been written on the causes, processes, and, in particular on the policy context of postcrisis restructuring, Mexico's willingness to impose strict austerity measures and diversify and liberalize its economy having earned it the reputation of model debtor.[2] Relatively little attention has been paid to the impact of fiscal restraint on the Mexican people, particularly those on the margins of the cash economy such as the peasantry, who are presumably among the most severely affected by the crisis.[3] Or are they? The net result of post-1970 federal agrarian policies and planned development projects in the countryside has been capital loss, stifled social initiative, and environmental devastation. Has the debt crisis provided the peasantry with the opportunity to escape the bonds of state paternalism by allowing them more freedom to farm productively? Has it compelled the government to discard old agrarian ideologies in its effort to restructure the troubled agricultural sector? What role will the peasants play in an open market economy?

This book examines the effects of austerity on Mexican peasants who had been enmeshed in a national agricultural crisis since the late 1960s.[4] At that time, the growing need to import basic foods (an inevitable consequence of the post-1940 import-substitution model) and increasing rural unrest had made it imperative for the government to attempt to

1

modernize the production of traditional peasants on *ejidos*, the unique corporate land tenure category generated by the 1910–1917 Revolution.[5] From 1970 until the onset of the debt crisis in 1982, public-sector expenditure on agricultural development programs was massive both in absolute terms and as a percentage of the national budget.[6] Rather than promoting an efficient, expanded productive base, however, this statist approach resulted in the institutionalization of an *industria de siniestros* (industry of disasters) in which crop failure, corruption, and chronic indebtedness have been the norm. By 1982, the majority of peasant beneficiaries of state-directed agricultural development programs constituted a modernized subsistence sector, a contradiction in terms of both production efficiency and the social justice promised by the 1917 Constitution.

Under the debt crisis, peasants have been particularly hard-hit by the widening gap between prices and wages and between production costs and profit margins. The debt crisis has, moreover, aggravated such ongoing problems of the agricultural sector as inappropriate cropping strategies, inadequate and high-priced credit, overcentralized state planning, bureaucratic malfeasance, the stranglehold of intermediaries, climatic vicissitudes, infrastructural bottlenecks, and the displacement of subsistence crops by export production and cattle in that they can no longer be offset by public-sector capital influx. Meanwhile, the peasants have borne the brunt of austerity measures under a continuing strategy of subordinating the interests of the countryside to those of the city. The outcome has been the deterioration of peasant agriculture to the point where in 1989 1 million of the nation's almost 3 million *ejidatarios*[7] fell into *cartera vencida* (default to the rural credit bank) as a result of government policies that have accelerated the decapitalization of the countryside while fostering an ethos of institutionalized failure.

In view of this convergence of agricultural failure and austerity, peasants tend either to subsume the debt crisis within the agricultural crisis as the most recent symptom of a now-chronic malady or to speak of the "double crises" with which they must cope on a day-to-day basis:

This crisis of external debt began with Cortés, the first foreigner to loot our resources. Today, exports to the gringos are the absolute priority of this government, which will bring the final ruin of the *campesinos*,[8] because the policy is to sacrifice the basic food producers in order to enrich agribusiness and the industrialists. (I-3, ejidatario, Pomuch, December 1989)

The government's fiscal crisis gives them an excuse to abandon the campesinos after despoiling our land. So we live with double crises, the crisis in agriculture, the product of the government's ineptitude, and the crisis of bankruptcy, the fault of the politicians who lined their pockets with our patrimony. (1-81, ejidatario, Yohaltún, March 1990)

Whether peasants identify the debt crisis as part of an ongoing process or as a discrete episode, whether it is seen as impinging directly on their lives or as an outside event of little immediate relevance, whether the crises have further eroded their ability to meet their subsistence needs or permitted them to profit from the increased farming flexibility consequent on government cutbacks and new agrarian policies are all highly contingent on specific historical and regional circumstances. This variation reflects the increasingly differentiated character of the peasantry that has resulted from more than two decades of extensive state intervention in the ejido, as part of the overall processes of rural modernization and national economic integration which have changed the face of rural Mexico to varying degrees over the past fifty years. However, the arrival of North American packaged junk food, transistor radios, pickup trucks, and bottled soft drinks in even the most remote villages has not offset the extreme regional and local diversity of the "many Mexicos" identified by Simpson (1941). Instead of becoming homogenized by forces toward national integration, peasants engage in increasingly complex and idiosyncratic patterns of interaction with the dominant economy, often resulting in considerable intra- as well as intercommunity variation at the local level. Consequently, it is not surprising that they have been affected differentially by both the agricultural crisis and the debt crisis and that they have responded with a wide range of coping strategies. These adaptations vary according to the nature and degree of the peasant household's insertion into the national and international socioeconomic nexus and the extent of involvement in government agricultural programs which have served, in many cases, to undermine rather than to enhance productive capacity.

Peasant adaptations to national crisis have taken on a new dimension since Carlos Salinas de Gortari assumed the presidency in 1988 and accelerated the pace of economic liberalization, which began to gain momentum after Mexico joined the General Agreement on Tariffs and Trade (GATT) in 1986 in a dramatic reversal of some forty years of extreme protectionism. In agriculture, Salinas has introduced an innovative package of reforms intended to restructure and recapitalize a sector that, with the exception of a few export enclaves, had been rapidly deteriorating for more than two decades. The new policies and programs are directed at opening agriculture to international competition by cutting tariffs and abolishing import licenses except for basic food crops, substantially reducing other supports and subsidies, selectively retreating from direct state intervention in the peasant sector, and promoting private investment in the ejido in an attempt to reintroduce market forces into agriculture. While efficient agribusiness exporters welcome further liberalization via the negotiation of a free-trade agreement with the United States and

Canada, the potential repercussions for peasants, particularly for the majority still dependent on marginal staple crop cultivation are enormous.[9]

This book will trace the evolution of Mexican agrarian policy and its cumulative impact on the peasantry, follow the progression of the agricultural crisis in the ejidal sector as a predicament caused to a considerable extent by state planning, illustrate the variety of peasant strategies for coping with the debt crisis as the latest phase in an ongoing process of rural decapitalization, and assess the potential of recent government initiatives for revitalizing agriculture and improving the peasant condition. In the process, three major and closely associated questions emerge. Is the Mexican state, which in many ways created both crises through its interventionist policies, likely to be able to plan its way out of them? More specifically, since the predominant outcome of state involvement in peasant agriculture has been the creation of a bankrupt, quasi-modernized subsistence sector operating on marginal lands often severely degraded by inappropriate farming technologies and adapted to an ethos of institutionalized failure, will organizational restructuring and economic liberalization be sufficient to redress the social and environmental as well as the economic balance? Despite this dismal legacy, will Mexican peasants, or at least some of them, be able to benefit from the relaxation of government paternalism in order to take advantage of local opportunities, or are they more likely to be overwhelmed by free-market competition? A corollary to all of these questions is the issue of whether the current reforms constitute a fundamentally new direction for Mexican agrarian policy or part of an ongoing process of refunctionalization of the peasantry in keeping with the evolving requirements of national and international markets.

Given the complexity of the relationships between the crises of agriculture and austerity, the difficulty of tracing the connections between agricultural policy and practice, and the extreme and increasing degree of regional and local diversity in the rural context, it is difficult to address any of these themes on a national scale other than in very general terms. Consequently, the book relies on an extended case study of the impact of the agricultural and debt crises on peasants in the state of Campeche, employing a subregional focus in order to bridge the gap between macro-level analyses of Mexican agricultural policy and detailed investigations at the village level. The product is a portrait of peasant adaptations to the crises in just one of the "many Mexicos" that nevertheless serves to ground national agricultural policy with regard to the ejidal sector and to provide a basis for assessing the implications of recent reorientations.

Campeche is particularly suitable for illustrating the discrete effects of the two crises on the peasantry, for demonstrating the connections between types and degrees of peasant incorporation into the national economy and specific household predicaments, and for isolating the direct impact of state agricultural policies and programs on the ejido. Only twenty years ago, most of this state was a sparsely populated tropical frontier, a virtual blank slate as far as modern agricultural development of any kind was concerned, having depended since the conquest on the export of one or two natural resources in a sequence of boom-and-bust cycles. Since the late 1960s, however, Campeche has been subjected to a barrage of government agricultural development projects aimed at transforming traditional Maya *milperos* (slash-and-burn maize cultivators) and transplanted colonists from the congested central Mexican uplands into efficient, mechanized farmers. The outcome has been, at best, only minimal increases in productivity achieved at high investment, opportunity, and social cost. In many cases, the direct transfer of technologies and cropping strategies developed for temperate latitudes has caused incalculable and irreversible damage to fragile humid tropical ecosystems. Meanwhile, the developmental risks of these experiments have been borne by the peasant "beneficiaries," who, by the onset of the debt crisis in 1982, had become almost totally dependent on inefficient and inappropriate state initiatives.

Thus it is possible to paint a "before-and-after" picture of peasant agriculture in Campeche that sharply delineates the role of state intervention in creating the contemporary crises in the countryside as part of a post-conquest history of increasing vulnerability to external economic forces. Variations in coping mechanisms are identified among diverse segments of the peasantry—milperos, frontier colonists, irrigation project members, mechanized rice growers, cattle ranchers, and Mennonite communities. Some have prospered under crisis, some continue to be insulated from it by their very marginality, while the main casualties are those who have become most deeply enmeshed in the network of dependency relations generated by two decades of state-directed agricultural modernization.

The implications of recent government strategies for recapitalizing agriculture are of central concern in evaluating alternative routes out of the crises. In general, they represent a tactic of economic triage that is likely to deepen the chasm between peasants considered to have viable commercial prospects and those relegated permanently to low-value staple production because of their failure to perform under past development initiatives. Thus, while the new policies represent, overall, an abrupt reversal of previous direct state interventionism in peasant agriculture, this retreat is highly selective, marked by a continued strong concentration on ejidatarios targeted as potentially successful commercial farmers. At the same time, ejidatarios who cultivate marginal lands in high-risk zones are, in essence, being repeasantized by the reduction in supports and subsidies or through inclusion in new relief programs of limited term and scope.

In the redefined commercial peasant sector, the emphasis is on confining official agricultural credit to ejidatarios with demonstrated productive capability and promoting joint ventures between agribusiness and the ejido. In these enterprises private initiative will assume the dominant position formerly occupied by the state, which will, however, continue to play a major role in facilitating contracts and establishing priorities. This new pragmatism may result in significantly improved income levels for a favored few, but it seems likely to ensure continued erosion of peasant control over the productive process as businessmen rather than bureaucrats call the shots. For the vast majority of producers dependent on staple food crops, government cutbacks, interim stimulus programs, and the overall winds of neoliberal change mean growing stress and uncertainty. These peasants are waiting to see whether the retreat of the state from the *in loco parentis* role will permit them to maximize local farming opportunities or abandon them to the forces of a free market in which they have no chance of competing on equal terms.

So far it appears that the peasants most likely to be able improve their condition in this rapidly changing context are those already favored in terms of access to prime lands or agricultural infrastructure, those possessing extensive experience with modern farming technologies, those able to recognize and take advantage of untapped local opportunities, and those intent on profiting at the expense of their peers. Many of the remainder have been severely demoralized by crisis austerity and participation in marginal government projects and programs. Apparently having lost the chance to become commercial farmers through their poor performance under previous state initiatives, they tend to see recent agricultural reforms as merely the usual empty rhetoric of the institutionalized revolution, masking an ongoing policy of subordinating the ejido to state, urban, and private interests.

At present, these ejidatarios appear to be facing increased pressures to abandon the land, to depend on wage labor on a supplementary basis, or to become repeasantized as self-sufficient staple producers under new government programs for the most marginal cultivators. Even this sector, however, has been empowered to a considerable extent by two decades of experience in the agricultural development business. Irrespective of project success or failure, many of the ejidatarios who have participated in the state-directed agricultural modernization process have acquired confidence in dealing with the agrarian bureaucracy, gained greater awareness of policies and programs, discovered how to use institutionalized corruption to their advantage, learned new technical skills, mastered strategies for negotiating a cut of the now-limited state resource pie, and, in general, become better able to defend themselves against manipulation by outside agencies. The stereotypical peasant of twenty years ago, struggling alone with ax and machete to wrest a corn patch out of the forest in order to feed his family, is now likely to be knowledgeable about hybrid seeds, fertilizer, pesticides, market prices, freight rates, and credit. Probably he can drive a tractor or pickup and is accustomed to completing forms in triplicate. In fact, the peasant of today may have to spend more time in town engaged in meetings with the agrarian bureaucracy than in cultivating his fields. He is also likely to be in debt, as government agricultural programs for peasants have tended to link credit with disaster and fostered a climate in which deception and fraud are regarded as essential for survival. Obviously, these attitudes and associations tend to operate against effective application of the new skills and capabilities acquired during the agricultural modernization process.

From this transformation of the peasantry derives a conviction widespread across the evolving commercial-subsistence agricultural spectrum—that ejidatarios should not be held in default, either specifically in terms of debts owed to the credit bank for failing to produce in misguided government projects or more generally as scapegoats for the failure of state policies. Rather, ejidatarios believe that the government has defaulted on its constitutional contract with the peasantry to provide social justice in the countryside, as part of "an equitable distribution of the public wealth . . . the balanced development of the nation and the improvement of the conditions of life of the population, rural and urban" (*Constitución Política de los Estados Unidos Mexicanos*, 1980: 1, cited in Zaragoza and Macías, 1980: 53–54, my translation). Peasants maintain that a fair settlement of this long-overdue debt should involve much more than mere restitution of lands via the ejido and a succession of state agricultural policies whereby the peasants subsidize the basic foods Mexicans consume while bearing most of the risk.

Whether this peasant conviction of unfair treatment by the state will inspire effective demands for the immediate reduction of rural-urban disparities, reinforce expectations of continued government subsidies for ejidatarios as the rightful due of the "favored sons of the revolution" (Warman, 1983 [1972]), an assumption which runs against the free market current, or promote increasing reliance on individual initiative remains to be seen. On the basis of the Campeche case study, it appears that the experience of coping with the crises and the abrupt reduction of public-sector funding for the ejidal sector have strengthened the capacity of at least some segments of the peasantry to cast off the historical and psychological chains of institutionalized dependency on state tutelage and take steps toward improving their condition.

The Winds of Change

In August 1982, with foreign-exchange reserves exhausted as a result of declining revenues in response to the 1981 world oil price collapse, high

interest rates abroad, accelerating capital flight, and more than a decade
of serious economic mismanagement, the government announced that it
was no longer able to service its $85 billion foreign debt and requested an
emergency loan from the International Monetary Fund (IMF). While the
roots of the 1982 debt crisis are far too complex to be examined here in
detail, in general terms it was a product of the post–World War II import-
substitution industrialization model and even longer-term forces promoting external dependence and internal disparities. The immediate
symptom of the vulnerability of an increasingly single-resource-based
economy was the petrolization of the economy in 1977—an overreliance
on hydrocarbons and the consequent direct connection between oil
wealth and foreign borrowing. Thus it was the 1981 plunge in oil prices
consequent on a global glut that precipitated the crisis, but the conjuncture itself had emerged over a decade earlier as the import-substitution
model generated serious bottlenecks militating against sustained, balanced growth.

When Miguel de la Madrid assumed the presidency on 1 December
1982, he inherited the world's largest foreign debt, a massive internal
public-sector debt, triple-digit inflation, escalating unemployment, and a
peso worth only one-quarter of the previous year's value. The fiesta of
petroleum-funded binge spending by both public and private sectors
under the previous president, Jose López Portillo, had ended in a rude
awakening to the fact that the debt crisis was not merely a short-term
adjustment in Mexico's impressive postwar growth pattern but a symptom of deep-seated economic distortions. Thus it became apparent that
Mexico's predicament was not an isolated instance of temporary in-
solvency but an exigency afflicting a number of Third World nations,
which appeared to threaten the stability of the international financial
system. In the eyes of the IMF the remedy, required as a condition for debt
restructuring, was major economic surgery via fiscal austerity and
economic liberalization.

These structural adjustments have resulted not only in an impressive
recovery from the immediate strictures of the debt crisis but also in rapid
progress toward a market-led economy. Since 1985 Mexico's economy
overall has exhibited a remarkable turnaround: "One of the world's most
protected economies has become one of the most open; one of the world's
most profligate governments has become one of the most frugal"
(*Economist*, 6 October 1990: 85). A concerted program of economic modernization hinges on retreat from state interventionism in virtually all
sectors. Major restructuring activities include deregulation, tax reform,
privatization of inefficient public enterprises, institutional rationalization,
elimination of trade barriers, and diversification away from reliance on oil
exports. In this scenario the former nemeses—the domestic private sector

and the United States—are to become the saviors whose investments will spur Mexico's entry into the twenty-first century as a First World nation, "a viable economy in a strongly competitive international environment" (Salinas de Gortari, 1990: 1).

In particular, Mexico is pinning its hopes of surmounting the debt crisis, promoting broad-based prosperity, and spurring political democratization on a free-trade agreement with the United States and Canada. Such an agreement could serve to stimulate economic growth in Mexico, stem the tide of migration to the north, and provide a regional trade safety net in the event of increasing protectionism in the world trading system. Thus, while the governments of all three countries appear to be firmly convinced of the advantages of a tripartite pact (despite the misgivings of North American interest groups concerned about lost jobs, perpetuation of poor working conditions in the Mexican labor force, and environmental repercussions), Mexico has the most at stake in an immediate sense and the most economic ground to make up, with a gross domestic product (GDP) only 3.6 percent of that of the United States in 1990.

While the results of this bold strategy thus far have been remarkable in terms of debt management and the rapidity of the transition toward industrial diversification and free trade, the Mexican people have yet to see the benefits of economic reform. Since the onset of the debt crisis, real wages have fallen for eight consecutive years to barely half of 1982 levels. Inflation in 1990 reached almost 30 percent, ten points higher than the 1989 figure. Despite the return to steady economic growth of almost 4 percent a year, many sectors continue to stagnate, with growth rates running at only 50 percent of those achieved in the late 1960s and early 1970s, while decreasing protectionism has severely affected the balance of trade (*Economist*, 6 October 1990). For most Mexicans, the burden of austerity appears to be increasing rather than decreasing, compounded by uncertainties generated by the wide-ranging economic reforms. In particular, living conditions have worsened substantially since the implementation of wage and price controls in December 1987, when annual inflation had reached 160 percent and the collapse of the nation's stock market in response to the October Wall Street crash had underscored the fragility of Mexico's apparent economic recovery.

Instead of freezing wages and prices unilaterally and indiscriminately, the Mexican control mechanism, initially named the Pacto de Solidaridad Económica (Pact for Economic Solidarity—PSE), is based on an agreement involving the state, organized labor, the formal peasant organizations, and private business sectors and allows for limited adjustments between frequent review periods. The first year of its operation saw a dramatic decrease in inflation, with the result that the agreement was renewed in December 1989 as the Pacto para la Estabilidad y Crecimiento

Económico (Pact for Stability and Economic Growth—PECE). While this strategy, originally intended as a limited-term shock tactic, has been relatively successful in keeping the lid on inflation, there are signs that it is working against further economic recuperation. Furthermore, official statistics indicating control over inflation fail to impress citizens who have had to cope, between December 1987 and February 1990, with official minimum-wage increases of 79.1 percent, while consumer prices climbed 123.3 percent (*Excelsior*, 23 June 1990).[10] These increases have been compounded by dramatic increments in public-sector prices; for example, in 1990 the government raised electricity prices by 300 percent and telephone rates by 400 percent as part of the continuing process of cutting subsidies to state-owned enterprises. The accelerating decline in purchasing power, with a 15 percent drop in real wages in 1990 alone, has been reflected in curtailed consumption in many areas, serious deterioration of nutrition, and increasing inequality in income distribution.[11]

In this context, Mexico's successes in economic reform domestically and in restructuring the external debt under the much-touted Baker and Brady plans tend to be regarded by ordinary citizens as "only a kind of international version of Monopoly played to impress the gringos" (I-132, businessman, Campeche, March 1990). Discontent with austerity and the compliance of organized labor and business organizations with wage and price controls has engendered an unprecedented level of popular protest: "These solidarity pacts just mean that the poor have to pay for the government's failures. So we campesinos, like all the other humble Mexicans, have been conditioned to condone our own exploitation. If things don't get better soon, they [the government] will find out what millions of votes can do" (I-82, ejidatario, Yohaltún, March 1990). This widespread discontent has been aggravated by the relatively slow progress toward democratization of Mexico's often blatantly corrupt political system, prompting divisions within the previously monolithic Partido Revolucionario Institucional (Institutional Revolutionary Party—PRI), Mexico's ruling party for over sixty years. Some gains have been achieved in terms of a new electoral law, occasional concessions of government defeat at the polls, sporadic attempts to reduce obvious manipulation of votes, increasingly visible opposition parties, a relative opening of the presidential selection process, and some attempts at decentralization.[12] Charges of fraud continue to cloud elections, however, and reforms within the PRI tend to be blocked by regional interests and old-guard politicians unwilling to eliminate structures on which their personal power depends.

Popular disaffection, the continuing burden of fiscal restraint, and the uncertainties generated by rapid economic restructuring were reflected in growing abstentionism and election results with increasingly slim government victory margins until the dramatic turnaround in the August 1991 midterm elections, when the PRI claimed to have captured more than 62 percent of the votes (*Economist*, 24 August 1991). Salinas maintains that economic reform must take precedence over political modernization, arguing that "if the people do not have bread, this leads to anarchy" and that "some countries have attempted all reforms at the same time and ended up without achieving even one of them" (*Newsweek*, 7 November 1990). A free-trade agreement will not, however, be a panacea. Furthermore, it is likely to be a decade or more before the benefits of such an agreement are felt by large segments of the population, particularly because major improvements will first have to be made in the country's decaying communications and distribution infrastructure. Without convincing signs of imminent relief from austerity, each stolen election undermines the foundation of the economic advances achieved to date by reinforcing widespread skepticism about the government's performance:

With respect to the democratic opening, few are naive enough to believe in it. The mass media are subject to severe self-censorship and abstentionism continues to grow as an unequivocal symptom of the Mexican's disillusionment and lack of interest in political issues. Even so, the majority of the recent state and municipal elections are the source of strong conflicts, bloody confrontations which exemplify the minimal real political will toward democratization. (I-129, professional, Mexico, D.F., February 1990)

So far Salinas has been unable to spur his party to a political opening commensurate with the pace of economic liberalization. Moreover, it appears that sweeping political modernization cannot be forced as long as a degree of unity and continuity in party structure is necessary to support the economic reforms and cushion the stresses they induce. In a Catch-22 situation, the president cannot eradicate political corruption as long as he needs the support of a viable party, but unless he does so the people are unlikely to believe that the PRI leopard has changed its spots.

The creation of a pluralist democracy may indeed be rendered even more difficult by the success (in terms of the return to sustained growth) of the Salinas economic reforms. The continuing decline of living standards has been offset to a degree by a shrewd strategy of extensive spending on highly visible social programs. The combination of these two elements apparently convinced many voters in the August 1991 elections, particularly the marginal urbanites who had turned away from the PRI in the 1988 presidential vote, that the ruling party could still deliver more than the fragmented opposition. This return to a virtual one-party system after a brief challenge in the depths of the debt crisis era is likely to undermine the process of democratization, particularly since Salinas's successes may have reinforced the already immense power of the presidency. Furthermore, the achievements to date owe much to his personal political, social, and economic acumen. Because presidents cannot be reelected there is concern that his successor will not be equally adept at balancing reform and dissent.

In spite of this recent tide of increasing confidence, the erosion of the PRI's popular base continues to be particularly noticeable among ejidatarios, traditionally in the ranks of its staunchest supporters (at least pro forma) because of the incorporation of formal peasant organizations into the official political structure and the dependence of this sector on government agricultural supports.[13] Given the record of peasant protest and rebellion in Mexico, widespread rural mobilization and protest might have been expected in response to the deepening agricultural crisis and the impact of austerity (Grindle, 1989). Instead, inflation and the massive cutbacks in state spending on the ejido have combined to generate increasing cynicism about government rhetoric as peasants concentrate on strategies for survival at the level of the individual household, rather than seeking solutions through collective action.[14] In particular, ejidatarios' mistrust of the government appears to have intensified in the wake of recent agricultural reforms.

Until the Salinas administration assumed office in 1988 Mexican agriculture had remained virtually untouched by the pressures for economic change, as a result of the depth of the crisis in this sector and the priority after 1982 of dealing with the foreign debt and implementing structural adjustment. The austerity measures quickly took their toll in the countryside, particularly afflicting the heavily subsidized ejido. Between 1980 and 1989, public-sector investment in agriculture fell by four-fifths, while rural credit was cut in half (*Economist*, 2 March 1991) and interest rates rose. Meanwhile, between 1982 and 1988, national guaranteed prices for the principal grains and staple crops fell 48.7 percent against the costs of agricultural inputs (Calva, 1988), which were excluded, by and large, from the price-control pacts. In other words, producers of the ten basic grains, many of them ejidatarios, were earning approximately half as much per kilogram in 1988 as they had at the onset of the debt crisis. In view of these and other long-standing disincentives to production in a sector riddled with inefficiencies, it is not surprising that agricultural output overall failed to keep pace with the net population increase over the decade of the 1980s, requiring continued massive food imports as agricultural production per capita in 1988 fell to the 1960 level (Hank González, 1990).

Against this backdrop of drastic decapitalization and stagnation, Salinas has been attempting one of his most difficult tasks in both economic and political terms, that of opening agriculture to international

competition. Global reconciliation of comparative advantage in agriculture is obviously a formidable undertaking, especially among nations
heavily committed to farm subsidies. For Mexico, currently competitive
in only a handful of agribusiness enclaves, in the process of substantially
eliminating farm subsidies, and unable to feed its own people, the
economic challenge of revitalizing agriculture on a broader basis is
enormous. This enterprise requires a reversal of traditionally paternalistic
and protectionist state policies involving long-standing explicit and
implicit subsidies, extensive restructuring of inefficient government agencies, intensification of production, and the development of a climate
conducive to the expansion of private investment, both foreign and
domestic. The goal of enticing national capital seems likely to prove particularly problematic, since the private sector has been conditioned by the
low profitability of agriculture overall and the fear of expropriation, preferring to invest in other sectors or abroad.

The political ramifications of opening agriculture to a free market are
even more daunting, particularly with respect to reforms involving the
stagnant basic-foods sector, such as maize growers, 70 percent of whom
are ejidatarios. The loss of self-sufficiency in maize is in itself a highly
sensitive area politically in that, as the staple food of a country that was a
hearth for its domestication, it remains at the core of national identity.
Policy with respect to the ejido is an even more delicate issue, involving
one of the most visible symbols of revolutionary reform and one that has
to a degree satisfied popular demands for social justice in the countryside.
Critics of the ejido, mainly politicians, economic analysts, and members of
the business community and of the agrarian bureaucracy, have long maintained that this institution is one of the main obstacles to agricultural
growth because of inefficiencies deriving from the insecurity of corporate,
usufruct tenure, ensuing underinvestment, marginal land, the contradictions of collective production, and the small size of individual plots.
Others argue that under comparable conditions ejidos are as efficient
as private farms and that low productivity derives primarily from ineffec-
tual state policies and lack of access to modern technology (see, e.g., Barkin and DeWalt, 1989; Calva, 1988; Heath, 1989; and Stavenhagen, 1970).
Peasants tend to insist that, despite its flaws, the ejido constitutes their
only defense against a return to a system dominated by *latifundia* (large
private estates), exploitation by private interests, displacement to the
cities, or full-fledged proletarianization.

As recently as the fall of 1991 it appeared that the otherwise economically audacious Salinas administration could not afford to take drastic
steps toward privatization of the ejido, considering the likely ensuing
political backlash from this key sector of the PRI's rural support base and
the broader symbolic ramifications of the revolutionary redistributionist

legacy. Neither can the logic of comparative advantage be pursued to the point of importing all staples from more efficient producers, given the dependence of the impoverished peasantry on these crops. Furthermore, because of the uncompetitive position, in particular, of Mexican maize growers, whose yields per hectare are only a quarter of those of their heavily subsidized counterparts in the American Midwest, it is likely that this crop will require substantial protection for the foreseeable future.

The Salinas agricultural reforms to date include cutting tariffs and abolishing import licenses for all except four basic products (maize, beans, wheat and powdered milk), phasing out subsidies on key inputs such as fertilizer, eliminating guaranteed prices except for maize and beans, privatizing state food-processing companies, restructuring institutions, establishing interim stimulus programs for subsistence producers, and encouraging collaboration between ejidos and agribusiness. The government views these reforms as responsible for the dramatic recuperation of agriculture in 1990, with a growth rate of 5.2 percent, almost double that of the population increment (*Excelsior*, 20 February 1991), in contrast to 1988 and 1989 when agricultural output fell by 3.2 percent and 2.1 percent respectively (*Economist*, 6 October 1990). Skeptics admit only that in 1990 the rain god was for once on the side of the farmers.

In the case of the ejido, these early initiatives seem to have represented a compromise between continued protectionism and outright privatization, but the PRI's relatively solid victory in the midterm election appears to have accelerated the opening of the ejido to capitalism. In November 1991, the president sent a "shock bill" to Congress proposing a halt to land redistribution and a radical change in ejidal tenure to allow individual ownership of parcels and thus their sale. This reform was also to legitimate the various leasing, renting, and collaborative ventures with private investors encouraged by his administration. Salinas insisted that the reform would mean the transformation rather than the end of the ejido, and that change would be gradual and a matter of choice; an ejido would be able to grant individual titles only if the majority of its members agreed, and the new owners would be free to do as they pleased with their parcels (*Wall Street Journal*, 29 November 1991). Critics denounced the proposal as counterrevolutionary and likely to concentrate land in the hands of *caciques* (rural bosses) and multinationals as uncompetitive ejidatarios would be dispossessed for a pittance. Leaders of the Confederación Nacional Campesina (National Peasant Confederation—CNC), the PRI's official peasant organization, cautiously endorsed the reform even though it would reduce their own power base, indicating that even in an era of rapid dismantling of corporatist structures the government still had control over a key institutional pillar (*Economist*, 16 November 1991). The initial response of many ejidatarios was mixed feelings—

welcoming the apparent move to give peasants more freedom, but fearing the abandonment of the government's revolutionary project.

Whatever the case, it appears that the winds of change are finally blowing through the Mexican countryside, if not yet at full hurricane force, as the state retreats from intervention in agriculture in favor of free-market dynamics. For the efficient agribusiness export sector, already highly capitalized from abroad, it appears that free trade will mean further growth and expansion into new crops despite existing phytosanitary restrictions and opposition from some U.S. lobbies. For many peasants, particularly ejidatarios dependent on low-value, low-yield staple production, a free market and the prospects of free trade are cause for alarm.

In this rapidly changing economic climate, ejidatarios are expected to become efficient farmers if they are to continue to receive supports and subsidies of any kind. For peasants, accustomed to the industry of disasters (an implicit subsidy) rather than to farming as a business proposition, this transformation requires both faith in the government's commitment to improving their condition and belief in their own capacity to increase production. Two decades of rapid agricultural decline and almost a decade of austerity have created a crisis of confidence on both counts. However, given the resilience that has brought them through centuries of crisis, it seems likely that peasants will be able to adapt to the new context. The direction of these adaptations will have significant implications both for the future of Mexican agriculture and for other Latin American peasantries as the free-trade winds blow south.[15]

Peasants, Proletarians, and the State

In recent years there has been considerable debate concerning the evolutionary direction of Latin American peasantries in response to the increasing integration of Third World economies into global markets. In particular, controversy has focused on the reasons for the unanticipated persistence of peasant forms of production alongside expanding commercial farming operations, the degree to which the pace of peasant dissolution is offset by forces for perpetuation of the sector, and the class nature of the increasingly differentiated rural population emerging under this uneven development. The lack of consensus about the extent to which growing participation in national and international economies has eroded and reshaped the peasantry is not surprising, given that it is "a very fluid concept, an abstract notion, a tendency, but not a clear statistical reality" (Bartra and Otero, 1987: 352).

In view of the complexity of contemporary transformations of traditional peasantries, it is important to distinguish between depeasantization— the gradual erosion of exclusive reliance on the land for subsistence—and proletarianization, whereby wage labor becomes the primary basis of household support (Paré, 1988 [1977]). In much of Latin America, the onset of depeasantization does not result in an immediate and complete transition to the proletarian end of a continuum. Rather, the expansion of commercial agriculture has maintained peasant subsistence cultivation, while increasing the numbers of rural people engaged, to varying degrees, in market production, the sale of their labor, or business operations, with the result that a heterogeneous, multifaceted, only partially proletarianized population has emerged composed of various categories of wage earners, farmers, craftspersons, and petty entrepreneurs in numerous and intricate permutations of activities. This diversification of rural household linkages to local, national, and international economic networks is particularly pronounced in Mexico, where peasant market integration accelerated after 1940 as a corollary of the government's efforts to stimulate commercial agricultural production by the private sector.

Mexican peasants with rights to land are designated officially as smallholders, ejidatarios or *comuneros* (members of indigenous communities). In addition, it is conventional to include landless agricultural workers within the broad category of campesinos, a degree of access to land being sustained by virtue of the insecurity of rural wage labor, ongoing ties to the family and the rural community, and the practice of sharecropping, tenant farming, and other, less formal subcontractual arrangements.[16] Thus peasants may share in the operation of small family holdings or individual ejidal plots (both often too small to sustain a household on a reliable basis) or participate in agricultural collectives, colonization schemes, and government development projects. They may experience some degree of commercialization of agriculture or may be virtually self-sufficient at the household level. At the same time, they may work sporadically or for extended periods for local landowners or in agribusiness, industry, tourism, or mining, produce crafts for the market, enter the drug trade, initiate small businesses, join the exodus to the cities temporarily, migrate throughout Mexico or to the United States as seasonal laborers and so on, in a constantly shifting network of activities. This means that peasants often sustain multiple relations with the dominant economy at varying levels of involvement as producers, wage laborers, and consumers while retaining many aspects of traditional peasanthood. In other words, any one peasant may engage in a wide range of partially overlapping economic endeavors as part of an increasingly complex strategy for survival at the household level that reflects the growing influence of national and international markets and of the state, as broker, on everyday life in the countryside.

The debate concerning the evolutionary direction of the peasantry in Mexico began to polarize in the mid-1970s around the *descampesinista* (proletarian) school, rooted in the Marxist perspective of articulation of different modes of production, and the *campesinista* (agrarian populist) school, strongly influenced by dependency theory and Chayanov's (1966 [1925]) perspectives on the peasant family economy. For example, Roger Bartra, one of the leading descampesinistas, states that rural Mexico is characterized by the particular historical articulation of a dynamic process of capital accumulation and a reconstitution of the small peasant economy, involving the integration of proletarianization and peasant reproduction (Bartra, 1974; 1982). Nevertheless, this "permanent primitive accumulation" portends the complete demise of the peasantry in the long run, and dissolution has already reached an advanced stage marked in particular by an erosion of the middle peasantry (Bartra and Otero, 1987). In contrast, the campesinista Gustavo Esteva, perhaps Bartra's strongest critic, maintains that the collective resistance of the peasantry to proletarianization has resulted in the peasantization of the rural population, strengthening peasant class consciousness and, in certain cases, even the objective conditions of the class (Esteva, 1978; 1980; Harris, 1978). In this scenario, even though the majority of peasants now depend to a greater or lesser extent on wages, effective proletarianization is prevented by the complementarity of commercial and subsistence production such that the essence of peasanthood is functionally retained (Esteva, 1978; 1980; Warman 1980; 1983 [1972]).

This polarization inevitably oversimplifies the evolving class structure in the countryside and fails to accommodate significant work that falls between the two extremes. Furthermore, increasing proletarianization and the persistence or growth of the peasantry can be seen as two sides of the same coin in that "if peasant expansion is on [land] units which are insufficient to maintain the family, the tendency toward proletarianization becomes more powerful, for the simple reason that the source which produces laborers is multiplied" (Astorga Lira, 1985: 126, my translation). In addition, with a few exceptions, the debate has inhibited empirical field assessments of the evolving diversity within agrarian society and of the actual circumstances operating for or against the eventual dissolution of the peasantry.[17]

By the early 1980s, the descampesinista-campesinista debate had bogged down in sterile polemics and the focus of attention had shifted to the impact of the internationalization of capital on Mexican agriculture under a new global division of labor (see, e.g., Astorga Lira, 1985; Barkin, 1978; 1986; 1990; Barkin and Suárez, 1981; Feder, 1977; Rama and Vigorito, 1980; and Sanderson, 1985; 1986).[18] At the same time, the accelerating deterioration of conditions in the countryside throughout most of the oil-boom years and into the debt crisis prompted renewed interest in analysis of the land invasions, rural political organizations, and protest movements that emerged in response (see, e.g., Alcantara Ferrer, 1986; Carr, 1986; Cartón de Grammont, 1986; Fox, 1987; Otero, 1988; Paré, 1988 [1977]; Rubio, 1987; and Warman, 1980). A central question was whether it was the peasant or the dispossessed agricultural laborer, the struggle for land or the battle to unionize the landless that presented the greatest revolutionary potential in the countryside (Paré, 1988 [1977]). This pre-occupation seems somewhat unrealistic given that independent political associations have tended to be promptly neutralized by the government through co-optation or stimulation of divisive forces. The difficulty of organizing peasants in terms of clearly defined interests is compounded by the contradictions created by the multiple roles of many contemporary ejidatarios, who may be at the same time effective owner-operators of land units, shareholders in a state agribusiness enterprise, employers, employees, petty entrepreneurs, and members of the state agrarian bureaucracy as political leaders. Furthermore, even in regions where wage labor is the predominant activity, rural social consciousness tends to remain more peasant than proletarian because of the insecurity of wage-earning employment and the consequent imperative of retaining ties to the land where feasible. The underlying peasant character of many agricultural workers has been underscored by the fact that when they do take collective action, the focus is often on demands for land rather than labor issues.[19]

In recent years, the polemic about rural revolutionary potential in Mexico has faded in the face of the deepening agricultural crisis and the inexorable daily reality of national austerity, as peasants are preoccupied with fending for themselves rather than seeking strength in union. Consequently, it is logical that individual household coping strategies should emerge as a central theme of studies of rural Mexico at this time, especially in terms of empirical investigations of peasant differentiation and the role of linkages between households and external economies and institutions. In particular, recent studies have focused on variations in household structure and the significance of extended migration and remittance income as part of the increasing diversification of peasant strategies for survival (see, e.g., Arizpe, 1979; 1981; 1985; Crummett, 1985; Dinnerman, 1982; Grindle, 1988; 1989; and Mines, 1981). On the whole, in responding to the recent crises peasant households have not sought new avenues for reducing hardship but rather intensified and extended long-term efforts to manage complex domestic economies squeezed by aus-terity and inflation (Grindle, 1989). Some peasant households have aban-doned the land altogether, leaving whole areas in the most marginal regions, such as the state of Oaxaca, virtual ghostlands. Many others designate one or two members to seek work in the United States, in the city, or on the rural labor circuit so that they can send back money. These remittances are now vital to the survival of many rural families rather than, as in the precrisis era, a bonus to be spent on nonessentials such as house construction materials, children's education, or small business investments (Grindle, 1989; Ostler, 1989). Other peasants have opted to join the often more lucrative if uncertain underground economy, engaging in such enterprises as growing narcotics, selling on the black market, transporting illegal immigrants from Central America, or resorting to banditry or individual crime. Less risky components of the informal economy such as unlicensed petty street vending are also flourishing in rural as well as urban areas, encouraged by the labyrinth of official regulations and taxes. Overall, the informal economy accounted for between a quarter and a third of the GDP by the late 1980s (Ostler, 1989).[20] However, extended migration, remittance income, and participation in the informal economy are significant options for only a relatively small proportion of peasant households. The remainder have coped with the crises primarily by retreating to subsistence cultivation if feasible, working harder, grasping casual labor when available, hoping that one of their offspring might attain well-paid professional employment, curtailing consumption of nonessentials, and tightening their belts in the traditional peasant response to recession.

Analyses of adaptations at the household level are closely associated with an increasing emphasis on the rural labor market for "human merchandise" (Astorga Lira, 1985)—agricultural workers drawn from the subsistence peasant sector and the ranks of the landless to serve commercial agriculture as a cheap work force on a seasonal basis, after which they must return to their marginal farms or seek further casual employment (see, e.g., Aguirre Beltrán, 1982; Astorga, 1985; Cartón de Grammont, 1986; Paré, 1987; and Rubio, 1987). Thus, proletarianization remains incomplete as commercial production partially restructures peasant agriculture so that the two can coexist in functional symbiosis (de Janvry, 1981), the peasant sector subsidizing agribusiness and ultimately urban living costs via the labor market's below-subsistence wages.[21] Consequently, although commercial agriculture and traditional peasant subsistence production may appear to be two totally separate systems, in fact they form a whole integrated by the labor market as mediated by the state.

The state has played an unusually dominant role in peasant agriculture legitimated in principle by the 1917 Constitution, which established that all lands and waters are part of the national patrimony subject to control by the government for the public good.[22] As a consequence of this assertion of the state's eminent domain and the emphasis on the social function of land, a distinctive relationship between state and countryside characterized by the apparently anachronistic coexistence of private and social (ejidal) property and by the explicit tutelary role of the government toward the ejido has evolved. State intervention in the ejidal sector has been expressed through political co-optation, direct and indirect manipulation of the rural labor market, and control of agricultural development projects, wages, commodity prices, distribution networks, credit, and other key production inputs. In view of the scale and scope of state-directed ejidal modernization initiatives and the minimal record of achievement of the majority of such ventures, it is not surprising that agricultural development project evaluations have proliferated, often in the form of "project pathologies" (see, e.g., Barkin, 1978; Barkin and King, 1970; Ewell and Poleman, 1980; Gates, 1988a; Poleman, 1964; and Szekely and Restrepo, 1988). However, quantitative measures of increased crop production reflect only one component of the state's agenda for accommodating the ejidal sector.

Overall, the state's highly centralized, bureaucratic, and paternalistic economic development strategy can be seen as directed toward a planned functional dualism—a deliberate slowing down of the dissolution of the peasantry in order to perpetuate a reserve pool of cheap labor, stimulate the lagging agricultural sector, and check the potentially politically explosive outflow of marginal masses from the countryside while sustaining the agrarian populist rhetoric engendered by the revolution. Thus, although the numerous peasant agricultural development projects initiated by the government over the past two decades have failed to raise production significantly, they have been functional in keeping at least some peasants down on the farm. In other words, while planned modernization of the ejido evidently has stimulated rural proletarianization, the process has proceeded only up to a certain point, the corporate land-tenure structure, insecurity of wage labor, state agricultural incentives, and family and community ties working together to make many peasants feel unable to sever their links to the soil.

Under national austerity and the transition from protectionism to an open market economy, this particular form of asymmetrical symbiosis is no longer advantageous. Mexico can no longer sustain massive and indiscriminate public-sector investments in ejidal agriculture merely to obtain minimal productivity increments, ensure a low-cost labor supply and pay lip service to rural social justice. Instead, at least some peasant agriculturalists must be transformed into efficient competitive farmers instead of indebted dependents of the agrarian bureaucracy, inured to institutionalized failure as pensioners of a long-ago revolution. In this context, the current agricultural reforms initiated by the Salinas administration can be seen as an attempt to refunctionalize the peasantry in adjustment to changing production imperatives under a global market. The reforms are intended both to spur economic dynamism among the most commercially viable peasants and to fortify the most marginal. While so far avoiding a direct attack on the ejido per se, these measures clearly involve a restructuring of the institution in terms of both form and function, as well as a dramatic change in the state-peasant relationship in the direction of a more laissez faire approach consistent with the evolving "market-friendly" emphasis of the international financial agencies (see, e.g., World Bank, 1991). The administration claims that opening the ejido to direct private investment merely legitimates and expands existing practices and gives peasants the opportunity to engage in the business of agriculture as competitive farmers rather than as marginals trapped in the subsistence struggle. However, ejidatarios tend to see this move as the thin end of the privatization wedge, throwing staple producers onto the mercy of the market either as individual owners of new infrasubsistence plots or as full-fledged rural proletarians.

At present, predictions of the imminent demise of the ejido or an immediate surge in the rate of proletarianization would appear to be premature in that the reforms introduced so far seem likely to keep ejidatarios in the service of the private sector and the state but through somewhat different mechanisms of integration. Nevertheless, the legitimation of individual ownership of ejidal parcels has major implications for Mexican agrarian structure and appears to signal the end of the era of agrarian populism by closing the revolutionary account.

After two decades of crisis, the pace of change in the countryside is accelerating beyond the level where it can be fathomed by armchair polemics. In view of the ever-increasing complexity and diversity of contemporary peasantries, it appears that detailed field investigations are necessary in order to assess the impact of changing agricultural policy on practice. In this way, we can obtain a more specific sense of peasant strategies for surviving the major economic crises of yesterday and today, so that a firmer basis can be established for evaluating likely adaptations to future transitions.

The Research Contract

At eight o'clock on a December morning, a much-abused pickup truck containing an anthropologist and her geologist husband bumps along a dusty field road leading to the Pomuch small irrigation project in the state of Campeche. The anthropologist has been visiting the Pomuch campesinos every few years over more than two decades, initially as a graduate student intent on demonstrating that ideology is significant in social practice, that peasant attitudes can be measured by means of a photographic projective technique, and that these attitude complexes can be related directly to development project performance (Gates, 1972;

1976). The Pomuch campesinos, like members of similar projects in neighboring communities in the Camino Real and Los Chenes regions of northern Campeche, were happy to oblige by looking at a set of photographs and telling stories evoked by the imagery, since these Maya peasants have a strong oral tradition, high verbal aptitudes, and a keen sense of humor, as well as an innate courtesy to outsiders.

On this particular day in 1989, the anthropologist was making her initial revisit of a new field season, with the usual butterflies in her stomach about reestablishing ties with old friends, making new ones, and probably making a fool of herself in the process, as on many occasions in the past when a careless remark reduced a whole village to tears of laughter. Ten minutes later, these fears are forgotten when familiar figures are spotted resting in the shade of a tree. Hugs and handshakes are exchanged: "You look stronger [fatter] daughter, with more little white ones [hairs]. We'll tell Alfredo and the other members this evening that you are back, so that everybody will be sure to come out and talk to you tomorrow" (I-3, ejidatario, Pomuch, December 1989). Then the campesinos proceed, unprompted, to recount the latest news of the project and its members, along with their perceptions of the most recent problems in the countryside under the double crises of agriculture and national austerity. This is the reason this book was written. These are the things that Campeche campesinos most like to talk about to a visiting anthropologist, or at least to this one, who has spent much of her life in fields chatting to farmers and is most at ease in that context.

This book is the product of an informal research contract—a personal commitment made over the years during repeated visits to agricultural development projects in Campeche and elsewhere in the Mexican tropics. Informants, both peasants and development agents, have talked to me out of friendship, a common love of farming, and shared frustration with the agrarian bureaucracy. Campeche peasants do not expect me to do anything to resolve their problems directly, but they appear to experience a degree of catharsis in talking about them, and a number have urged me to write their story in detail in the hope that someone will listen, understand, and perhaps change something, someday.

Not all days in the field proceed as smoothly as the one described above. Twenty years ago, if one wanted to locate a particular Campeche campesino between dawn and mid-afternoon, he was sure to be in his field every day of the year except Sunday and perhaps Christmas Eve, unless struck down by a serious illness or accident. Today, ejidal leaders and perhaps whole groups of ejidatarios engaged in formal production programs are as likely to be found in the offices and meeting rooms of government agencies as cultivating their land. Thus, while my preferred locus and mode of interview is out in the field with an individual campesino, some had to be conducted en masse while waiting for meetings to begin or while transporting project members to town on ejidal business. I abandoned the practice of interviewing in campesinos' homes long ago, except for social visits, because of the distractions created by ambient noise and routine household activities, as well as because, by and large, farmers want to talk about farming in the field, where they can point to their successes and failures. Using these procedures, fieldwork days tend to be long, hot, hungry, and full of uncertainties as the interviewer has to fit in with the informants' schedules and preferences. For example, one should not interrupt farm work in the cool of the early morning, when campesinos are rushing to get as much done as possible before the full heat of the tropical day. Also, interviewing on weekends and during holiday periods can be a difficult business, since drinking is a widespread recreation among the non-Protestant rural population.

The perspective is a longitudinal one, based on ongoing fieldwork to monitor the transformation of the peasantry and the progression of the agricultural crisis, but the detailed profile of the impact of the debt crisis in the Campeche countryside was compiled during a sabbatical-leave field season from November 1989 to April 1990. During this period, I conducted in-depth, open-ended interviews with 115 campesinos from seven communities in diverse regions of the state concerning the definition and perceived causes of the crises and their impact on such matters as yields, agricultural inputs, profit margins, household budgets, out-migration, wage labor, and supplementary income sources. Informants included Maya campesinos from the villages of Pomuch (20), Tinún (16) and Nilchi (14 project members and 10 milperos), Mennonites from new settlements near Hecelchakán in the northern Camino Real district (8), and colonists from other parts of Mexico in Bonfil (20), Yohaltún (10) and the Candelaria (8 from Monclova, 4 from Estado de México, 3 from Venustiano Carranza, 2 from Nuevo Coahuila) in the center and south of the state (Fig. 1.1). Most informants were ejidatarios and members of government-directed agricultural development projects, although not always currently engaged in production for the market. In addition, I interviewed 400 campesinos from other Campeche ejidos at a more general level in order to gain understanding of the range of socioeconomic differentiation among peasants in the state today. Informants were male heads of families, because agriculture is definitely a man's business in Campeche; women work in the fields only at harvest time, although care of plants in the *solar* (house yard) is within their purview. On occasion, however, I was referred to a wife or other household members for additional details on the domestic budget. A further 100 development agents, politicians, businessmen, urban workers, and representatives of other sectors were

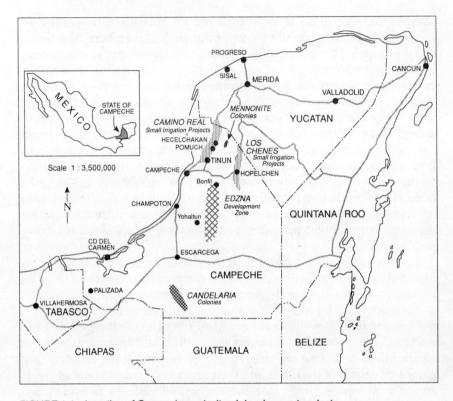

FIGURE 1.1   Location of Campeche agricultural development projects

interviewed about broader aspects of the crises and the implications of recent economic restructuring.

In a fieldwork-based undertaking such as this, ethical considerations are always paramount, particularly since agriculture tends to be a particularly sensitive area in the Mexican psyche and is an innately political topic in this context. As a result, campesinos are identified by ejido or community but not by name, while agricultural development agents, professionals, and businessmen are designated by broad occupational category to protect informants from potential career prejudice. Campesinos throughout Campeche were eager to talk about the crises, the changes in their lives to date, and their hopes and fears for the future. (In the one instance where this was not the case, because of cultural and linguistic barriers with Mennonite women, interview attempts were abandoned immediately.) Development agents also were anxious to talk about the crises, particularly with reference to the frustrations they have added to their jobs and their lives.

The information collected from these interviews and from government agricultural records is displayed in tables or graphics where possible.[23] Data on household income and expenditures are presented in aggregate form by type of producer, since within the collective production units investigated profits and debts are distributed more or less equally.[24] In other words, within the modernized ejidal sector, households tend to be differentiated in economic terms according to whether they cultivate maize or mangos, whether they are ranchers or rice growers. Thus, in many cases, relative prosperity is derived as much from the largely fortuitous circumstance of participation in a viable project devoted to high-value agricultural activities as from the industry or initiative of individual peasants.

The book is organized as follows: Chapter 2 examines the record of state intervention in Mexican peasant agriculture in the context of the evolution of national agrarian policy over the course of this century. In particular, it addresses the content and direction of the agricultural reforms introduced by the Salinas administration and the changing nature of state-peasant relations. Chapter 3 begins with a historical analysis of the "development of underdevelopment" in Campeche (Frank, 1967; 1969), dependent since the conquest on the export of natural resources in a sequence of boom-and-bust cycles, such that the local economy stagnated. The chapter goes on to characterize the rhythm of life in urban and rural Campeche as a backdrop against which the impact of the debt crisis can be examined. Chapter 4 outlines the condition of agriculture in Campeche in 1970, prior to the initiation of the concerted government effort to modernize the ejidal sector. It concludes by setting the institutional stage for the emergence of the agricultural development "business" as a new economic boom that became a way of life for bureaucrats and peasants alike as slash-and-burn milpa cultivation gave way to mechanized production. Chapter 5 follows the progression of planned agricultural development in Campeche as the industry of disasters through case studies of four projects representing different models of state intervention in the ejido. The chapter closes with a profile of agriculture in Campeche today that can be compared with the 1970 baseline presented in chapter 4 to show the limited results of two decades of state-directed ejidal modernization. Chapter 6 concentrates on the specific impact of the debt crisis on agriculture in Campeche since 1982 and identifies the adaptations of peasants to this latest phase of the agricultural crisis. Chapter 7 assesses the cumulative impact of state intervention in agriculture in Campeche in the context of current changes in national policy and discusses the potential implications of peasant survival strategies in this state for the peasantry as a whole.

The outcome of this exercise is essentially a forum in which peasants, development agents, and other concerned individuals criticize the agricultural system, evaluate the toll taken by the crises, assess the current transformations, and express their hopes, doubts, and expectations about the future. Rather than dwelling on past mistakes, it highlights the growing determination of peasants to control their own destiny while simultaneously fearing abandonment by a government that, for the past twenty years, has regulated virtually every aspect of agricultural life. If economic logic now dictates that the revolutionary account still pending in the ejido be closed once and for all or if the state decides that rural social justice can be achieved only through a free-for-all in an open market economy, what will life be like for the Mexican peasants of tomorrow?

> The government made the Mexican campesinos dependent to the point where this is now central to our identity. So what will happen if the government abandons us? With no one to depend on, will we cease to exist? That would be the ultimate injustice, the final breach of the revolutionary contract. You see, the government thinks we are in debt to them because they screwed up our agricultural base, but in reality they owe us because they still haven't brought justice to the countryside. If they destroy the ejido, that would be the end of any hopes of a better future for the campesinos . . . Perhaps it is time to take our destiny into our own hands. (I-21, ejidatario, Tinún, February 1990)

Notes

1. This book contains verbatim excerpts from interviews I conducted in the Mexican state of Campeche in 1990, 1989, 1985, 1982, 1981, 1975, 1970, and 1969. The majority come from the November 1989–April 1990 field season, involving quotations from 54 peasant informants out of a total of 115 interviewed in depth and from 26 civil servants, professionals, businessmen, and citizens-at-large out of a total of 100 informants in this category. Excerpts are identified by the informant's number, occupation, place, and date of interview.

2. For overviews of the debt crisis in Latin America see Bray (1989), Canak (1989), Dietz (1989), Griffith-Jones and Sunkel (1986), Guillén (1989), Hartlyn and Morley (1986), Inter-American Development Bank (1984), Pastor (1986; 1989), Smith and Cuddington (1985), Stallings and Kaufman (1989), Thorp and Whitehead (1987), and Wiarda (1987). On the Mexican case, see Barkin (1990), Carr and Montoya (1986), Cordero and Tello (1983), Guillén (1984), González Casanova and Camín (1985), Looney (1985), and Pastor (1987).

3. While a number of studies have focused on the implications of austerity for the Mexican urban consumer (e.g., Lomelli, 1991), there are still relatively few detailed regional and local examinations of the impact of the debt crisis per se in rural Mexico, apart from preliminary surveys such as those by Beaucage (1991), Carr (1986), Cook (1988), Fox (1987), Grindle (1989), and Prieto (1986).

4. General studies on the agricultural crisis in Mexico include Austin and Esteva (1987), Barkin and Suárez (1982), Barkin (1990), Barkin and DeWalt (1989), Brannon and Baklanoff (1987), Echeverría Zuno (1984), Goodman et al. (1985), Grindle (1977), Johnson et al. (1987), Moguel (coordinator) (1989), Rama and Rello (1982), Rello (1985), Sanderson (1981, 1986), Yates (1981), and Yúnez Naude (1988). Detailed em-

pirical studies of its most recent phase are still relatively scarce (see, e.g., Calva, 1988; Cárton de Grammont, 1986; Grindle, 1988, 1989; Paré, 1987, and Scherr, 1985).

5. The ejido combines communal title vested in the state with usufruct rights to land worked individually or collectively. Thus, ejidal lands cannot be sold or mortgaged. Despite the low productivity of many ejidos, the institution remains entrenched as a visible symbol of revolutionary social justice.

6. Mexican public-sector investments in agriculture increased only from 13.4 percent of total public-sector investment in 1970 to 18.1 percent in 1975, declining to 16.6 percent by 1980 (Barkin and Suárez, 1982: 64), but total government revenues and public-sector spending increased dramatically over this period as a result of the oil boom and an associated upsurge in foreign borrowing.

7. An ejidatario is a peasant who has legally recognized individual or collective rights to farm land belonging to an ejido and is obliged to participate directly in the productive process on such lands. In order to apply for ejidal rights, individuals must be Mexican by birth and older than sixteen years or responsible for a family, must cultivate land personally as a habitual occupation, must have resided for six months in a community comprised of twenty or more applicants (if a new ejido is solicited), may not possess personal title to more than a small parcel of land (equivalent to the minimum grant size) or own substantial capital in industry or commerce, and may be male or female (*Ley Federal de Reforma Agraria*, 1971). In practice, the majority of ejidatarios are male; relatively few women cultivate the land directly or participate actively in the general assembly of members which governs the ejido.

8. Generally, peasants refer to themselves as campesinos (people of the countryside) rather than ejidatarios unless the specific institutional context is under discussion.

9. In 1991, Mexican agricultural exports were still subject to U.S. tariffs of up to 36 percent. Phytosanitary restrictions covering pests and diseases in specified crops as well as use of carcinogenic fertilizers and pesticides provided additional protection for U.S. growers.

10. Most Mexicans have been faced with consumer price increases substantially greater than those represented in official figures, which are based primarily on the prices registered in large urban department stores and supermarkets. In the small and middle businesses excluded from the "pacts" that account for some 60 percent of national trading activity, prices are 30–40 percent higher, and thus the poor have to pay much more for basic commodities than do the urban middle and upper classes (Lomelli, 1991).

11. Since 1982, consumption of meat in Mexico has fallen by one-third, that of total animal protein by over half, and staple intake by 20 percent. It is estimated that between 65 percent and 75 percent of the population suffer some degree of malnutrition, 30 percent in acute form, particularly in the rural areas and urban squatter settlements. In 1989 it was estimated that 20 percent of the total Mexican population possessed 50 percent of the nation's wealth and 18 percent had incomes less than the minimum wage, while 33 percent were dependent on the minimum wage of approximately $3 a day, 90 percent of these being rural dwellers (Instituto Nacional de Estadística, Geografía e Información, 1990).

12. The relative opening of the political process has accelerated under Salinas, whose determination to pursue significant reforms in his party's modus operandi

was reflected initially in the unprecedented concession of defeat by the PRI in the July 1989 Baja California governorship race. After the August 1991 midterm elections, a second opposition governor assumed office on an interim basis in Guanajuato, appointed by the state legislature after the previously proclaimed PRI victor declined the office consequent on widespread accusations of fraud. It is widely assumed that Salinas orchestrated this reversal (*Economist*, 7 September 1991).

13. This support has tended to be underlain by political apathy and cynicism that appear to have deepened over the past two decades as peasants have become increasingly aware of the extent to which they have been manipulated, cheated, and abused by both the formal political organizations and the government agencies responsible for rural development initiatives (Grindle, 1977; 1989).

14. Significant collective rural protest has, however, occurred in some areas, generally in connection with broader-based popular mobilization in response to economic concerns and demands for political reform, though rooted often in demands for land. For example, the Coordinadora Nacional Plan de Ayala (the National Plan de Ayala Coordinating Committee) drew together regional groups of agricultural wage laborers, ejidatarios, and women concerned about access to state-subsidized household supplies (Carr, 1986). Other important movements include attempts to organize agricultural workers nationally and the struggles of wage laborers in tomatoes in Sinaloa and coffee in Chiapas. Most rural protest, however, tends to be short-lived and focussed on a single agrarian issue, generally related, in recent years, to specific austerity hardships such as low guaranteed crop prices and credit default, although organized land invasions still occur from time to time, for example, in Veracruz in 1991.

15. On 26 March 1991, Argentina, Brazil, Paraguay, and Uruguay signed an agreement to create a Southern Cone Common Market, involving a common external tariff and free movement of goods and services within the zone, by the end of 1994. The United States is negotiating the framework of a free-trade agreement with this market (*Economist*, 30 March 1991).

16. According to the 1980 census, agricultural wage laborers numbered a little over 3 million persons, constituting almost one-third of the total economically active population in Mexican agriculture, with only 20 percent of paid workers classified as permanent employees. An additional category of unpaid nonfamily laborers totaled 1,111,383. Because a separate unspecified employment component of 982,262 individuals is also likely to be engaged in agricultural labor (Paré, 1988 [1977]) and underreporting of casual wage labor is common, an estimate for 1980 of over 5 million laborers appears reasonable. According to Schejtman's (1981) analysis of the 1970 census, the campesino sector overall comprised 87 percent of all Mexican agricultural producers, of which 72 percent were compelled to engage in some degree of off-farm labor because their plots did not produce enough to cover household subsistence needs.

17. With some exceptions (e.g., Téran, 1976; Paré, 1988 [1977]) the descampesinistas tended to focus on broad economic class indicators such as size of landholding, value of production, and the extent of wage labor. Although important, these elements are not always the most critical indices of peasant differentiation, particularly where the state has assumed the dominant role in agricultural

development. Furthermore, until relatively recently the ejido has tended to neutralize the potentially divisive effects of variations in holding size and quality. The campesinistas have been more inclined to grass roots studies (e.g., Scherr, 1985), but these have not been plentiful and have tended to emphasize the economic success stories that are far from the norm in most parts of rural Mexico (Spalding, 1988).

18. For more general studies of the evolution of the New International Division of Labor (NIDL), as the latest stage in relations between First World and Third World nations wherein the latter are increasingly integrated into the world market see, e.g., Becker (1987), Frobel et al. (1985), and Marcusson and Torp (1982). From the perspective of the NIDL, events such as the Third World debt crisis of the 1980s do not, in fact, constitute a threat to the fiscal stability of the first world core, but are instead a manifestation of the evolving logic of capital accumulation in the world system, where the transformation of Third World economies is sustained by the integration of dominant class interests in the core and the periphery, and conditioned by the disciplinary authority of supranational agencies over national regimes (Canak, 1989).

19. For example, the massive land invasions in the Yaqui and Mayo Valley in Sonora in 1975 and 1976 resulted in the expropriation and reallocation as ejidos of over seventy thousand hectares, more than half of which was prime irrigated farmland (Cartón de Grammont, 1986; Otero, 1988).

20. The dimensions of the informal and underground economies obviously are difficult to quantify. However, together they appear to be a significant sector in many countries today, particularly where heavy tax burdens, excessive regulation of economic activities, prohibitions and bureaucratic corruption are the norm, as in Mexico (Centro de Estudios Económicos del Sector Privado, 1987). The Mexican government is mainly concerned about the growth of the informal economy as tax revenues lost, but attempts to regulate it may be counterproductive in terms of loss of sectoral dynamism, especially as recent fiscal reform appears not to have gone far enough towards deregulation and increased flexibility.

21. See de Janvry and Garramón (1977) for a succinct elaboration of this "functional dualist model". Where the majority of peasant households operate at the infrasubsistence level, production must be supplemented by wage labor, largely in commercial agriculture, which pays below-subsistence wages for limited seasonal requirements only. At the same time, peasant agriculture increasingly loses the ability to produce commodities as control of the means of production is eroded. Thus, peasant production effectively subsidizes commercial production through surplus extraction via the labor market and supplies cheap foodstuffs for the urban sector, where low wages can also be sustained.

22. See, e.g., Austin and Esteva (1987), Calva (1988), Esteva (1980), Grindle (1977; 1985; 1986), Hardy (1984), Sanderson (1981; 1986), Sanderson (1984), Warman (1983) [1972], Wessman (1984), and Zaragoza and Macías (1980). Grindle (1986) and Sanderson (1981) emphasize the significance of relative state autonomy in the articulation and implementation of Mexican rural development strategies. For a more general discussion of the evolving role of the Mexican state, see Cockcroft (1983), Hamilton (1975; 1982; 1984), and Hamilton and Harding (1986).

23. I have tried to use the most authoritative and reliable sources available, but even here frequent discrepancies occur as a result of a general lack of analytic precision and the manipulation of data for political purposes. Where possible I use data only after having cross-checked several sources and matching them with field estimates.

24. Within collective ejidal production units there is some small variation in the incomes of members depending on the number of labor days each puts into cultivation.

2

Codifying Marginality: Agricultural Policy and the Peasantry

We are proud to be campesinos, men of the country, producers, because life is still clean here. I mean that the campesinos are the heirs of Zapata, the sons of General Cárdenas, the bearers of the revolutionary banner in a dirty world. (I-22, ejidatario, Tinún, March 1990)

Peasants, politicians, bureaucrats, we are all part of the same system, we all feed off it to serve our own interests, even those at the bottom. You can do very well in agriculture, and I don't mean from the crops. (I-130, civil servant, Campeche, October 1985)

Mexican agrarian philosophy has been characterized by remarkable consistency over the seventy years since the revolution despite drastic changes in the overall economic context. For many Mexicans the symbols of revolutionary reform—"land and liberty," Zapata, and the ejido— persist untarnished. *El agro* (agriculture) remains a highly sensitive area shrouded in the mystique of past social struggles, with the result that present-day options are tightly constrained by the legacy of previous development decisions.[1]

The distinctive relationship between state and countryside established by the 1917 Constitution has been a dominant motif in agrarian policy and its implementation. Thus postrevolutionary reform legislation has until recently reflected ever-increasing state intervention not only to spur productivity but also to accommodate the agrarian populist concerns about social justice in the countryside on which its legitimacy rested.

This reform process has created a cumbersome institutional structure that is incapable of coping with harsh contemporary economic realities. The petrolization of the economy and the ensuing revelation of the full extent of the debt crisis compounded the ongoing agricultural crisis associated with demographic pressures, chronic rural poverty, sluggish growth in many crop complexes, increasing reliance on export crops, and the correlative loss of self-sufficiency in basic foods. Effective programs for stimulating domestic food output are urgently needed, but the government has been unable to combine the imperative of spurring production with its constitutional commitment to improving the peasant condition. Agricultural needs and agrarian institutions seem to have been operating at cross-purposes (Yates, 1981).

Key agricultural policy reorientations since 1971 have emphasized first the social welfare component and more recently productivity. To date, these efforts have achieved at best only modest gains at great cost, and the government has been unable to achieve a rational balance between export-dollar-earning cash crops and staples such as maize, the "salary" of the campesino. Rather than generating an efficient expanded productive base, the new policies have created an institutionalized modern subsistence sector reflecting the growing breach between the social necessities of the people and the incapacity of the productive apparatus to satisfy them. Thus the agricultural crisis is in many ways the product of the very policies designed to alleviate it in that the modernization strategy pursued has effectively codified peasant marginality. At the same time, private enterprise has been bridled by direct state intervention in the process of capital accumulation, which has severely limited the possibilities for productive forces to advance at their maximum momentum.

Since 1980, when the Ley de Fomento Agropecuario (the Agricultural and Livestock Production Promotion Law—LFA) legitimated the further expansion of state control of agriculture, enclaves on both private and public lands that are virtually state-managed farms using underemployed rural labor have been allotted an increasing share of the now-limited national resources at the expense of the subsistence sector. This single-focus strategy for increasing staple crop production has proved insufficient under the strictures of debt crisis austerity and inflation, and since 1985 Mexican agriculture has slumped into the worst phase of its twenty-year crisis.

The Salinas administration has introduced a package of reforms since 1988 to restructure and recapitalize the agricultural sector in keeping with the dramatic "opening" of the economy overall. Despite a recent resurgence of government programs with strong populist overtones, the general trend in policy progression is pro-production rather than pro-peasant in response to a complex of national and international economic forces

that appears to be radically altering Mexican agrarian structure. To understand the extent and implications of the current transformation of peasant
productive organization it is necessary to trace the evolution of agricultural policy in some detail. In particular, this chapter focuses on the
impact of changing policies on peasants in the ejido (Table 2.1 at end of
chapter), showing how increasing direct state intervention has transformed the lives of traditional peasants through the credit mechanism,
collectivization, the introduction of modern farming technologies, and
the promotion of dependency relationships in an attempt to legislate a
productive base which is both economically efficient and socially just.

The Ejido: The Base of the Pyramid

The ejido has attracted special interest because of its unique and apparently contradictory position as a potentially socialist alternative to private
landownership within a capitalist framework. Despite extensive government attempts to inject capital and technology and thus economic dynamism into the ejido over the past two decades, however, the sector has
never demonstrated conclusive evidence of providing a viable alternative
to private enterprise in terms of productive efficiency. Although collectivization has been a central component of modernization efforts, the majority of ejidos still operate individually with separate plots generating a
bare minimum of subsistence, virtually indistinguishable from *minifundia*
(sub-family holdings). Plots are frequently very small (58 percent of the
parcels consisted of fewer than four hectares in 1980), located on marginal
land, and cultivated with traditional technology (Gordillo de Anda, 1990).
These problems are compounded by the inflexibility of ejidal tenure, internal organizational weaknesses, and the lack of effective infrastructural
support from the public sector, keeping productivity low even though
overall economic performance has been surprisingly high in relation
to the limited resources available.[2] In general, the ejido can be seen as a
holding device or tranquilizing factor, providing minimal subsistence for
a large sector of the rural population and thus serving to defuse social
tensions (Bartra, 1974). Although it is recognized as the most important
achievement of Mexican agrarian reform in that it satisfies, to a degree,
popular demands for social justice, it is still a long way from fulfilling its
promise of comprising the foundation of a more efficient and equitable
productive base.

Many of the ejido's problems were caused by the Mexican government's preoccupation with mere land redistribution as opposed to integral reform for some fifty years after the revolution, with the exception of
some limited experiments with collectives during the Cárdenas administration from 1934 to 1940.[3] Until the late 1960s the state made only mini-

mal investments in the ejidal sector beyond the formal mechanics of processing claims, and completion of these legalities is often delayed for many years. Land redistribution was only piecemeal after the massive reforms of the Cárdenas era (Fig. 2.1)—when the number of private holdings also increased dramatically—and failed to keep pace with the increase in the peasant population, resulting in drastic growth in the ranks of landless laborers (Cockcroft, 1974). A frontier safety-valve mentality developed after President Manuel Avila Camacho called for a "march to the sea" in 1941, concerning the potential for relocating peasants from the particularly congested areas of the central uplands to presumably fertile underutilized coastlands, principally in the tropical southeast. However, sporadic colonization and a few grandiose river-basin development schemes such as the ill-fated Papaloapan project (initiated in 1947) could hardly be regarded as comprehensive reform measures (see Barkin and King, 1970; Ewell and Poleman, 1980; Poleman, 1964). The government continued to assume that redistribution per se would eventually promote broad-based agricultural progress. For the time being it was considered sufficient to integrate the peasantry via the ejidos firmly into the base of the ruling PRI's organizational pyramid.

The "Mexican Miracle": A Dual-Track Strategy

From 1940 to 1965 the government pursued a strategy of heavy federal investment in rural infrastructure (dams, irrigation works, roads, electri-

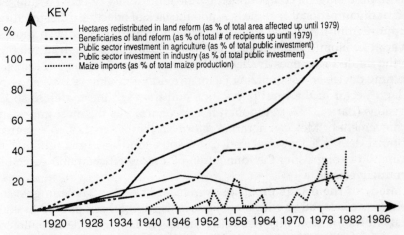

FIGURE 2.1   Mexican agricultural policy and practice (SOURCES: Zaragoza and Macias, 1980; Barkin and Suraez, 1982)

fication, etc.) on high-potential lands primarily in the northwestern states of Sonora and Sinaloa, la Laguna, the Rio Grande borderlands, and the western Bajio region to create a climate conducive to private investment in large-scale irrigated commercial agriculture. This was part of what was essentially a dual-track agricultural policy, separating social justice considerations from productivity objectives and establishing two clearly defined farm sectors, commercial and subsistence, which were, however, linked through the agricultural labor market (Bailey, 1981). This approach worked reasonably well for a while; modest peasant aspirations were accommodated to a point, and the country made significant gains in food production and the promotion of agribusiness, contributing to the "Mexican miracle" of unprecedented growth and diversification.[4] A dual-track approach was also characteristic of the initial adoption of the import-substitution model of economic modernization; in contrast to many Third World countries at that time, Mexico maintained a rough balance between agricultural and industrial development until the late 1950s.[5]

Much of this impressive agricultural growth was due to the government's early emphasis on Green Revolution research in cooperation with the Rockefeller Foundation and the subsequent diffusion of the new hybrid seeds and a supporting modern technological and credit package in the irrigation zones, where farmers could afford to take advantage of the costly inputs. Increased yields together with the expanded irrigation hectarage enabled the country to become a modest grain exporter after 1963 (Barkin and Suárez, 1982), agriculture helping to generate foreign exchange and to provide low-unit-cost food supplies for the growing industrial labor force.[6] The ejidos and peasant smallholdings were regarded primarily as pools of cheap labor both for commercial agriculture and for the expanding urban areas. Thus agriculture essentially subsidized industrial expansion through a deliberate strategy to keep the urban cost of living low—a decision which has constrained agrarian policy until the present.

Internationalization of the Economy and Emergence of the Agricultural Crisis

By the late 1960s it had become clear that the "Mexican miracle" was seriously flawed. Critical economic bottlenecks began to emerge as the strategy of rapid industrialization at all costs exacerbated preexisting problems such as rural-urban drift, city mushrooming, skewed income distribution, increasing regional disparities, and inefficient, overprotected industries biased toward import substitution and often predicated on foreign capital inputs (Street, 1981). The agricultural sector lost its overall growth dynamic after 1965 in response to the state's industry-first approach and the levelling off of the initial effects of Green Revolution innovations. Public investment in agrarian infrastructure declined as the pace of expansion of irrigation slowed. At the same time, market forces were reshaping production as changing dietary patterns, particularly in urban areas, increased the demand for meat, poultry, and processed and imported luxury foods, domestic food and industrial crop-processing industries required increasing quantities of sugar, cotton, and soybeans, and the international market (principally the United States) sought feeder cattle, fruits, and vegetables (Bailey, 1981).

The net result of these increasing pressures was the dramatic displacement of subsistence crops such as maize and beans by modernized livestock production and associated forage crops such as sorghum (which had not even been grown in Mexico prior to 1958), the principal ingredient in custom foods for poultry and pig rearing.[7] Meanwhile, wheat in irrigation zones gave way to higher-value crops such as fruits and vegetables primarily for export and, more recently, oil seeds also used for feed after the extraction process. What has been termed the "cattle-ization" of agriculture has had particularly severe implications for maize production. Competition from more lucrative operations in both rain-fed and irrigated farming areas, the impulse of agribusiness, low government-guaranteed prices, reduced official supports, and the relative lack of research enticed commercial farmers to abandon this basic crop wherever the opportunity arose.[8] Maize once again became predominantly a campesino crop, cultivated traditionally on the least productive land primarily for household consumption, as the commercial farm sector became increasingly unable to satisfy the country's need for this and other food grains.[9] From 1970 on, Mexico was forced to import large quantities of basic foods as the agricultural crisis became an acknowledged fact. As Barkin and Suárez (1982) point out, it is ironic that it was technical progress in the countryside, the fruit of the internationalization of the economy, that provoked the productive changes threatening the nation's capacity for self-sufficiency.[10]

Self-Sufficiency and Social Justice

By 1970, the logic of the economic growth model and the incompatibility of the industrialization drive with continued reform and social welfare considerations in the countryside made it imperative for the state to intervene more directly in peasant agriculture and reorganize the relations of production (Edelman, 1980). Besides the food crisis, growing symptoms of rural discontent expressed in land invasions and violent conflicts between peasants and landowners, together with the symbolic significance of increased dependence on external resources for the daily tortillas and bread, required a basic reorientation of agricultural policy in order to stimulate commercial production of basic foods by ejidatarios and smallholders. New, more restrictive federal agrarian reform and water laws were implemented in 1971, and throughout the Echeverría administration (1970–1976) the government engaged in reformist deficit spending based on heavy foreign borrowing and monetary expansion in an effort to promote agricultural growth and provide extensive social programs for Mexico's poorest.

In the peasant sector the emphasis was on massive land redistribution[11] and the modernization of subsistence agriculturalists on the margin of the cash economy. Rather than just turning over the land to campesinos as in the past, programs were expanded to provide the high-yielding seeds, the fertilizers and agrochemicals, and the equipment, credit, and technical backup considered essential for the transformation from traditional to modern farming. A variety of federal agencies initiated comprehensive rural development programs intended to promote long-term social and economic development and spur a more equitable distribution of the social product so that peasants would be content to stay down on the farm. A developmentalist onslaught of new organizations, commissions, subagencies, and plans proliferated in a maze of acronyms, the inevitable bureaucratic concomitant of increased state initiative in Mexico. An umbrella agency, the Proyecto de Inversiones Públicas para el Desarrollo Rural (the Public Investment Project for Rural Development—PIDER), was set up in 1973 under the Ministry of the Presidency to coordinate the numerous national projects, with components as diverse as the construction of feeder roads and small irrigation works and the fostering of peasant organizations, training, and welfare. PIDER constituted the world's largest World Bank-funded rural development program, reflecting that institution's policy at that time of channeling the bulk of its aid strategically to "middle poor" nations (Edelman, 1980).

The ejido provided a natural framework for implementing this diffusionist model of improving the peasant condition in situ. From 1970 to 1979 private agricultural property declined from 91 million to 82 million hectares, while ejidal and communal land increased from 70 to 85 million hectares, of which 6 million were national and frontier lands (Zaragoza and Macías, 1980: 467). The planners' "agrarian horizon" was to include all underutilized lands. Fearing expropriation and perturbed by excessive state regulation, many private farmers shelved expansion plans and reallocated their capital, often abroad.

In particular, the ejidal collectivization movement gained momentum on a level unparalleled since Cárdenas, because of the perceived advantages of economies of scale, ease of mechanization and coordinated planning, and the elimination of the parasitic *comprador* (merchant middleman). Certainly the new collectives, together with credit societies formed on individual ejidos for commercial crop production (which constituted de facto collectives), seemed to offer the most efficient mechanism for the management of resource inputs, human and other. Cooperative labor and specialization were encouraged, while dependence on official institutions for credit, technical assistance, and physical infrastructure intensified. The greater the degree of modernization attempted, the more directly government supervision replaced local decision making. Credit, especially, became a tool for manipulating the campesinos as they became increasingly part of the agrarian bureaucracy. Everything was supposed to go according to plan on orders from outside, even though effective farming requires on-the-scene responsiveness rather than faithful adherence to a script. Consequently, collective ejidos since 1970 have exhibited characteristics of what Singelmann (1978) has termed "controlled collectives," in which peasants effectively "sell" their labor to an enterprise that is only nominally theirs in that a credit bank or some other sponsoring agency essentially takes over the organization of production.

On the whole, the results of these efforts to modernize the ejidal sector through collectivization have been disappointing.[12] Expenses are often so great in relation to output that, given the subsidies involved, the result is de facto deficit production. For the majority of the peasants involved, the large debts incurred via relatively short-term loans for acquisition of capital goods mean that substantial crop and livestock dividends rarely reach their hands. Instead, they subsist on *diarios* (cash advances) paid by the bank out of the total credit package for daily labor on their own lands. Furthermore, most collectives have not in fact expanded legitimate peasant employment opportunities, as the number of labor-man-days available rarely exceeds those on individual ejidos. The problem of rural underemployment persists, and only the more enterprising ejidatarios become relatively well-off through their own initiatives—independently producing nonofficial crops beyond the control of the bank, hiring out as farm laborers during the slack season, starting small businesses, and performing nonagricultural work often using skills acquired in the collective experience such as heavy-machine operation—sometimes to the point of becoming absentee farmers in violation of the agrarian code.[13] Others, especially among the leadership, become wealthy at the expense of their peers through graft and corruption. The main beneficiaries, however, are outside the peasant sector—the merchant middlemen, the distributors of fertilizer, farm machinery, and other new agricultural inputs, purchasing agencies and processing industries, together with the government officials, independent brokers, and large landowners, who are in a prime position to benefit in both the formal and underground economies from the numerous opportunities for personal enrichment offered by rural developments on this scale.

Thus the most "successful" collective ejidos tend to be those in which proletarianization is most advanced and the peasants have opportunities to develop a variety of adaptive strategies to increasing market participation. In those cases, the ejido is usually heavily involved in agribusiness subject to the imperatives of national and international capital. Plan Chontalpa, a large-scale integrated river-basin development initiated in 1966 in the state of Tabasco, and the Edzná agricultural and resettlement zone, which began operations in Campeche seven years later, are prime examples of this complex symbiosis between state capitalism and the peasantry on collective ejidos. In both cases, economic "success" is marked by almost total dedication to cash crop production and cattle rearing, although some members continue to practice traditional cultivation on the side because of the limited returns from inefficient project activities. Internal economic differentiation among project participants has become sharply accentuated, with new classes of rich, middle, and poor peasants emerging as people respond differently to the various opportunities and constraints consequent on increasing involvement with the capitalist sector. Those who work regularly outside the projects or have developed independent business activities may acquire color television sets, stereos, freezers, and pickup trucks. Others become full-time peasant politicians. For the majority of simple farmers who rely solely on the projects to survive, life-styles are little different from those of the traditional peasantry; unless one is a friend or relative of the current ejidal leadership there is no year-round steady work in the projects. Charges of corruption abound, involving government officials and outside merchants as well as ejidal officers.

Daily work is available during the cash crop season but only for a limited period because of the high degree of mechanization. Consequently, many ejidatarios prefer to fulfil their collective obligations by hiring cheap labor from peasant communities outside the projects. Meanwhile, they wait to be paid their profit dividends, being, paradoxically, at the same time landlords who lease their lands to the government sugar mill (in the case of the Chontalpa) or to the rice mill (in Campeche), *patrones* (employers) who hire *peones* (day laborers), and underpaid workers in their own enterprises. As one Chontalpa ejidatario put it: "We are still in chains to the government, even more so than before, sitting around waiting for our pay" (I-116, poblado 28, Plan Chontalpa, November 1981). An ejidatario from the Edzná project was even more blunt: "Here there is a real chance for the ambitious campesinos to rise to the top by standing on the backs of the others" (I-61, Bonfil, October 1985).

The modernized subsistence sector created by this government intervention in the ejido has been a convenient mechanism for visibly dispensing welfare—housing, education, health, and related programs in rural areas, but the extent to which these measures constitute a real increase in social justice is debatable. All too often, new collective ejido programs fall into what might be called *proyectismo* or "project fever," characterized by a preoccupation with physical infrastructure, expressed in an excessively eager compulsion to proliferate large-scale costly developments serving primarily as a monument to the developers (Gates and Gates, 1976). This phenomenon is expressed in an initial announcement of overambitious goals followed by a succession of expensive errors, declining official interest, and eventual neglect or abandonment of the project. Then government enthusiasm turns to the next grandiose scheme, not heeding the lessons of past mistakes, while the peasants are left to go on as best they can.

Petrolization and Global Planning

By the time President López Portillo assumed office in 1976, the "Mexican miracle" seemed to have evaporated in financial crisis. Echeverría's expensive reforms had left the nation with a huge deficit that was compounded by the 1974 recession and the petroleum price increase as import costs rose (Mexico was still importing some petroleum products at that time) and export earnings and tourist revenues declined. The adverse shift in the terms of trade had had a devastating effect on Mexico's balance of payments. The deficit had tripled between 1972 and 1975 while external public debt had quadrupled (Street, 1981). There was massive capital flight in anticipation of López Portillo's 42 percent devaluation of the previously stable and overvalued peso in 1976, followed by unprecedented inflation (*Economist*, 5 September 1987).

In the agricultural sector, the previously positive balance of trade attributable to commercial agricultural exports had become negative by 1974 because of increasing imports of maize, beans, and oil seeds. Maize imports rose from 2.2 percent of production in 1972 to 31.1 percent in 1975 (Barkin and Suárez, 1982) with no radical change in consumption (Centro de Investigaciones Agrarias, 1980). The failure of the Echeverría strategy to increase agricultural production significantly was evident. However, López Portillo was unable to come to grips immediately with the imperative of restructuring agricultural policy, because of the exigencies of managing Mexico's monetary problems and placating the World Bank and the IMF with respect to its already substantial foreign debt.

Meanwhile, vast oil discoveries in the southeastern states of Campeche, Tabasco, and Chiapas appeared to offer an eventual solution to Mexico's chronic problems. In 1976, the country's revenues from petroleum exports were modest, and in fact new discoveries made in the latter part of the Echeverría administration had been concealed for fear that the president would use them irresponsibly (Bizarro, 1981). By 1982, Petróleos Mexicanos (PEMEX, the state oil monopoly) was producing 2.5 million barrels per day of which about half were sold abroad, making Mexico fourth in the world in oil production capacity and fifth in proven oil and gas reserves. These reserves increased elevenfold to nearly 80 billion barrels from 1976 to 1982, with impressive estimates of additional, undeveloped potential (Rummerfield, 1984). Oil was to be Mexico's savior, fostering a climate of unbridled optimism and developmentalism that might deflect peasant and urban marginal discontent by translating oil revenues into better living standards, income, and employment opportunities, while accelerating industrial development, controlling inflation, and improving the balance of payments. The oil boom provided the foreign exchange to purchase massive food supplies from the United States, contributed important agricultural inputs such as fertilizers, and appeared to buy the government time to devise longer-term solutions to the agricultural crisis (Bailey, 1981).

Oil exploitation has, however, proven to be a mixed blessing for many nations because of the danger of "petrolization" of the economy, with concomitant growth in capital and luxury imports, increased foreign indebtedness as a result of the attractiveness of oil wealth to foreign bankers, inflation, and a skewed income distribution (Grayson, 1981). In agriculture, petrolization

> implies the avoidance of difficult reforms and the continued reliance on exports to buy food from abroad and to subsidize agricultural processing, production, and consumption at home. This is the grim lesson of Venezuela, with its increasingly serious lag in agricultural production. Above all, the oil boom heightens expectations about actually resolving age-old problems of want and injustice. Failure in face of hopes aroused is doubly serious. (Bailey, 1981: 358–59)

Unfortunately, many of these negative side effects of dependence on oil exploitation were already problems for the Mexican economy, and, having inherited the Echeverría debt, López Portillo had little choice but to "petrolize" the economy (Fig. 2.2).

By 1981, oil provided three-quarters of export earnings and nearly one-third of government revenues (Grayson, 1981). Petrodollars, together with large supplementary foreign loans, were used to purchase oil and steel industry equipment and technological inputs from abroad to continue expansion of PEMEX operations in the hope that Mexico's oil export

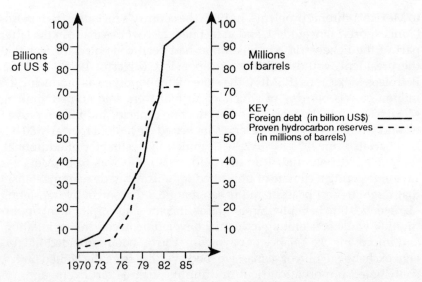

FIGURE 2.2   Petrolization and the Mexican debt crisis (SOURCES: IMF, PEMEX)

capacity could be used to alleviate recession and restore economic growth. Oil export earnings were also used to finance the continued food imports, which rose to all-time high levels in 1980 following the 1978 cold spell and the disastrous 1979 drought.[14] Only a relatively small proportion of the oil-based foreign exchange earnings were used for productive investments generating income and employment, such as new refineries and agricultural developments. Meanwhile, over the six years of López Portillo's term, public- and private-sector borrowing abroad reached $60 billion.[15]

Internally, economic conditions became increasingly chaotic as inflation spiraled, unemployment worsened, and public spending mushroomed. The presence of oil had permitted an economy that was foundering in the mid-1970s to show an annual growth in the gross national product (GNP) of more than 7 percent by 1980 (Grayson, 1981: 379). However, living conditions had not improved overall and the peasant condition had actually deteriorated, while corrupt elements in the public sector, such as in PEMEX, appropriated a lion's share of the spoils. Something had to be done to promote wiser use of energy resources and channel petroleum revenues more productively in order to spur domestic agricultural and industrial development and alleviate social ills.

The Plan Global de Desarrollo 1980–1982 (Global Development Plan) represented an ambitious attempt to put oil wealth to work for all sectors of the public by means of an integrated set of programs for industrial, agricultural, rural, educational, and infrastructural development. It was impressive in its comprehensiveness and pinpointing of strategic development needs, though obviously unrealistic in its time frame. In agriculture it emphasized productivity and exports, giving priority to restoring self-sufficiency in basic food production while providing social assistance to the rural poor.

The Sistema Alimentario Mexicano (the Mexican Food System—SAM) was set up as a comprehensive approach to regaining self-sufficiency in staples and thus reducing imports; it aimed at a balance between production and welfare considerations by focusing on previously neglected regions. The goal was self-sufficiency in maize and bean production by 1982 and in rice, wheat, soybeans, and sorghum by 1985. Peasant nutrition and income levels were to be improved along with productive efficiency. Departing from tradition, the SAM emphasized rain-fed areas, underutilized lands, and production for the domestic rather than the export market. Ejidatarios and smallholders were encouraged to avoid the temptations of more lucrative cash crops and concentrate on staples by sizable increases in the credit available from the Banco Nacional de Crédito Rural (the National Rural Credit Bank—BANRURAL) and substantial increments in government-guaranteed prices, and by a new policy of "shared risk" whereby the government would compensate campesinos in rain-fed areas for a portion of the profits lost through a failed crop instead of merely covering credit input costs as before. In collaboration with the Coordinación General del Plan Nacional de Zonas Deprimidas y Grupos Marginados (the Coordinating Commission for Marginal Areas—COPLAMAR), the Compañia Nacional de Subsistencias Populares (the National Basic Foods Company—CONASUPO) was to play a key role in creating incentives for basic food production by expanding availability of subsidized foods in the most depressed zones, increasing supplies to processing industries, and providing a technological package of seeds, agrochemicals, and commercialization services to campesinos with production and sales contracts (Barkin and Suárez, 1982). Massive resources were allocated to the SAM, and investment in the COPLAMAR component was scheduled to increase to $4 billion between 1979 and 1982, representing the first direct injection of significant oil revenues into the most needy sector and, indeed, rural spending on a scale unparalleled in Mexican history (Street, 1981).

The SAM was billed as a renewal of the revolutionary alliance between state and campesino wherein the former would serve as "guide, nurturer and promoter . . . in developing an improved form of campesino organization for generating more dynamic production" (*Plan Global de Desarrollo 1980–1982*, 1980: 287). Despite this grandiose rhetoric, essentially it was little more than a system of subsidies to production, agribusiness, and consumption aimed at expanding rural employment and purchasing power through a concentrated attack on poverty. It can also be seen, however, as a nationalistic reaction to the increasingly direct equation between U.S. grains and Mexican petroleum—part of a broad campaign to reduce vulnerability to pressures from international capital. As Wessman (1984) has pointed out, the choice of acronym is itself significant with reference to Mexico's attempts to regain basic food self-sufficiency at a time when "food power" and U.S. hegemony were virtually synonymous.

The development strategy implied by the SAM required critical changes in the federal agrarian reform law, and these were elaborated in the Agricultural and Livestock Production Promotion Law passed by Congress in December 1980 after unprecedented debate and opposition (Bailey, 1981). The new law was officially proclaimed merely as a codification of the SAM, but whereas the SAM ostensibly sought a balance between productivity and social justice it was explicitly geared to increasing agricultural production, emphasizing the precedence of public interest in self-sufficiency over private advantage.

The 1980 law substantially increased direct state involvement in farming, legitimating and expanding existing activities. Specifically, the key ministry, the Secretaría de Agricultura y Recursos Hidráulicos (the Ministry of Agriculture and Water Resources—SARH) was given the ultimate authority in setting national and local production goals and in recommending expropriation of underutilized lands for reallocation to ejidos or other groups for productive use with subsidized credit and other state supports. In practice, this meant that SARH, together with BANRURAL, controlled agriculture in the production zones down to the level of who grew what in which field for how much money—a difficult if not impossible task. In an attempt to reduce the obvious potential for corruption, the law contained nominal sanctions against officials failing to denounce owners of expropriable lands and more substantial fines for uncooperative landlords. It also set out to avoid atomization of minifundia by declaring subdivision illegal and promoting consolidation of units where possible.

The most controversial article of the law provided for the formation of "production units" in which ejidos were encouraged to associate with landowners or other ejidos for agriculture and cattle production under SARH supervision, with privileged access to credit, mechanization, and other modern technical inputs and "shared risk" insurance coverage in rain-fed areas. In this way, the law effectively established another land-tenure category combining private and public property, supposedly without alienating either but marking a remarkable departure from agrarian reform tradition. In response to concerns that the opening up of the ejido to private investment would threaten its cherished inviolability, the government contended that this measure merely regularized existing coalitions between ejidos and private enterprise and that it contained effective provisions for protecting ejidatarios from exploitation (Bailey, 1981). Opponents argued that ejidatarios would have to further subordinate their interests to those of commercial farmers in the push for the recapitalization of staple production. Furthermore, there was considerable skepticism as to the ability of SARH to assume such a critical role in planning and administering production and reshaping the land-tenure map in view of that ministry's record of inefficient *proyectismo*. Utilization of cattle lands was another contentious area of the law, as ranchers were permitted for the first time to improve sizable portions of their holdings for growing forage crops for their own herds and for regulated sale without being subject to expropriation. Although the government's intent was to stimulate domestic production, decrease imports, and reduce the pressure of competition on staple cropland, critics predicted a return to large private estates and the further internationalization of the economy (Bailey, 1981).

While the SAM was a limited-term strategy for increasing productivity within a popular framework, the agricultural promotion law was overtly pro-production, emphasizing capital-intensive and modern technological solutions to the agricultural crisis. It was essentially a pragmatic rather than an idealistic approach to a chronic problem, and as a law rather than an interim system it was likely to have a more profound effect on agrarian structure. Agricultural policy had developed a nationalistic insistence on the basic food production imperative no matter what was required to achieve it (Wessman, 1984). On a quantitative level, the SAM initially made rapid progress toward self-sufficiency in basic foods. It appeared that maize and bean targets had been met in 1981, a year earlier than projected, but in January 1982 it was announced that the 1981 record bean crop was so high in moisture content that it fell below the minimum nutrition standards for consumers, while part of the bumper maize harvest was contaminated by unidentified toxins. The proclamation of self-sufficiency was the result of a "prematurely triumphant spirit" (*Tribuna de Campeche*, 26 January 1982). CONASUPO refused to buy any more beans from the 1981 crop, leaving the campesinos to find less profitable outlets with no mention of "shared risk." It was officially acknowledged that while productivity increases were generally impressive, insufficient progress had been made in organizing and strengthening the rural social sector.

Meanwhile, the campesinos generally reacted to the SAM with their usual skepticism about new government initiatives, complaining about the state's use of coercion to condemn them to continuing poverty by confining support systems to low-value staples. In practice, it appeared that a significant portion of the SAM subsidies were captured by the more advantaged farmers, including well-organized peasants and large export-oriented growers, who saw the chance of making a quick profit from staple production incentives (Grindle, 1985). Thus, it seems likely that much of the SAM's initial success was due to the participation of farmers outside the primary target group of small peasants, with the result that existing inequalities in the agricultural sector, both between commercial and subsistence operations and among subsistence producers, were reinforced. Furthermore, the emphasis on drought-prone rain-fed agriculture for subsistence crop production, even with substantial World Bank support involving a $280 million loan from 1983 to 1985, raised doubts as to whether self-sufficiency could be maintained even if achieved (Walsh, 1983). As Bailey (1981: 392) points out, "SARH [the Secretaría de Agricultura y Recursos Hidráulicos] can mulch every plant in the nation with 1,000 peso notes, but unless the rains are sufficient and timely, self-sufficiency will be unsustainable."

Agriculture Under Austerity: Opening Up the Ejido

The de la Madrid Administration: Dealing with the Debt Crisis

The 1981 oil glut and the subsequent revelation of the full magnitude of the debt crisis in 1982 and the ensuing economic restraint meant that Mexico would be unable to continue spending at the level considered necessary to maintain wide-ranging programs such as the SAM, which was scrapped shortly after Miguel de la Madrid assumed office. Under his administration (1982–1988) Mexico made considerable progress in recovery from the immediate strictures of the debt crisis as a result of drastic cuts in public expenditures and the government's willingness to yield to external pressure for trade liberalization and to initiate innovative debt-restructuring strategies. This external pragmatism was not, however, translated into effective tactics for reducing the massive internal debt and spurring growth in stagnant domestic production. The people continued to pay a heavy price for their government's relative success in renegotiating the external debt and containing inflation.

The impact of inflation, public-sector cutbacks, reduction of subsidies, and government austerity measures such as wage and price controls has been particularly severe for those on the margins of the cash economy such as the majority of campesinos. However, these effects tended to be muted during the early years of the crisis; agriculture performed somewhat better than the weakened economy at large from 1982 through 1986, in part because of improved exchange rates for agricultural exports, favorable weather, and a small increase in government-guaranteed prices for staples. An additional factor in this temporary upswing was increased direct government intervention in staple cultivation on the production units made possible by the 1980 agrarian reform legislation.

The intent of this legislation had been to stimulate the establishment of joint ventures between the private sector and ejidatarios. The onset of the debt crisis eliminated any possibility of enticing significant spontaneous reinvestment of private monies in agriculture, the few entrepreneurs who had risked investments involving the ejido having been quickly driven out of business by the devalued peso (particularly if they owed money in dollars). Instead, the production units became essentially state-managed farms on ejidos or on the lands of small property owners associated in collectives for credit purposes, both of which received the lion's share of the now-limited public resources available at the expense of subsistence-level peasants and independent private property owners. These farms were integrated into the national supply system under implicit regional production quotas, while collective ejidatarios and other underemployed rural laborers served as low-cost manpower with no input into decision making and minimal income gains. Many of the units involve land in the raw, requiring expensive clearing, leveling, drainage, and irrigation improvements together with large-scale mechanization. Resource-base abuses such as the mining of ground water where recharge is inadequate and the rapid deterioration or salinization of tropical soils are common. The payout for these projects will be only on a long-term basis, especially since many of the crops are extensively cultivated and the farming systems have not been tested in these harsh environments. Under this strategy, productivity gains were made only at great expense and without a noticeable increase in economic efficiency.

By the mid-1980s the relatively strong performance of the agricultural sector under austerity had proved illusory. Attempts to increase production foundered in a sea of debt because of drastic increases in production costs, soaring interest rates, continued low official purchase prices for staples, and the long-term downward trend in world market prices.[16] De facto deficit production had become the norm in many state-directed agricultural projects over a decade earlier as massive government investments had turned out to be expensive mistakes. With the debt crisis, many ejidatarios in these inefficient projects fell into default, unable to repay their high-cost loans. In this climate, corruption flourished under what has become widely known as the industry of disasters. Unscrupulous members of the agrarian bureaucracy, in particular from BANRURAL and the Aseguradora Nacional de Agricultura y Ganadería (the National Agency for Agricultural and Livestock Insurance—ANAGSA), acting alone or in collusion with ejidal authorities, initiated elaborate schemes to defraud government agencies. Frequently these swindles involved arranging credit and insurance for fictitious operations or obtaining compensation for actual crops declared a *siniestro total* (total loss) when in fact the majority was harvestable. For many ejidatarios at marginal levels of production, the latter deception has become the only way to avoid repeated default and consequent ineligibility for credit. Furthermore, many peasants feel that they are entitled to credit and other subsidies, irrespective of the harvest outcome, as ejidatarios promised social justice under the 1917 Constitution and still awaiting payment in full. As a consequence, an ethos of institutionalized failure has developed wherein deficit and debt have become the norm and deceit the only reliable economic strategy. Such a mentality, once established, is hard to alter and obviously militates against the success of future developments.

These problems have been compounded by extensive cutbacks in the agrarian bureaucracy after years of unchecked state growth. In the Ministry of Agriculture and Water Resources (SARH), the lead agency in the agricultural development sector, the majority of affected jobs involve middle-and lower-level administrative, secretarial, technical, and support staff. In addition to generalized restraint, austerity budgets resulted in the immediate elimination of many projects and programs, including the closure of key research institutes such as the Instituto Nacional de Investigaciones de Recursos Bióticos (the National Research Institute for Biotic Resources). As a consequence, many development agents now lack the resources or the motivation to supervise the remaining field activities, and much of the already inefficient agricultural, distribution, and transportation infrastructure has deteriorated to the point that an estimated 30 percent of harvests fails to reach the consumer (*Excelsior,* 3 March 1988). Meanwhile, for many ejidatarios, accustomed to the constant influx of new government funds to compensate for the failure of past development strategies, the abrupt withdrawal of official supports acted as a major disincentive to production in an already unprofitable and inefficient system.

By 1988, agriculture was widely acknowledged to be in chaos, in sharp contrast to the impressive recovery of the national economy overall, as the gross value of production fell by 3.2 percent to the lowest value in a decade (*El Financiero,* 4 April 1989). The crisis was particularly severe in the staple food sector as a result of a prolonged drought throughout much of the country, compounding the long-term relative debasement of government-guaranteed prices for such crops[17] and soaring agricultural input costs under inflation. The dream of restoring self-sufficiency became increasingly remote with each disastrous crop cycle. Imports of basic foods rose from 8.5 million tons in 1981 to 10 million tons in 1988 (*Excelsior,* 11 April 1989), and the population grew by some 7 million.[18] Meanwhile, international market prices of key agricultural imports such as maize rose also, tying up public-sector funds that otherwise could have been employed in social programs or invested in economic infrastructure and other sectors neglected since the onset of the crisis.

The deepening of the agricultural crisis between 1986 and 1988 reflected the low priority given to the sector by the de la Madrid administration, which was preoccupied initially with renegotiation of Mexico's vast external debt and implementation of domestic austerity measures. In midterm, its reform horizons broadened as it became clear that the logic of restructuring required the abandonment of petroleum dependence and an opening to foreign trade.[19] The pace of economic liberalization, gradual at first, accelerated after Mexico entered GATT in 1986, but these initiatives had little immediate effect. Inflation rose, the economy continued to stagnate, and the internal debt burgeoned to 15.6 percent of GDP despite extensive efforts to cut government costs (for example, through the sale of inefficient state enterprises). In response to these worsening conditions, the de la Madrid administration introduced a comprehensive anti-inflationary program. Its 1987 Pacto de Solidaridad Económica succeeded in reducing inflation to 52 percent by the end of 1988, but economic activity remained weak; real GDP grew by only 1.1 percent in 1988, despite increased private-sector investment activity, and consumption rose by less than 1 percent in real terms (*IMF Survey*, 10 July 1989).

The Salinas Administration: Modernization, Restructuring, and "Solidarity"

In the midst of this struggle to attain a balance between short-term measures to contain inflation and initiatives to stimulate economic growth (which tend to act at cross-purposes), Salinas, who had been de la Madrid's budget minister, took over the presidency in 1988. Even though the successor is hand-picked by his predecessor, such political transitions tend to be characterized by abrupt discontinuities in policies and programs, largely because of the enormous personal authority vested in the chief executive office and the desire of each incoming president to place an individual stamp on the *sexenio* (six-year term). No such hiatus took place this particular transition as a result of the fiscal exigency and because both individuals belonged to the new breed of *técnicos* (technicians), foreign-educated professionals adept at economic management, rather than being old-style politicians preoccupied with orchestrating the traditional worker and peasant alliances with the state. Consequently, continuity became the hallmark of the Salinas regime.

Differences in presidential style did, however, become apparent. Whereas de la Madrid administration had been cautious, reform under Salinas was bold and rapid. De la Madrid had talked about moral renovation, but Salinas embarked upon on a tough and comprehensive anti-corruption campaign that resulted in the apprehension of the leaders of two of Mexico's strongest unions, a drug czar, a top financier, and other significant public figures, often political allies. De la Madrid had held state agencies to austerity budgets, Salinas trimmed the government fat to the bone in many sectors, introduced significant state decentralization, streamlined economic procedures via extensive deregulation and tax reform, and initiated a privatization effort resulting in the sale or closure of more than four hundred public enterprises.

Rapid and comprehensive measures to continue the economic opening via relaxation in the foreign investment law and tariff reduction became an overall program of national economic and political modernization explicitly designed to "strengthen [Mexico] in the global context and improve coexistence among Mexicans . . . to generate employment and opportunities for all . . . to forge a more just, more generous, more valuable society for each one of us, more respected in the world" (Salinas de Gortari, 1990: 1, my translation). In the political domain, Salinas envisioned a "democracy consubstantial with the economic modernization of our country . . . a public service which serves rather than being served by power . . . a new political culture." At the same time, the de facto return in August 1991 to a one-party state has permitted him to propel Mexico rapidly toward a free market economy and the negotiation of a free trade agreement with the United States and Canada. Most tariffs have already been cut extensively[20] and therefore a hemispheric free trade agreement at this point has little to do with trade per se. Rather, it concerns the attraction of the foreign investment desperately needed to create new jobs for the ever-increasing numbers of unemployed and underemployed (*Economist*, 6 October 1990), reaching, by some estimates, over 50 percent of the active work force in the 1980s as 1 million new workers entered the labor market each year (Ostler, 1989).

Another high-profile area during the first eighteen months of the Salinas administration was the further renegotiation of the foreign debt under the Brady Plan.[21] This March 1990 agreement cut Mexico's debt-service payments by $4 billion a year. Although less than was anticipated originally, it has been sufficient to boost private-sector and foreign investor confidence in the economy and bring interest rates down to their lowest level since 1981.[22] Most important, the savings, together with rising oil prices, appear to have given Salinas the impetus to devote attention to Mexico's chronic social problems and to devise specific initiatives to promote the recapitalization of agriculture, the Achilles heel of the Mexican economy.

In the agricultural sector, between 1982 and 1988 public sector investment fell by more than two-thirds in real terms. At the same time, official guaranteed prices for staple crops dropped 49 percent against the agricultural input cost index (Calva, 1988), reflecting the government's ongoing urban bias as arbitrarily cheapened foods were used as an anti-inflationary device (Gordillo de Anda, 1990; Tellez Kuenzler, 1990). Ejidatarios growing staples at a marginal level of production were overwhelmed by rising credit rates, particularly after the initiation of wage and price controls in 1987. At the same time, the combination of inflationary pressures, the crop pricing policy, and reduced government incentives provoked an accelerating outflow of private-sector capital from agriculture. All in all, structural adjustment measures under austerity exhibited a definite antiagrarian slant.

Efforts of President Salinas to promote economic dynamism in agriculture were initially directed at eradicating corruption and improving the efficiency of the agricultural development agencies. Late in 1989 it was announced that BANRURAL would cease to employ field inspectors, who had been in a prime position to initiate insurance and other frauds. At the same time, ANAGSA was abolished and replaced by a new agricultural insurance company, a parastatal affiliate of the Aseguradora Mexicana, which will operate with only one-third of the personnel and no field inspectors. Although this cleanup campaign has uncovered hundreds of major frauds at all levels, petty swindles appear to have increased in the latest phase of the debt crisis, largely in response to a decline in real wages to little more than a half of 1982 levels. With average salaries of less than $300 a month, agrarian bureaucrats often feel compelled, at the very least, to cheat on their gasoline allowances, to extort boxes of produce from the ejidatarios and to rob their employers of time by padding their work sheets. As one government employee put it:

> As long as the government pays the bureaucracy like janitors and keeps the price of basic crops down to an absurd level, people working in agriculture will have to find ways to look after themselves. Salinas can't stamp out a necessary part of our income, especially when the government, the party, everybody is doing the same thing. (I-131, civil servant, Campeche, February 1990)

Anticorruption measures were paralleled by a major restructuring of BANRURAL, which is to become a normal banking institution after two decades of paternalistically supervising deficit production and will now grant credit only to crops, regions, and producers that virtually guarantee an adequate return to investment. Thus the majority of peasants will be excluded from these supports in future. To reduce this delinquency and provide increased production incentives, BANRURAL interest rates were slashed 15.75 percentage points to 28 percent in 1990.

The formal agricultural strategy of the Salinas administration has been articulated piecemeal in the second and third years of its term, but the emphasis is clearly on the recapitalization of agriculture via a more flexible, balanced, and heterogeneous development model attuned to the differential needs of various types of producers, crops, and regions. This will involve deregulation and disaggregation of the preexisting policies with regard to pricing, incentives, subsidies, credit, insurance, investment, technical assistance, organization, and training. Important elements in this strategy include institutional and legislative reform, intensification of production through high technology, promotion of agribusiness in regional development corridors, restructuring, trimming, and decentralization of government development institutions, the liberation of most crops (except staples) from official price controls, and the creation of an agricultural commodities exchange. The intent is to open agriculture to the external market gradually and selectively, to extend the linkages between the peasant and commercial sectors, and to provide support programs for marginal producers with "productive content which will give them economic viability in the medium term, moving away from 'the administration of poverty' in any shape or form" (SARH, 1990: 1). Thus producer initiative and participation in policy generation is to be encouraged through dialogue as the state selectively withdraws from direct intervention in peasant agriculture. These goals are to be pursued by the various agrarian agencies, collaborating in committees comprised of representatives from all the institutions and interest groups involved including formal peasant organizations and ejidal delegates, operating at national, regional, and local levels.

While the new watchword *concertación* (working in harmony) sums up Salinas's style, the content of agrarian policy is dominated by the productivity imperative. This preoccupation with the restructuring of agriculture first and foremost as a business enterprise rather than a social category was reflected in the unexpected appointment of Carlos Hank González as minister of agriculture in December 1989. Hank had been a tough and efficient public-sector manager as Salinas's minister of tourism and previously as governor of the state of Mexico. In the past, Hank had made no secret of his conviction that the ejido was an anachronism that Mexico could no longer afford.

A core component of the recapitalization strategy is the Plan Nacional de Modernización del Campo 1990–1994, which gives additional impetus to associations between ejidatarios and the private sector. Such production units had been legalized in 1980, but few had been created as a result of the financial exigencies of the debt crisis and a continuing lack of clarity with respect to constraints imposed by the corporate ejidal system, wherein usufruct tenure officially prohibits alienation of land. Under the new "alliances for production," contracts between ejidos and private investors can be very flexible, permitting ejidatarios to receive income from the outright rental of lands, from wage labor on the agribusiness enterprise, and from profit dividends. These kinds of arrangements are not new, having been the norm (though technically illegal) for U.S. agribusinesses operating on ejidal lands in the north since 1950 as well as in the government's own large-scale agricultural projects in the 1960s and 1970s, but they can now be engaged in by any portion of the ejidal sector that can attract private capital. The new system also calls for a greater degree of production responsibility on the part of ejidatarios, with the aim of fostering a business ethos in that sector as well as encouraging domestic in addition to international investment. Within a few months of announcement of the initiative, several major Mexican agribusinesses signed contracts with ejidos. Gamesa, a corporation mainly concerned with food processing, in June 1990 formed the first such association, the Vaquerías project in the state of Nuevo León, to produce beans collectively on twenty-five hundred hectares of irrigable land, funded equally by the enterprise and the government.[23] Later that year, the company was acquired by Pepsico.

Although agricultural policy has been oriented toward promoting productivity, profitability, and recapitalization, increased producer responsibility has been a recurrent theme underlying the reforms. This motif has come to the fore in a dramatic new program, the Programa Nacional de Solidaridad (the National Solidarity Program—PRONASOL), announced in 1990 to channel resources toward alleviating poverty and stimulating productivity among the most disadvantaged, both rural and urban. Four general principles guide PRONASOL: community initiative, popular participation and organization, shared responsibility, and "transparency, honesty, and efficiency in the management of the resources" (Salinas de Gortari, 1990: 6, my translation). The intention is to stimulate self-sustaining economic and social dynamism by demonstrating the concern of the state with the needs of the people through funding for specific productive and welfare initiatives. In many respects, PRONASOL seems to represent Salinas's personal agenda for promoting the nation's social as well as economic recovery, which evolved from specific requests and suggestions made to the president during the course of his official visits to communities all over the country. The approximately fifty thousand activities undertaken in the first phase of the program included construction of 516 clinics and hospitals, electrification of 3,500 rural communities and urban squatter settlements, provision of drinking water and sewage systems to 1,600 settlements, distribution of 350,000 land titles (equivalent to the number extended over the past fifteen years), initiation of 1,256 rural road projects, and delivery of 45,000 low-cost housing units. It is estimated that 10 million Mexicans have benefited in this initial phase (Salinas de Gortari, 1990).

In agriculture, under the new slogans of *Confianza y esfuerzo proprio* (Confidence and one's own effort) and *Pagar es corresponder* (To pay is to reciprocate) (Gobierno Constitucional del Estado de Campeche, 1990), the Fondo de Solidaridad para la Producción has supported more than four hundred thousand peasants in 1,350 municipalities. The program is intended to benefit peasants who cultivate lands of low productivity in high-risk zones, who are no longer eligible for BANRURAL credit, and are not in default to the bank through personal delinquency at the time of application. Under PRONASOL, individual peasants can receive interest-free credit for up to four hectares of crops, at 300,000 pesos a hectare (a total of $451)[24], requiring no guarantees other than the promise of the producer: *Palabra ofrecida, palabra cumplida* (Word offered, word kept) (Salinas de Gortari, 1990: 7). The program is managed autonomously by local-level committees and campesinos receive credit directly from the municipal government. Additional incentives for loan repayment are that the funds collected will be allocated to "works of social benefit" at the discretion of each municipality and that lists of defaulters will be published locally at the end of the agricultural cycle (Gobierno Constitucional del Estado de Campeche, 1990).

PRONASOL marks a radical departure in its degree of decentralization and interagency consultation, its emphasis on agent-producer collaboration rather than old-style paternalism, and its focus on individual rather than collective liability for debt, which had been the foundation of the official bank credit system and the cause of much default. Furthermore, the campesinos who receive PRONASOL funds are not compelled to grow a particular crop or employ a stipulated technical packet of agricultural inputs. Rather, the program aims "to stimulate incursion into new activities which recognize the experience of the campesinos" and to help break "the vicious circle that has linked agricultural credit to disaster and default, while promoting corruption, deception, and paternalism" (Salinas de Gortari, 1990: 7, my translation). This bold move underscores the government's commitment both to increasing productivity without the chronic waste and diversion of funds endemic to past such attempts and to promoting individual responsibility and an ethos of success within the constraints of the ejidal system. It is still too early, however, to judge whether PRONASOL will succeed on either count on a sustained basis in view of the depth of the agricultural crisis.

Critics of PRONASOL, including many campesinos, see the program as little more than a typical populist attempt to boost flagging support for the PRI, and it is often referred to as *PRINASOL*. It does, however, differ in a potentially crucial way in that direct credit contracts established between the state and individual producers bypass the crumbling corporatist structures of the ejido and the Confederación Nacional Campesina that have integrated peasants into the PRI hierarchy as a co-opted class (Gerardo Otero, personal communication, May 1991). In addition, although PRONASOL is supposed to be supported by new funds, there is suspicion that in fact monies that would have been allocated to public works in any event will be recirculated via this fresh route, with the same likelihood as before of loss due to default and corrupt appropriation. From this perspective, the program appears to be designed to provide jobs for bureaucrats while offering yet another placebo to the disadvantaged and disaffected. Despite official assertions that PRONASOL is neither a charity nor a subsidy, the government seems to be falling back on its traditional paternalism, albeit with fewer strings, a more explicit focus on efficiency, and a lot more time spent in meetings in the name of producer participation and agency collaboration. For skeptics, it will take much more than one program, even if successful, to give the government any real credibility:

> The government has given us no reason to be convinced that "modernization" and "solidarity" are anything more than the usual empty slogans to buy our silence. Social solidarity has never existed in Mexico: history shows that is the case. Who are we supposed to have "solidarity" with? The government? Why should we? Each other? How can we? The party has made sure that we are divided in our misery so that there is no "we." (I-62, ejidatario, Bonfil, March 1990)

In a structural sense, the terms of reference of PRONASOL's agricultural activities seem likely to harden the boundary between peasants with possibilities for commercial agriculture and those relegated to subsistence production on a permanent basis. Officially, PRONASOL loans are not tied to basic crops, but, in view of the continuing government emphasis on promoting staple production, the lack of real alternatives in most regions, the high cost of fertilizer and other agricultural inputs, and the greatly reduced allocation of funds per hectare compared with official bank credit, most campesinos will have no option but to continue to grow them. Consequently, even with interest-free loans and slight increases in guaranteed rates, profits will be strictly limited as long as staple crop prices remain debased.

Thus, the overall implication of PRONASOL together with the restructuring of BANRURAL and the renewed encouragement of "alliances for production" appears to be the repeasantization of those who have failed to perform under previous misguided government strategies for modernizing ejidal agriculture. The majority of peasants will be eligible, at best, for incentive programs likely to recreate household subsistence units with little or no economic surplus through a return to reliance largely on low-value staples cultivated via traditional practices. At the same time, the few ejidatarios possessing good production records with priority crops in high-yield regions are to become full-fledged, high-technology farmers for whom agriculture will be a business rather than a marginal way of life, in collaboration with the state via the bank credit mechanism or the private sector by means of contracts. The government maintains that this opening up of the ejido constitutes neither a license for private enterprise to despoil the social sector nor a step toward the imminent dissolution of this previously sacrosanct land-tenure institution. Whether these favored campesinos will become truly independent competitive farmers or de facto rural proletarians remains to be seen. As far as PRONASOL is concerned, irrespective of whether it turns out to be genuine reform or populist palliative, the lamentable fact is that some such program is desperately needed at this time, in order to bring a degree at least of immediate relief to those millions of rural Mexicans who are sinking daily into deeper poverty. The swing back to the PRI in the August 1991 midterm elections has been credited in part to PRONASOL's success in targeting effective social welfare programs (*Economist*, 24 August 1991), even if many peasants remain skeptical of the social justice implications of its agricultural strategy.

The proposal of optional privatization of ejidal plots, submitted to Congress in November 1991 on this wave of popular support, has increased peasant misgivings about the long-term implications of the reoriented agricultural development strategy. The president of the PRI insists that "choice" is the operative word in this radical reform: "If they [ejidatarios] want to remain as members of the ejido commune, that would be fine. But if ejido members prefer to operate as a joint venture with a large company that can better exploit the farmland, so be it" (*Wall Street Journal*, 2 December 1991). This significant step toward outright privatization of the social property established by the revolution underscores the apparent end of the era of state tutelage over the ejido, and the government's determination to remove a principal obstacle to increased foreign investment in agriculture. It seems doubtful, however, how much "choice" ejidatarios in prime agricultural zones will have under pressure from agribusiness giants. At the same time, it is highly unlikely that any major investor, foreign or domestic, will be interested in "alliances for production" on the marginal lands of the majority of ejidos in southern Mexico, and here such traditional predators on the peasantry as rural bosses and merchant middlemen are likely to make a killing from sales of newly privatized parcels. Thus it appears that the quasi-privatization of the ejido will inevitably accelerate socioeconomic differentiation and proletarianization among the peasantry. For the heirs of Emiliano Zapata's battle for "land and liberty," the fruits of the revolution have been continuing subordination in a progression from the old *hacendados* (landlords) to the PRI *caciques* (local political bosses), and, more recently, the agricultural development bureaucracy. The future now seems to hold the "choice" of either accepting yet another set of masters, the CEOs of agribusiness, continuing the subsistence struggle on the most impoverished land without the benefits and costs of state paternalism, or abandoning farming altogether.

Repealing Marginality?

In evaluating agricultural policy since the revolution, Warman (1978) has distinguished between *política agrícola* and *política agraria*, the former implying a technocratic production orientation emphasizing mechanization and state-controlled modernization and the latter stressing the social function of land and redistribution to the landless. These two facets, both deriving from the 1917 Constitution, have interplayed in different ways at different times, each constraining the other. The outcome has been a highly distinctive relationship between the Mexican state and the countryside, particularly as expressed in policies affecting the ejido.

While política agrícola and política agraria have been regarded as flip sides of the same coin, in recent years the productivity orientation has become paramount, marked, until the consolidation of the debt crisis, by ever-increasing state intervention in the ejidal sector. The ejido has evolved from the initial revolutionary reform, which effectively tied peasant labor to land, through five decades of infrastructural neglect to the recent period of concerted modernization initiatives. This phase, lasting from 1970 to the early 1980s, when it ended abruptly under debt crisis austerity, was characterized by massive government intervention in peasant agriculture to stimulate basic food production via controlled collectivization, credit societies, large-scale development projects,[25] infrastructural investment, and a variety of incentive programs and subsidies. The cumulative effect of these agricultural policies has been the progressive loss of peasant production autonomy, the consolidation of the ejido at the base of the ruling party pyramid through the bureaucratization of agriculture right down to the grassroots level, and two decades of intensifying agricultural crisis. In particular, the effects on agriculture of the internationalization of the economy, including the increasing emphasis on exports, domestic agribusiness, and cattle rearing, have displaced basic foods production commercially and increased pressures on staple crop land. For ejidatarios, this has often meant either designation as cheap part-time labor for capital-intensive cash crop production or relegation to low-value staple-producer status. The outcome was the creation of a quasi-modernized sector of heavily subsidized, yet marginal peasants, wherein social justice has been redefined in terms of production tons instead of rights to land.

Despite its high cost-benefit ratio, government spending on agricultural modernization programs in the ejidal sector has served the interests of both the state and the private sector by keeping at least some peasants tied to otherwise infrasubsistence holdings. A pool of relatively stable and semiskilled cheap labor has been created for commercial agriculture that remains dependent on traditional subsistence activities because of the limited remuneration accruing from state projects and temporary wage work. In other words, a rural semiproletariat has been consolidated as the peasantry has been reshaped by the labor market in an evolving relationship of asymmetrical complementarity between commercial and peasant agriculture (Kearney, 1980).

From 1940 until 1970, this implicit subsidy of commercial agriculture by the peasantry was paralleled by a net transfer of value from the agricultural sector to industry through production of cheap food for urban areas where low wages could also be sustained. This direct transfer was reversed after 1970 with the injection of state funds and other agricultural supports, but the continued repression of crop prices and the inefficiencies and discontinuities of state programs have acted as a disincentive to both private and ejidal investment and fostered an ongoing outflow of resources from the countryside. This long-term rural decapitalization has been accentuated under debt-crisis austerity by the sharp reduction of government agricultural subsidies, while the official crop pricing policy became, once again, a device for masking inflation. The recent wage and price control pacts have underscored the state's implicit antiagrarian bias by excluding the majority of agricultural inputs from regulation.

At this juncture, the ongoing agricultural crisis, the continuing need for restraint in public-sector spending, and the rapid transition to a free market economy are transforming the previous modus vivendi between the state, the private sector, and the peasantry. Current overriding concerns with productivity are constrained by budgetary limitations. The 1980 legislation promoting agricultural and livestock production might be seen as laying the foundation for a new economic realism in agricultural policy, but it does not accommodate the legacy of concerns with the social function of land and the current political imperative of dealing with an ever-increasing marginal rural population.

The Salinas administration has placed an even greater stress on política agrícola, but with a major retreat from state intervention in peasant agriculture in keeping with the dramatic opening of the economy. Reform in agriculture is much more difficult, however, than in other sectors given the depth of the two-decade-old crisis, the extent and complexity of the structural imbalances, the existence of politically sensitive areas such as the ejido and food subsidies, and problems with reconciling comparative advantage in this sector both internally and externally. Mexicans at large have yet to enjoy the fruits of economic liberalization despite an economic growth rate of 4.8 percent in the first half of 1991, the highest figure in a decade (*Economist,* 24 August 1991). The peasantry in particular has seen little evidence so far that market forces per se will be directly equated with improved social conditions, especially given the uncompetitive position of much of Mexico's agricultural production in the world arena.

Consequently, the main agricultural question for the government at this time is whether, even if the nation can be returned to self-sufficiency in basic foods, the correlative processes that have impoverished the peasantry can be reversed. More specifically, since increasing state intervention has been one of the main causes of the agricultural crisis and the intensification and codification of peasant marginality, the question is whether the state is likely to be able to legislate or, rather, create through deregulation a productive base that is both economically viable and socially and politically just.

The administration seems confident that it can do so and has initiated a number of bold reforms, but the task of reestablishing economic dynamism in agriculture is enormous. The sector made an unexpected recovery in 1990, the best production year in more than a decade, possibly reducing by as much as 25 percent basic foods imports for 1991 (*Excelsior,* 12 October 1990). Yet this improvement appears to have been due as much to timely and abundant rains as to the impact of government reforms.[26] Furthermore, it will take much more than the mere fact of a free market economy and a handful of new programs to reverse the effects of fifty years of favoring the city over the countryside.

Despite recent populist overtones, the Salinas strategy for reversing the agricultural crisis appears to boil down to little more than continuing the reduction of agricultural supports and subsidies in most peasant sectors while increasing stimuli in the targeted most viable areas. It essentially amounts to economic triage—a purge of producers to spur production through free market competition and erase the legacy of the state-created industry of disasters with its endemic default and deceit. This in itself, however, constitutes a major reorientation of agricultural policy in terms of the curtailment of the paternalism toward the peasantry which has been the revolutionary legacy. The rapidity of the transition toward a free market and continental free trade, together with the changing role of the state from direct farmer and overseer of the peasantry to an "arm's length" approach to agriculture compel an accompanying modification in the forms of peasant production exemplified in the 1991 move toward private property rights to ejidal land.

So far it appears that the outcome is likely to be further socioeconomic differentiation of the already divided peasantry, militating against reversal of the ethos of failure for the majority, severely decapitalized in social as well as material terms. Specifically, the opening up of the ejido to associations with agribusiness seems destined to promote de facto proletarianization as ejidatarios become the servants of the private sector rather than wards of the state, probably enjoying more prosperity than before but still functioning as laborers on their own land for a new breed of masters. It is doubtful that programs such as PRONASOL for the most marginal peasants will be able to fortify low-value staple crop producers against the forces of international competition. Rather, contrary to the government's proclaimed intent, the net result of this type of individual incentive program appears, in the short term at least, to be the inadvertent repeasantization of a sizable segment of the ejidal sector. It will likely return those ejidatarios who had failed to perform adequately under state-directed agricultural modernization programs to household subsistence units producing little or no economic surplus. In the long term, given the uncertainties of staple production on the subsistence margins, it appears that this strategy will further accelerate proletarianization, whether or not free trade produces the promised increased employment opportunities and better wages. In the interim, some ejidatarios have been able to profit simply from the increased farming flexibility with respect to local conditions and opportunities permitted by the dwindling state presence. Nevertheless, from the peasant perspective overall, the winds of neoliberal change mean increased uncertainty and stress, as they wait to see if the new era of free market forces means life after debt via fulfillment of the government's constitutional commitment to improve their social condition or de facto abrogation of any state responsibility for their destiny:

> Agriculture today is like a waiting room, where we guess what will be the outcome of this sudden outburst of energy Salinas is turning on the countryside. This is quite a shock after years of tortoise-like bureaucracy. Is it real reform? We don't know. If it is, can he get away with it? And what will happen to Mexican peasants after the free trade tornado? (I-63, ejidatario, Bonfil, February 1990)

Notes

1. Part of this chapter originally appeared in somewhat different form in Gates (1988b), included by permission of the *Journal of Latin American Studies*.

2. Only 16 percent of Mexico's land (32 million hectares) is considered suitable for agriculture, and only 20 million hectares are currently under cultivation, with 18 million hectares actually harvested (Santos de Hoyos, 1990). Over half of Mexico's potential farmland is under ejidal tenure. In 1989, ejidos produced 67 percent of the nation's maize and beans, 36 percent of the wheat, 70 percent of the

rice and 35 percent of the sorghum. However, 65 percent of the nation's 28,000 ejidos are regarded as units of low productivity (SARH, 1990).

3. Collective ejidos were established in 1936 in the Laguna area of the north-central states of Durango and Coahuila in an extensive land reform intended to subdue rural unrest. Despite initial promise, the majority of these dissolved because of land and water shortages, credit allocations, internal factionalism, corruption, mismanagement, and political opposition to the collectivization principle after the end of the populist Cárdenas administration (see Eckstein, 1966; and Stavenhagen, 1975).

4. Economic growth in Mexico averaged 6 percent per annum during the period 1955–1970 (Bailey, 1981).

5. M. Pastor (1987) succinctly characterizes the import-substitution industrialization model as a strategy of encouraging domestic enterprises to assume the market for which there is a known demand, that for imported consumer goods. Domestic substitutes are then protected by high tariffs while overvaluation, dual exchange rates, and subsidies cheapen the imports (raw materials and capital equipment) required for final goods production. Meanwhile, the state takes an active role by managing demand and constructing infrastructure, often financed by foreign borrowing. Import substitution got off to an early start in Mexico under Cárdenas. Manufacturing was further encouraged by World War II and boomed in the postwar years accompanied by increasing foreign investment in selected sectors.

6. Between 1940 and 1965 total land under cultivation increased by more than one-third and irrigated land doubled. Total agricultural production doubled between 1950 and 1965 (Walsh, 1983).

7. Sorghum occupied 9.2 percent of the total cultivated area in grains in 1958 and 59.6 percent of the total in 1980. Correspondingly, while virtually no grains were destined for animal consumption in 1957, by 1980 more than half of all grains produced were for nonhuman use (Barkin and Suárez, 1982: 58).

8. Maize began to lose ground in cultivated area after 1967 when it occupied 51 percent of the total. In 1979 it covered only 37 percent of the cultivated area, an all-time low (Barkin and Suárez, 1982: 58). Prices are controlled by La Compañia Nacional de Subsistencias Populares (the National Basic Foods Company—CONASUPO), which froze guaranteed prices from 1963 to 1972 while the growers' real income declined 14 percent, an obvious disincentive to production although an ongoing subsidy to urban consumers (Centro de Investigaciones Agrarias, 1980: 66). However, substantial increases in the guaranteed price after 1972 did not result in significantly increased harvests, partly because of rising production costs and deteriorating terms of trade internationally, the natural hazards of rain-fed agriculture, the primitive technology employed, and the high degree of family consumption by producers in the subsistence sector (Centro de Investigaciones Agrarias, 1980). Furthermore, research into improved varieties of maize has been hampered by the lack of adaptability of the crop to Mexico's wide variety of growing conditions (Walsh, 1983).

9. As a result of declining infant mortality rates and an official pro-growth policy, the population increase rate was 3.5 percent in 1970. Recognition of the

social implications of a demographic explosion spurred the initiation of a family planning program in 1973. Meanwhile, agriculture had decreased its contribution to total production to 11 percent in 1970 compared with 21 percent in 1940, despite the booming export sector (*IMF Survey*, 27 June 1988).

10. An extensive literature exists on the deleterious results of the internationalization of peripheral economies in terms of increasingly skewed export-dependent structures, highly vulnerable to world market fluctuations, and plagued by dysfunctional specializations, unequal development, income concentration, and growing regional disparities as part of the expanding international division of labor. For example, Barkin (1978) examines the shifting fortunes of Plan Chontalpa, a large-scale, state-directed river-basin development in the Mexican state of Tabasco, in response to the changing dictates of national and international capital.

11. During the last months of his presidency, Echeverría expropriated sizable areas of large estates in Sonora and Sinaloa, many belonging to descendants of notable revolutionary politicians and military heroes, and hurriedly turned them over to peasant invaders—often before the necessary legal procedures had been formally concluded. The next president, López Portillo, was forced into an extended legal battle over the legitimacy of these expropriations by the powerful interest groups affected, resulting in dispossession for many campesinos and extensive indemnification payments for landlords (see Bartra, 1982: 58–60).

12. More success in terms of increased crop yields, self-management, and democratic organization has been achieved by semi-proletarian direct producers, for example in the Coalición de Ejidos Colectivos de los Valles del Yaqui y el Mayo (Coalition of Collective Ejidos of the Yaqui and Mayo Valleys), as a result of conscious efforts to achieve a degree of independence from both the state and private capital (Otero, 1989). These achievements, however, have been under increasing stress since the onset of the debt crisis.

13. Ejidatarios must work the land personally, fulfil collective labor obligations, and derive only limited income from nonagricultural pursuits, and cannot possess other landholdings equal to or greater than the ejidal allocation. If labor is hired on ejidal lands, the fruits of such labor are to accrue to those worker. Violation of the code is widespread, particularly in the large-scale development projects, heavily oriented to agribusiness, in which the proletarianization process is most advanced.

14. In 1980 food purchases from the United States amounted to $2 billion, more than double the 1979 figure (Street, 1981: 375). Meanwhile, domestic per capita consumption of maize declined (Redclift, 1980).

15. It is significant that one-third of this debt was contracted in 1981, as "panic borrowing" intended to shore up the economy against the effects of a softening world oil price, declining revenues, high interest rates abroad, world recession, and rising inflation (*Economist*, 5 September 1987: 7). Meanwhile, over the course of the López Portillo administration (1976–1982), capital flight was estimated at $25.3 billion (Cumby and Levich, 1987).

16. This trend dates from the early 1950s. The main effects have been on export crops for which global overproduction triggered price declines, for example, cotton. For staple crops, prices are conditioned primarily by the internal market,

where state intervention has acted to debase official guaranteed rates in the interests of urban consumers. The official price operates as a ceiling rather than a minimum, because the government freely imports staples whenever the equilibrium prices rise above the domestic guarantees. Therefore, staple growers are unable to benefit from temporary shortfalls in supply (Heath, 1989).

17. This debasement was particularly acute from 1963 to 1972 and from 1982 to 1986 (Tellez Kuenzler, 1990). Thus, between 1965 and 1986 controlled prices declined by almost 25 percent in real terms and failed to be offset by inefficient subsidies such as credit and infrastructural development (*Excelsior*, 12 December 1990).

18. The increase in population from 66.8 million in 1980 to 81 million in 1990 was some 4 million less than had been anticipated (*Excelsior*, 16 October 1990), but basic grain imports represented 30 percent of national consumption by the end of the decade (*Excelsior*, 20 May 1990).

19. The value of Mexico's exports from oil and mining was 78 percent in 1982, dropping to 38 percent in 1986 (*Economist*, 5 September 1987). The greatest annual growth in non-oil-related industries occurred in the iron and steel complex, the manufacturing of chemical products, and transportation equipment. At the same time tourism boomed in response to favorable exchange rates.

20. The average tariff on imports from the United States in 1990 was 11 percent; the United States's average tariff on imports from Mexico was 4 percent (*Economist*, 6 October 1990).

21. Under this plan, debtor nations that implement structural reforms meeting the approval of the IMF qualify for partial debt forgiveness by their foreign commercial-bank creditors and, under some circumstances, for new money. The 1990 Mexican restructuring package was the first agreement under the plan, but three years earlier the IMF had allowed Bolivia to use borrowed money to buy back most of its commercial-bank debt at 11 percent of face value, cutting its total bank debt by over 80 percent. Subsequent Brady Plan agreements have been reached with Costa Rica, Venezuela, and Uruguay (*Economist*, 5 January 1991).

22. This innovative agreement gave each of Mexico's five-hundred-plus creditor banks a choice among three options—exchanging old loans for thirty-year bonds to cut the debt principal by 35 percent, exchanging old loans for thirty-year bonds with the same face value but reducing the interest rate to 6.25 percent, and providing new loans (or recycling interest received from Mexico) for four years with guarantees against default by the IMF and the World Bank (*Economist*, 29 July 1989). The outcome was restructuring of 43 percent of the debt by principal reduction, 47 percent through decreased interest rates, and only 10 percent by new money (Salinas de Gortari, 1990).

23. Funding of the Vaquerías project was based on a formula of $2 million contributed by the state of Nuevo León, $4 million provided from debt-for-equity Swaps and an investment of $6 million by Gamesa. It was estimated that participating ejidatarios would receive dividends equivalent to 8 percent of the processed harvest (Santos de Hoyos, 1990).

24. An average exchange rate of 2,660 pesos to U.S. $1 is used for the period from August 1989 to July 1990.

25. It has been estimated that half of Mexico's 28,000 ejidos currently are

involved in some kind of production association on an inter-or intra-ejidal basis, or in collaboration with private property owners and agribusiness (Gordillo de Anda, 1990).

26. Maize production was estimated at about 12 million tons for 1990, 1 million tons above the 1989 figure. The bean harvest was on the order of 1 million tons in 1990, double the 1989 yield. However, 1990 production figures for rice, wheat, and sorghum were significantly lower than 1989 levels (*Excelsior*, 28 November 1990), and the maize increment was offset by the disastrous 1990–1991 winter agricultural cycle, with a projected harvest only 50 percent of the antici- pated 4.4 million tons (*Excelsior*, 6 March 1991).

TABLE 2.1 The Evolution of Mexican Agricultural Policy

Policy Phase	Key Policy Component	Impact on Commercial Agriculture	Impact on Peasant Agriculture
1910-1917 Revolution	1911-Emiliano Zapata's *Plan de Ayala*—"Land and Liberty." 1915 *Land Reform Law*—provision for restitution of alienated communal lands. 1917 *Constitution*—Article 17 provision for agrarian reform via legal dissolution of the *hacienda* and debt peonage and redistribution of expropriated lands to landless peasants in *ejidos*. All lands, waters, and minerals including subsoils declared part of the national patrimony subject to control by the state for the public good.	Many *hacendados* (large landowners) killed or exiled. (In 1910 1% of the population had owned 97% of the land).[a] Destruction of much of the commercial agrarian economy.	Divided and "defeated"[b] peasantry pinned hopes on the *ejido*, combining communal title vested in the state with usufruct rights to land worked individually or collectively. Redistribution remains rhetoric from 1915-1920 (167,935 hectares allocated to 46,398 *campesinos* or 1.6% of the total beneficiaries up until 1979).[c]
1917-1934 Post-Revolutionary Restructuring	Land redistribution. 1926 *Colonization Law* promoting development of under-utilized lands. Cultural nationalism ("mestizoism" and "neoindigenism"). Literacy campaign. Economic modernization thrust. Formation of labor unions. Increasing dependence on foreign capital despite new nationalism.	Rebuilding and expansion of large estates by surviving *hacendados*. Emergence of new "revolutionary landlords." Expansion of mechanized commercial agriculture in center and north. Lengthy appeals delay expropriations.	Slow start on modest *ejidal* land redistribution (7,549,678 hectares from 1920-1934 for 736,932 *campesinos* or 25.3% of the total beneficiaries up until 1979).[c] Emphasis on mere land redistribution rather than integrated reform and provision of infrastructural support. Subsistence-level individual *ejidos* predominate. Increased number of private "sub-family" *minifundia*.

(continues)

TABLE 2.1 (continued)

Policy Phase	Key Policy Component	Impact on Commercial Agriculture	Impact on Peasant Agriculture
1934-1940 The Cárdenas Era: Nationalist and Populist Reformism	Massive land redistribution. Populist social reforms. Nationalization of selected industries (including foreign-owned oil industry, 1938). Federal price controls introduced. Increasing state economic intervention. Organized labor permitted strike protest, but peasant organizations not allowed to join central workers' movements. Continued external dependence.	Commercial enclaves flourish in center and north despite farm labor unrest. Foreign corporate expansion on mechanized lands (eg in the irrigated areas of La Laguna). Largest and most prosperous holdings untouched by expropriation. Number of privately owned farms increased 44%.[d]	More than twice as much land redistributed than in previous post-revolutionary administrations (17,906,430 hectares redistributed to 811,157 campesinos or 27.83% of the total beneficiaries up until 1979).[c] Limited experiments with collective ejidos (less than 10% of total ejidos) e.g. in La Laguna, after frequent farmworker strikes and generalized agrarian unrest. Increasing numbers of ejidatarios hire out as peónes (day laborers) or "rent" their lands to commercial farmers (alienation of ejidal land forbidden under the agrarian code but de facto crop contracting a common practice).
1940-1965 The Mexican Economic Miracle	Dual-track policy: -ejidal subsistence sector (social justice through land redistribution) -private commercial sector (productivity objectives). Escalation of commercial agriculture modernization thrust favoring private sector through public sector infrastructural	Counter reform: private landholding sizes increased. Heavy federal investment in irrigation infrastructure in north, northwest, and Bahio favoring large-scale mechanized farms through promotion of "Green Revolution" inputs. Increased agribusiness and cash	Ejidos and small holdings served as pools of cheap labor for commercial agriculture and expanding urban areas. Sporadic land redistribution unable to keep pace with population increase (27,086,508 hectares redistributed to 79,161 campesinos between 1940 and 1964 or 27.0%

investment hinging on "Green Revolution" and irrigation inputs. Import substitution and agricultural export emphasis (with an "industry-first" priority after the late 1950s). 1947 *Federal Colonization Law* favored spontaneous private colonization of under-utilized lands.

1965-1970
The Internationalization of the Mexican Economy

Continued strategy of rapid industrialization at the expense of agriculture, while critical economic bottlenecks emerge. Increasing centralization and state economic intervention. Growing direct foreign investment and overall internationalization of the Mexican economy. Extensive promotion of agribusiness and export crops. Declining public investment in agrarian infrastructure.

cropping (eg fruits and vegetables) primarily for export. Agriculture subsidizes industrial expansion by providing low-unit-cost foodstuffs for growing urban-industrial labor force.

Agricultural sector lost overall growth dynamic in response to decreased federal investment, leveling off of initial Green Revolution impact and slower pace of expansion of irrigation. Progressive displacement of subsistence crops by modernized livestock production, forage, industrial, and export crops in response to changing dietary patterns and the needs of the international and national markets. "Cattle-ization" of the countryside and expanding export and agribusiness enclaves threaten Mexico's self-sufficiency in maize after 1967. Neo-Latifundism increases (re-emergence of large land-holdings) operated by both domestic and U.S. capital.

of the total beneficiaries up until 1979.[c] Rapid increase in numbers of landless laborers. Limited tropical frontier spontaneous colonization and large-scale integrated river basin development, e.g., Papaloapan Project.

Land invasions and overall widespread symptoms of rural discontent. Increased day labor and "renting" of *ejidal* lands for cash crop enterprises. Growing number of landless laborers (14,139,574 hectares redistributed to 216,695 *campesinos* between 1964-1970 or 7.4% of the total beneficiaries up until 1979).[c] Peasant sector increasingly responsible for national staple crop production. Expansion of large-scale government-sponsored agricultural development planning (with foreign aid loans) e.g., Plan Chontalpa.

(continues)

TABLE 2.1 (continued)

Policy Phase	Key Policy Component	Impact on Commercial Agriculture	Impact on Peasant Agriculture
1970-1976 The Echeverría Era: Modernizing Peasant Agriculture	The "rediscovery of the peasantry." Reformist deficit spending based on heavy foreign borrowing and monetary expansion to promote agricultural growth and social welfare programs for Mexico's poorest. Emphasis on land redistribution and modernization of subsistence peasant agriculture to stimulate commercial production of staples to reduce food imports. Overall "neo-Cardenist" populist strategy purported to rectify the social justice imbalance. 1971 *New Federal Agrarian Reform Law.* 1972 *New Federal Water Law.* 1973 *PIDER* established—a rural development umbrella program (World Bank funded) coordinating numerous new development agencies. 1976 *COPLAMAR* established—an agency for integrated development in the most depressed areas.	Massive capital flight as landholders shelve expansion plans fearing expropriation and peso devaluation. Continuing internationalization of commercial agriculture through "cattle-ization", export crops and expanding agribusiness. Decreasing capacity to supply Mexico's basic food needs. Hectarage under private holdings decreases.[e]	16,814,350 hectares redistributed to 284,870 *campesinos* between 1970-1976 or 9.7% of the total beneficiaries up until 1979.[c] Planned modernization of *ejidal* agriculture through government controlled collectives hinging on credit and technology transfer (with foreign aid loans). Rampant *proyectismo* (project fever). Increasing dependence of *ejidatarios* on development agencies, accentuated internal differentiation, and accelerated rural proletarianization. Bureaucratization of peasant agriculture. Resettlement projects on underutilized and tropical frontier lands (e.g., Edzná project). Hectarage under *ejidal* and communal land tenure increases.[e] Land invasions continue. Trend towards creation of a "modernized subsistence sector," with the principal beneficiaries of developmentalism outside the peasant sector.

1976-1982 Boom and Bust: Petrolization and Global Planning

Financial crisis management (1976-1979). (1976: 42% devaluation of peso followed by unprecedented inflation.)

"Petrolization" of the economy after discovery of new S.E. oil fields leading to oil-based developmentalism based on heavy foreign borrowing (and rapidly increasing foreign debt).

Petrodollars financed continued staple food imports (reaching an all-time high in 1980).

Nationalistic policies devised to channel petroleum growth more productively, to regain self-sufficiency in staple crop production, and improve the deteriorating peasant condition through welfare programs.

1980 *Global Development Plan* to use oil revenues for integrated development.

1980 *Mexican Food System* (SAM)—a strategy for regaining self-sufficiency through a balance of productivity and social welfare objectives emphasizing rain-fed areas and "shared risk" between state and peasant.

1980 *Law for Promoting Agricultural Production* legitimating increased direct state intervention in

Increased basic food production by large commercial farmers capturing a significant proportion of the SAM subsidies and incentives (aimed at peasants).

Promotion of rain-fed rather than irrigated areas.

Expansion of cattle ranching after 1980 agricultural law provision encouraging growth of forage crops on ranchlands.

Private-sector operation of *ejidal* lands for staple crop production legitimated (after 1980).

Increased capital flight after 1980 law expropriation threats.

Deterioration in peasant living standards due to increased costs of agricultural inputs, continuing low market prices for subsistence crops (government-subsidized), and overall inflation.

Oil-funded welfare programs for marginal groups have only limited effect.

SAM subsidies increase staple production by peasants, but benefits outweighed by low crop value and galloping inflation.

De facto "renting" of *ejidal* lands to government agencies and private interests for state-managed "production units," Increasing peasant bureaucratization, proletarianization, and overall dependence on state initiative. (Only 1,799,939 hectares redistributed to 26,667 *campesinos* between 1976-1979 or 0.9% of the total beneficiaries up until 1979).[c]

(continues)

TABLE 2.1 *(continued)*

Policy Phase	Key Policy Component	Impact on Commercial Agriculture	Impact on Peasant Agriculture
1976-1982 Boom and Bust: Petrolization and Global Planning *(continued)*	agriculture to spur productivity, opening up the *ejido* to private investment in "production units," and authorizing widespread expropriation of under-utilized lands for redistribution to *ejidos* or other groups for productive use. Pro-production rather than pro-peasant legislation. 1981 oil glut and rapid fall in barrel prices reveal foreign-debt-based foundation of petrolized Mexican economy. Full scale debt crisis ensues.		
1982-1988 The de la Madrid Administration: Dealing with the Debt Crisis	Priority to renegotiating debt service. Ensuing economic restraint spells demise of global planning, public-sector spending cuts, and emphasis on sectoral recovery. Cutbacks, inflation, and rising unemployment feed political dissent and widespread public discontent. 1986 debt negotiations with IMF and creditor banks conclude in US $12 billion rescue package to permit continued debt service with economic growth.	State attempts balance between export and staple crops on commercial farms (through incentives). Private cattle ranching continues to expand, often in frontier areas cleared for *ejidal* use. Continued collaboration with government agencies in new "production units."	Greatly reduced public investment in modernization of *ejidal* agriculture. Focus on selected more viable production units under strict government agency control— *ejidatarios* serve as low-cost labor with no input in decision making and minimal income gains. Peasants are increasingly "resources to be managed" as partial proletarians and/or low-value staple producers. Peasant marginality effectively

(President de la Madrid fails to win special concessions linking repayment terms to future oil prices).

Agricultural policies to generate productivity under austerity and reduce food imports. Staple emphasis continues with continuing farm price supports. Increasing direct state intervention in agriculture (eg regional production quotas and state-managed farms). 1986 Mexico enters GATT. December 1987 *Pact for Economic Solidarity* introduced (wage and price controls).

codified in agricultural policy while agrarian crisis continues.

1988-1994
The Salinas Administration: Modernization, Restructuring, "Solidarity"

Continuation and intensification of debt restructuring and austerity. Acceleration of "economic opening" via pursuit of North American Free Trade Agreement (NAFTA).

A degree of electoral reform and political democratization.

Agricultural crisis deepens with continued low staple prices and rising input costs leading to widespread loan default by *ejidatarios*.

National Plan for Modernization of the Countryside emphasizes "agricultural opening" and recapitalization via retreat of the

June 1990 Vacquerías Project initiated as pilot "alliance for production" between Nuevo León *ejidos* and GAMESA (Mexican food processing company subsequently taken over by Pepsico).

Foreign agribusiness awaits *ejidal* reform (privatization) before committing major new investment. Mexican agricultural export sector favors NAFTA. Domestic private sector still reluctant to invest in agriculture beyond selective participation in least risky "alliances for production."

Epidemic of loan default by *ejidatarios* disqualifies majority from further BANRURAL credit. *Campesinos* with low production in high risk zones eligible for *PRONASOL*—an agrarian populist resurgence to boost flagging PRI popularity.

Overall, *National Plan for Modernization of the Countryside* and free market thrust constitute a strategy of economic triage—a purge of producers presaging privatization of the *ejido* and the end of the state revolutionary project.

(continues)

TABLE 2.1 (continued)

Policy Phase	Key Policy Component	Impact on Commercial Agriculture	Impact on Peasant Agriculture
1988-1994 The Salinas Administration: Modernization, Restructuring, "Solidarity"	state from the *ejido*, deregulation, anti-corruption campaign, institutional reform, credit rationalization, promotion of agribusiness. 1990 *PRONASOL* program offers direct credit to *campesinos* "on one's word" to promote increased production, producer participation, and individual responsibility. Encouragement of "alliances for production" between *ejidos* and agribusiness by November 1991 initiative for optional privatization of *ejido*.		

[a] Stavenhagen, 1970:227.

[b] Cockroft, in Chilcote and Edelstein, 1974:256. Although the peasantry was symbolically the driving force of the Revolution, Zapata's forces had limited direct regional influence and his assassination in 1919 left the peasant movement divided and without a leader.

[c] Zaragoza and Macías, 1980:457 based on data supplied by the Secretaría de la Reforma Agraria elaborated by the Centro Nacional de Investigaciones Agrarias.

[d] Cockroft, 1974:268.

[e] Zaragoza and Macías, 1980:467 based on data from the *IX Censo General de Población de 1970* elaborated by the Centro Nacional de Investigaciones Agrarias.

3

Tradition and Change in Campeche

Ah Campeche! So far from Mexico [City] and so close to Mérida. (I-132, businessman, Campeche, March 1990)

When I get off the plane from Mexico [City], I feel as if I were in another country, another century. This is not just an accident of history and geography but the product of the economic forces that enriched the world while Campeche slept. (I-133, civil servant, Campeche, February, 1990)

In a nation of extreme diversity, the regional personality of the Yucatán Peninsula is particularly distinctive, forged by an interplay of geographical, cultural, and historical factors. Closer and more accessible to Cuba than to the nation's capital in the colonial era, oriented to the Gulf of Mexico and the Caribbean rather than to the interior, the peninsula has remained isolated because of the difficulties of overland communication with the rest of the country. The Chiapas mountains form a formidable barrier to the southwest, while travel westward along the Gulf to Veracruz involved a series of ferry trips across numerous rivers and lagoons until the completion of the peninsular highway in 1967. The deficiencies of the national railway system and inadequate highway maintenance budgets still make a trip to the Yucatán Peninsula a significant undertaking for the majority unable to afford the airfare.

This physical separation has been reinforced by the persistence of the region's Maya heritage. The Classic Maya civilization had disintegrated over five hundred years before the Spanish conquest, but the Yucatec Maya had retained their basic cultural integrity despite invasions in the tenth century by the Itzá, a tributary group of the Toltecs (Mexicans), which effected considerable reorientation in political, social, artistic, and religious forms but had little effect on everyday life (Henderson, 1981; Moseley, 1980). The Spanish conquest, in contrast, left an indelible stamp on the region and its inhabitants, although the Maya continued to defy colonial domination in uprisings as late as the 1847–1848 War of the Castes. As a result of this resistance and the integrity of the pre-Columbian legacy, Maya language and culture continued to evolve in a uniquely Yucatecan syncretism rather than being overwhelmed by the institutions of Spanish rule. Although the distinctive cultural identity of the peninsula is still vital, it is increasingly threatened by the outside influences brought both by foreign tourists in search of sun, sand, and archaeological sites and the modernization of everyday life to which no Mexican province is immune. The traditional *huipil* (embroidered smock) and *pibipollo* (chicken tamale) are losing ground to jeans and hamburgers. Nevertheless, the modernization of the Maya has so far proceeded relatively slowly, selectively, and with a modicum of dignity, perhaps because of the peninsula's relative lack of currently desirable economic resources and the tradition of resistance to external forces which continues to provide a counterbalance to homogenizing trends.

The identification of an unique macroregional character does not imply similarity and unity throughout the area and, in fact, masks considerable underlying diversity. Of the three states comprising the peninsula, it is often said that "Yucatán got the people and the infrastructure, Quintana Roo got the beaches and the bandits, and Campeche got the soil." The resulting differences and inequalities have provoked a variety of interregional rivalries and jealousies. Thus, for example, factions of Campeche's mercantile elite have at various times competed against, collaborated with, or firmly opposed their northern neighbors, oscillating between envy and emulation. These diverging allegiances continue down to the subregional level. Although five physiographic, cultural, and economic regions can be identified in Campeche, the overriding distinctions are coast versus interior, as the narrow littoral strip has always turned its back on its hinterland, and the Maya north versus the frontier south. The northeastern third of the state, composed of the more densely populated Camino Real and Los Chenes regions (often referred to together as the "Maya maize zone"), seems much like adjacent Yucatán in its cultural and physical aspects. The southwestern low-lying plains and swamps of the Candelaria-Palizada "river zone" blur with neighboring Tabasco. The sparsely populated southern interior forests of the Río Bec region form part of the Guatemalan Petén in geologic and physiographic terms. Only the central, transitional section appears to be "frankly Campechano" (Lanz, 1937).

Perhaps because the strong regional personality overpowers local identity, native Campechanos, Maya and non-Maya, rural and urban, tend to define themselves by what they are not rather than what they are. Campeche, one often hears, is "not Mexican, not Yucatecan, not a tourist attraction, and not industrialized." It is a somewhat sleepy and peaceful province, proud of its Maya heritage, noted economically only for its shrimp and offshore oil, and still largely dominated by families who achieved prominence during the colonial and independence eras. Despite having played a transcendental role in the history of the peninsula, Campeche has often deliberately insulated itself from it as well as from the rest of Mexico, at the same time jealous of more successful regions and guarding the very lack of progress that has served to maintain traditions.

The Place of the Snake and the Tick

The city of Campeche has the distinction of being the first settlement occupied by the Spaniards on the peninsula and is said to have been the site of the first mass performed on the continent (Lanz, 1937). The earliest recorded Spanish-Maya contact occurred in 1511, when a shipwreck stranded thirteen sailors on the peninsula's east coast. This accidental encounter was unfortunate for both parties: the Spaniards were eaten or enslaved, and the Maya contracted a lethal pestilence, probably smallpox (Henderson, 1981; Landa, 1978 [1566]; Morley, 1956). In 1517 Hernández de Córdoba's expedition sailed west from Cuba in search of new lands to conquer and fresh Indians to enslave, that island's indigenes having been decimated in the 1511 conquest. It landed at several places on what was still believed to be the island of Yucatán, including a water stop at a sizable community of some three thousand palm-thatched huts known as Kin Pech, "the place of the snake and the tick" (Peña Castillo, 1986: 13). The settlement was the capital of the *cacicazgo* of Ah-Kin-Pech, one of the many small and often warring chiefdoms into which centralized governance had disintegrated after the fall of Mayapan in 1441.[1]

In contrast to the hostile reception encountered at the subsequent port-of-call at the town of Champotón to the southwest, in Kin Pech the members of the expedition "were well received by the chief and the Indians marveled at seeing the Spaniards, touching their beards and persons" (Landa, 1978 [1566]: 5). The Spaniards in turn were impressed by the town and its inhabitants, noting in particular a temple dedicated to Kukulcán, the Toltec plumed-serpent god, where evidently human sacrifice was practiced.[2] They enjoyed the lavish hospitality of their hosts for three days before suddenly being asked to leave in no uncertain terms: "By signs they told us to leave their country before they lighted the wood they had piled up and finished burning it. If not, they would make war on us and kill us" (Díaz del Castillo, 1942 [1527]: 63). The Spaniards departed with dispatch after naming the settlement San Lázaro in honor of the saint on whose name-day it was discovered.

San Lázaro was rebaptized Salamanca de Campeche by Francisco de Montejo in 1531 and became the first Spanish settlement as the base for the conquest of the peninsula. In 1540, two years prior to the foundation of Mérida on the site of the Maya city T-Hoo, Don Francisco's son and namesake changed the name yet again to San Francisco de Campeche and conferred on it the title of *villa* (chartered town), which it retained until awarded the formal status of *ciudad* (city) in 1777. By March 1547 the conquest was virtually complete after a twenty-year bloody struggle in which more than five hundred thousand Indians may have perished (Moseley, 1980). However, in the northeastern and southeastern regions Spanish control remained very tenuous throughout the colonial era, as many Maya rejected Christianity and other "civilizing" influences.

In fact, the colonizers must have wondered at times if the conquest of the peninsula had been worth the effort. The Spaniards were first attracted by early explorers' reports of rumors of the Indians' wealth and splendor. In reality they found neither gold nor silver mines and no dazzling cities such as Aztec Tenochtitlán but instead a harsh environment with modest natural resources that supported a productive agricultural civilization because of the skill, ingenuity, and adaptability of its inhabitants. The Franciscan Diego de Landa reported on this contradiction in 1566, referring to the northwestern portion of the peninsula:

> Yucatán is a land of less soil that any I know, being all live flat stones with very little earth, so that there are few places where one can dig down a fathom without meeting great banks of large rocks ... The country is excellent for lime of which there is much; it is a marvel how much fertility exists in the soil on or between the stones, where is to be found all there is. (Landa, 1978 [1566]: 93)

Another observer remarked about the same area that "there is not one piece of land the size of a hand's span which has not been cultivated," so extensive was the mark of centuries of Maya occupance (Relación de Cancacabo, 1580: 196, quoted in Moreno Toscano, 1968: 114).

Much of the Yucatán Peninsula consists of a thick karst (limestone and dolomite) platform with very limited areas of agricultural soils in scattered solution hollows and depressions and in an area of alluvium from the Usumacinta River drainage basin in southwestern Campeche.[3] Consequently, most of it has no surface water, and until the advent of modern well-drilling technology settlement location was constrained largely, by the occurrence of *cenotes* (natural openings formed by the collapse of superficial limestone exposing subterranean waters) or perched water tables. The water-supply problem is compounded by the climatic regime, which in most of the peninsula is hot savanna or tropical wet-and-dry, with little temperature fluctuation throughout the year and heavy summer rains followed by a variable three- to five-month dry season.[4] Erratic rainfall patterns are further complicated by considerable sub-regional microclimatic variation. The Classic Maya coped by developing complex, locally adapted water management systems, including cenotes, *chultunes* (underground cisterns) supplied by the mining of cave water, *aguadas* (shallow soil-lined ponds) sometimes maintained as reservoirs, *bajos* (seasonal wetlands), drains, and possibly canals in various combinations.[5] However, dry-season stress and the scarcity of agricultural soils were and continue to be major constraints, particularly in the rocky, semi-arid northwestern portion of the peninsula now occupied by the state of Yucatán, where, paradoxically, the population has been concentrated for the past thousand years or more.

The area now comprising the state of Campeche must have been a particular disappointment to the Spanish colonizers, at least before the value of its tropical-forest products was established. Its population at the time was sparse, mainly confined to the coastal strip, where rich marine resources, including salt, as well as agriculture and commerce were sufficient to support the inhabitants in some degree of comfort. In addition to cacicazgos such as Ah-Kin-Pech, the Spaniards found the province of Acalán, an important cacao production region in the Candelaria River basin to the southwest. Here, the Chontal Putún Maya had developed a flourishing and extensive trading network in the Postclassic involving Mexican peoples of the Gulf Coast to the north and west as well as northern Yucatán and Maya groups to the south and east. Also, Nahuatl-speaking merchants affiliated with the Aztec empire had established an important trading outpost at Xicalango on the vast Laguna de Términos. All in all, this coastal zone had a decidedly cosmopolitan character, testifying to the extent to which the syncretized Postclassic Maya retained functional unity despite apparent fragmentation (Henderson, 1981).

Cortés and other early Spanish visitors found Itzamkanac, the capital of Acalán, to be a large and prosperous town with significant temples and hundreds of fine houses, but there were neither any really impressive cities or ceremonial centers along the coast nor rumors of spectacular remnants of past glories inland. In any event, exploration of the interior would have been a daunting proposition, particularly in southwestern Campeche, where higher rainfall and sizable rivers created dense rain forests and impenetrable swamps. Calakmul, one of the largest Classic Maya urban centers, which may have supported sixty thousand inhabitants at its apex (Folan, 1984), was located within the current bounds of Campeche, close to the Guatemalan border, but had been abandoned over five hundred years before the conquest and remained forgotten in the jungle until its rediscovery in 1931. The Classic site at Edzná was only some fifty kilometers inland from the city of Campeche but was apparently unknown except to local peasants until the beginning of this century and did not attract the attention of archaeologists until 1927. More recent excavations suggest that the importance of this city has been underestimated in that it was occupied continuously from the Preclassic to the Late Classic and probably later, sustaining a significant population via a highly developed agricultural base in the largest valley of deep soils in the peninsula, supported by a sophisticated artificial water-management system, possibly including large canals (Matheny et al., 1983) or drains. However, these impressive accomplishments and the distinctive architectural styles of the Classic Río Bec, Chenes, Petén, and Puuc sites further inland would probably have been of little interest to the Spaniards even if they had seen them, since the colonial objective was to eradicate Maya tradition.

The Spanish pacification of the peninsula involved the infliction of "unheard-of cruelties," which were considered a necessary evil in that "being so few in numbers they [the Spaniards] could not have reduced so populous a country save through the fear of such terrible punishments" (Landa, 1978 [1566]: 25). The Spaniards became obsessed with the eradication of "heathenisms" associated with the Maya religion such as human sacrifice and self-mutilation and conducted a systematic campaign to wipe out idolatry and associated beliefs and practices. Since in the Maya universe religion permeates virtually every aspect of daily life, this meant that almost everything was suspect. The principal agents in this campaign were the Franciscan friars, who quickly established a virtual monopoly over ecclesiastical affairs (Moseley, 1980). As self-proclaimed defenders of the Indians, they played a key but somewhat contradictory role. They condemned Spanish atrocities, learned the Maya language, acted as mediators, and converted the Indians, often protecting them from the worst abuses of the colonial *encomienda* (guardianship) system. At the same time, they were intent on stamping out every vestige of heathen influence, initiating one of the most brutal inquisitions in the Hispanic realm. The ultimate paradox was Bishop Landa's destruction of the majority of the ancient Maya books and records in the name of Christianity in 1562 while preserving invaluable information on Maya culture and history in his own writings.

Meanwhile, "the Indians took the yoke of servitude grievously" (Landa, 1978 [1566]: 24). Many Maya were congregated forcibly into nucleated villages to facilitate their conversion, making it difficult if not impossible for them to cultivate their ancestral lands. A particularly effective conversion method involved collection of the children of the Maya elite in special houses around the monasteries and employing them as informers on their parents' idolatries. Nevertheless, many Maya continued the old practices in secret, while some committed suicide rather than submit to the inquisition. As a result of this repression, sporadic revolts, and European diseases, as well as general anomie, the Maya population declined drastically. By the end of the sixteen century its customs had been greatly changed and syncretized with European beliefs and practices, at least in the core northern area of Spanish colonization (Moseley, 1980).

In outlying regions such as most of Campeche, Spanish control was very weak except in a few major administrative and economic centers. Consequently, a number of Maya refugees from northern Yucatán relocated in the Campeche interior. Despite the efforts of the Franciscans, who established forest missions after 1604, many Maya persisted in their rejection of Christianity and continued the old religious and social practices under their traditional *h-men* (spiritual leaders). Many Indians fled from "civilization" altogether, seeking refuge in the forests and retreating south and east as frontier settlement advanced. For those who stayed, incorporation generally was gradual and accomplished through tax and tribute as well as through the missions.

At the beginning of the colonial era Spanish attention in Campeche was focused on the coast. Since the Spaniards visited the area repeatedly after 1517 and the city of Campeche had served as the base for the conquest of the peninsula, there was little need for local pacification. Only the Chontal Putún province of Acalán required subjugation, and its inhabitants were relocated from the Candelaria River basin to the coast south of Champotón (Morley, 1956; Scholes and Roys, 1968). The former ruler of Acalán was quickly assimilated into the new regime by marriage and administrative employment and played a key role in the gradual incorporation of the countryside into the colonial sphere.

Although waters are shallow for considerable distance offshore, the city of Campeche initially gained prominence as the peninsula's premier port since its location on the Gulf close to Veracruz and Cuba facilitated communication with Spain, the lifeline in the early colonial years. Campeche soon became the most important commercial center in the region receiving imports of essential supplies, particularly manufactured products, and exporting goods from as far away as Tabasco, including tobacco, sugarcane, cochineal, indigo, salt, cacao, and dyewood (*Haematoxylon campechanium*). The latter, which became known as palo de Campeche, was the key to the city's early prosperity. The shrub grew abundantly in southern Campeche and neighboring Tabasco in areas of periodically inundated clay soils, and the extract obtained from the heart of the wood was consumed in vast quantities by the textile industry of

Europe. Given the volume of maritime trade, it was natural that in 1573 Campeche became the home of the only shipyards on the Gulf of Mexico, where exceptionally durable vessels were built of the local hardwood *jabín* (a type of quebracho) and the naval fleet was second in importance only to that of Veracruz (Peña Castillo, 1986). Colonial Spanish visitors praised Campeche as "an example of the Latin good life," with a democratically stratified population, hardworking without being frenetic, who knew how to set a good table: "rich and poor regaled themselves with Moorish rice, laced with saffron and native shark served with tomatoes on maize bread" (Vasconcelos, 1936, cited in *Tribuna de Campeche*, 14 January 1990). The city was laid out tidily in the standard New World grid-pattern with the central Spanish villa, the Maya *barrio* (quarter) of Campechuela (later known as San Francisco) to the north on the site of the original Indian settlement of Ah-Kin-Pech, and the southern barrio of San Román, originally populated by Aztecs brought by the Spaniards to assist in the conquest of the Yucatán Peninsula.

These halcyon days of Campeche's economic primacy were not to last long, however. A major factor in Campeche's decline was constant threat of piracy along the coast, initially mainly from the French but by the late sixteenth century from the English and the Dutch, linked to inter-metropolis rivalry for supremacy in the Caribbean (Moseley, 1980). Strategically located and prosperous Campeche was a choice and easy target as a result of its calm waters and lack of fortification. The roster of Campeche's pillagers until the beginning of the eighteenth century reads like a buccaneers' Hall of Fame. Campeche's citizens offered valiant resistance, but could do little except rely on an elaborate escape system of caves and tunnels constructed under the city. They had clamored for the construction of defensive installations since the earliest raids, but the *cabildos* (municipal councils) of Mérida and Valladolid were reluctant to allocate major revenues to the port city (Moseley, 1980). In 1686 work finally commenced on an eight-meter-high wall around the entire city core that was only completed in 1704. Forts were constructed on hilltops immediately north and south of the city and with the outlying batteries along the shore comprised one of the most modern and complete defense systems in the New World. Despite these measures, piracy continued to be a threat until 1708.

By this time Mérida had consolidated its position as the administrative, economic, and cultural core of the peninsula. In the area now occupied by the state of Campeche, outside of the port city, which boasted 20,646 inhabitants by 1810 (Magana Toledano, 1985: 52), the only population concentrations were the small coastal towns of Champotón and Ciudad del Carmen and a strip of Maya villages inland along the Camino Real (the royal road to Mérida). Agriculture was minimally developed, and from early on Campeche relied on staple food imports from Yucatán, concentrating instead on its trading role.

The economic marginalization of Campeche accelerated after 1810 with the construction of the port of Sisal only fifty kilometers from Mérida. As Campeche's star declined, Sisal became known worldwide for its massive exports of the Yucatec henequen fiber with which, by the middle of the century, the new port's name was synonymous. The commercial interests of Campeche naturally resented this preemption and demanded the cessation of trade with Cuba through Sisal. This demand was rejected outright by Mérida, adding an element of hostility to the political and economic rivalry between the two principal peninsular cities. Under Spanish rule, this animosity was largely held in check, subsumed under the division of labor imperative. After independence was achieved in 1821 and Yucatán joined the new federation of Mexican states it erupted into open conflict on a regional scale (Moseley, 1980).

Initially Campeche remained preoccupied with attempts to recoup the port's losses, apparently oblivious to the broader conflicts between liberals and conservatives, centralism and federalism, that were sweeping the country. By the late 1820s, however, local interests had begun to coalesce with wider political currents as the internal dissensions between the peninsular cities took on the color of national-level struggles. In 1829 a military force in Campeche revolted and proclaimed José Segundo Carvajal political and military ruler of the peninsula. The Mérida garrison supported the scheme and overthrew the constitutional state government. Carvajal then moved the seat of government to Campeche, and a series of attacks and counterattacks continued for the next four years. In 1834, General Francisco de Paula Toro announced in Campeche that he supported the centralized government of Antonio López de Santa Anna, crushed federalist elements in the northern Campeche town of Calkiní, and marched triumphantly into Mérida. Toro subsequently became governor and ruled Yucatán as part of the centralized Mexican state for the next two years. The intercity clash of interests became even more acute in 1840 when the Campeche federalist Santiago Mendez was elected governor and the staunch regionalist, Miguel Barbachano, a Campechano whose principal support was in Mérida, became vice-governor at the same time (Moseley, 1980; Reed, 1964).

Hostilities between Campeche and Mérida continued sporadically until attention was diverted by the outbreak in 1847 of the War of the Castes, the last great Maya uprising, which continued for two years and resulted in the loss of half the population of the peninsula. The Indians, at their peak, occupied four-fifths of the peninsula, with the whites clinging to Mérida, Campeche, and a few other urban centers. Many Campechanos sought refuge in the island city of Carmen, which was defended by three hundred U.S. Marines after its citizens petitioned the United States for protection (Reed, 1964). Then, suddenly, the Maya abandoned the struggle and went back to plant their *milpas* (cornfields). The son of one of the Maya leaders explained this abrupt departure as follows:

> All at once the *sh'mataneheeles* [winged ants, harbingers of the first rain] appeared in great clouds . . . all over the world. When my father's people saw this they said to themselves and their brothers, "Ehen! The time has come for us to make our planting, for if we do not we shall have no Grace of God to fill the bellies of our children." . . . Thus it can be clearly seen that Fate, and not white soldiers, kept my father's people from taking T-ho [Mérida] and working their will on it. (Reed, 1964: 99)

The rebellion continued sporadically until 1855, mainly in the eastern peninsular forests, where the Maya had rallied around the "Speaking Cross" at Chan Santa Cruz (now Felipe Carrillo Puerto in Quintana Roo). Here, for the rest of the century, the Maya pursued their traditional defense: retreat, interrupted periodically by raids and skirmishes.[6]

The war accelerated Campeche's decline vis-à-vis Mérida. The economy of the entire peninsula had been disrupted by the rebellion, but Campeche in particular had been devastated by the loss of the sugar crop, which, along with tropical hardwoods, had replaced dyewood as the main source of capital. Mérida, less dependent on sugar in particular and trade in general, with a large hinterland and the personal wealth of the old landed creole families to spur recovery, was damaged less seriously (Reed, 1964). Old grievances were exacerbated by the sharp contrast between the growing prosperity of Mérida and the virtual bankruptcy to the south. In 1857 a separatist movement emerged under Pablo García, and after some years of bitter negotiations statehood was ratified by presidential decree in 1863, followed by a brief period of reunification (1864–1867) after the 1863 French blockade. Political division of the peninsula did not, however, put an end to the rivalry, which continues to be a dominant motif in regional relations.

Boom and Bust: From Dyewood to Petroleum

Since the beginning of the colonial era, the export of one or two natural resources has constituted Campeche's economic base. While many other regions of New Spain were in a similar situation as a result of the insatiable greed of the crown, the majority of these former colonies have since been able to diversify to some extent, at least in terms of staple products for the domestic or local market. In contrast, Campeche has made no serious attempt to broaden its range of economic activities, content to allow the dynamics of boom-and-bust cycles to run their course, confident that a new exportable substance will materialize whenever the market or resource base for its predecessor is exhausted. While there are some signs that this exploitative attitude is beginning to change, so far the inertia of the Mexican system, the dynamics of peninsular relations, and Campeche's adherence to tradition have combined to militate against a significant economic reorientation.

In many ways, this restricted resource dependence is understandable, given both the riches of the humid tropical environment with which Campeche is blessed and the early focus on trading. Dyewood and tropical hardwoods dominated Campeche's exports from the early colonial era until the beginning of the twentieth century, when artificial dyes such as aniline displaced the former and the forests began to run out of easily accessible, precious woods. Fortunately, by this time a demand had developed for chicle, a product of the *chicozapote* (*Achras sapota* L.) used for chewing gum. Santa Anna had introduced James Adams to chicle in 1860, and by the turn of the century it was being exploited mainly by foreign companies on large land grants conceded by the government of Porfirio Díaz. After the revolution, the reformist Cárdenas administration allotted these lands to ejidatarios as forest reserves, and chicle cooperatives were promoted. The boom continued until the early 1950s, when once again technology challenged a raw material in the form of synthetic latex. Campeche continues to export chicle, mainly to the United States, Japan, and Italy, but on a greatly reduced scale, compounded by poor forest management (Otañez Toxqui and Equihua Enríquez, 1981).

Henequen, like dyewood and chicle, was a product long known to the ancient Maya. It was particularly well suited to the thin, rocky soils and semiarid climate of the northwestern peninsula, where the dense population satisfied the heavy labor requirements except during the peak years of the boom at the turn of the twentieth century, when large numbers of Yaqui from Sonora, Chinese, and Koreans were imported. The first commercial henequen plantation was established in 1833. Consequent on an expanding world market for twine and cordage and increased prices and political stability under the Díaz dictatorship (1876–1911), Yucatán entered its glory age of "Green Gold" as the state's economy was transformed into a monoculture. Because henequen fiber must be extracted within a day after cutting, it requires processing in situ, and as a result Yucatán developed a reasonably efficient industrial and transportation infrastructure and exported manufactured products such as rope, hammocks, matting, and ships' rigging as well as raw fiber. During this period it enjoyed a global henequen monopoly, and the immense fortunes made by the landholding elite were reflected in the ostentatious mansions lining the Paseo de Montejo in Mérida. For the Maya, however, the henequen era meant virtual slavery as their lands were absorbed by the expanding plantations and the brutal debt peonage of the hacienda system became entrenched (Baklanoff, 1980; Joseph, 1980). In fact, by the turn of the century the "going rate" for a henequen worker was determined by world market fluctuations (Joseph, 1980).

Early in the twentieth century, prices fell because of the increase in production and the slowing of world demand. World War I offered a brief reprieve, but the slump continued in the postwar years, when for the first time Yucatán faced effective competition from foreign plantations, mainly in East Africa and Java (Baklanoff, 1980). The world market continued to contract in the 1930s as the reaper was replaced by the combine harvester, which does not use twine. Yucatán's production was further dislocated by Cárdenas's 1937 agrarian reform, when more than half of the henequen lands were turned over to collective ejidos while the rest remained in private hands on the vestiges of the plantations remaining after the expropriation of the haciendas.[7] This reform effectively disrupted the functional agricultural-industrial unity of the henequen hacienda (Chardon, 1963). World War II provided another respite, but afterwards profits on the henequen ejidos continued to fall, plagued by state management errors, an inefficient and often corrupt official credit system, and the total absence of production autonomy for ejidatarios. This was paralleled by the declining performance of the processing industry, under public-sector management since 1961, and the increasing substitution of cheaper synthetic fibers. Meanwhile, economic depression grew increasingly more acute. Over the course of a century, Yucatán had become one of Mexico's richest states and then fallen into poverty again by virtue of its dependence on a monocrop export cycle.

At the same time, the henequen era's legacy of a relatively efficient transportation net centered on Mérida and a nucleus of industrial plants (albeit now often obsolete) has facilitated recent attempts to diversify Yucatán's economy. In contrast, Campeche, on the fringes of the henequen boom, was less devastated by the bust but had the correlative misfortune of missing out on the laying of the foundations for a modern industrial infrastructure. Instead, while henequen and chicle were in decline, Campeche found itself yet again in possession of a new commodity prized by the world market—shrimp. Exploitation of the Gulf of Mexico's rich and diverse marine life had always been an important activity locally, but until the late 1950s commercial development was strictly limited by the lack of freezing, processing, and transportation facilities. Since then, Campeche's shrimp capture has increased dramatically, with exports generally exceeding 4,000 tons per annum, worth over $55,000,000 in 1988 and representing the bulk of the state's nonpetroleum revenues (Gobierno

Constitucional del Estado de Campeche, 1989). With production and processing costs inflated by the debt crisis, Campeche has recently lost ground, however, to countries such as China, Thailand, and Ecuador in the competition for the lucrative U.S. market. At the same time, the transfer of Campeche's shrimp fleet from the private sector to fishermens' cooperatives in 1981–1982 resulted in organizational dislocation and inefficiency that brought much of the sector to the verge of bankruptcy (*Excelsior*, 22 May and 3 July 1990). This situation is compounded by a downtrend in the world market price of shrimp, overfishing, and marine pollution, with the result that the shrimp industry appears to be "at a technical and social crossroads" (Gobierno Constitucional del Estado de Campeche, 1986: 127). If these problems are not soon resolved or offset by revenues from the new private-sector shrimp farming enterprises encouraged by federal legislative changes in December 1989, Campeche's shrimp industry seems headed for an imminent bust.

Campeche's latest resource export boom is undoubtedly its biggest but, paradoxically, perhaps the one from which the state has received the fewest benefits and the most negative repercussions. The discovery of vast oilfields offshore in the Sound of Campeche was announced in 1976, making Campeche one of the richest petroleum regions in the world. Currently, the state accounts for some two-thirds of Mexico's petroleum, almost one-third of the natural gas, and the lion's share of reserves (Gobierno Constitucional del Estado de Campeche, 1989). It sees nothing of these riches, however, because of the offshore character of exploitation and the absence of any industrial spillover, the oil being piped directly out of state. Thus, the immediate effects of the oil boom are confined to the southern coastal city of Ciudad del Carmen, which serves as the base for PEMEX operations in the area. This once sleepy fishing port has been transformed into a typical petrolized enclave, where the influx of highly paid oil workers and migrants hoping for casual employment has dislocated the regional economy and also occasioned social disruption through stress on public services and infrastructure and increasing crime. While these social pathologies are largely restricted to the oil enclave itself, side effects of petrolization ranging from environmental contamination to exacerbation of regional inflation have spread throughout the state. Meanwhile, close proximity to oil money has fostered a demand for consumer goods on the part of the local population at a time when the debt crisis has drastically curtailed purchasing power. Thus, as in many other oil-boom areas, petrolization in Campeche has served both to accentuate existing regional distortions associated with an export-skewed economic base and to aggravate social tensions without providing the means to correct them.

In Campeche today, the legacy of almost five hundred years of dependence on one or two exports at any given time is obvious. With less than 1 percent of Mexico's population and 0.5 percent of the national GDP there is virtually no economic dynamism outside the sector producing the current global boom commodity. Particularly in the case of tropical-resource export economies such as Campeche's, subordination to the demands of the international market is compounded by vulnerability to the vagaries of nature. When an additional, unanticipated complication, such as the national debt crisis, occurs, there is no flexibility in the local economy, no fallback position except retreat to subsistence agriculture, the informal sector, or an additional job if one can be found. The advent of the debt crisis has planted the seed of the diversification imperative in the minds of some elements of Campeche's establishment, but the obstacles to such reorientation are myriad, particularly in an era of restraint and retrenchment, because the infrastructural prerequisites for alternatives are minimally developed.

Tourism is frequently mentioned as an attractive option, but the Gulf waters lack the turquoise clarity of the Caribbean, the only sandy beaches are near the southern oil enclave, developed archaeological sites are few and far between, and the climate is generally too hot and humid to entice the visitor to more than cursory exploration of the city of Campeche's colonial charms. Furthermore, the seas are too shallow for most cruise ships, ecotourism in the Calakmul Biosphere Reserve's forests would, by definition, attract only a few visitors, and, at present there is only one tourist-grade facility outside the two major cities of Campeche and Ciudad del Carmen.

Expansion of fishing would seem to be another logical option, but it would require a substantial investment in boats, refrigeration, and processing facilities. The fishing cooperatives established in 1981 are plagued by inefficiency. High interest rates, mounting debts, the ineptitude of the national fisheries bank, poor organization, and deteriorating equipment have combined to keep one-third of the fleet out of the water, and cooperative production has decreased by 70 percent since 1982. Furthermore, poor communications in the interior of the state and with the rest of Mexico remain an obstacle to the distribution of perishable products. As a consequence, the local market is confined mainly to the coast, and demand is met by existing activities, as the numbers of small fishermen have increased along with the expanding urban population.

In a spirit of optimism three industrial parks have been set aside, but they are minimally developed, and because "the capital-poor Campechano elite don't even have the money to start a cement plant" (I-134, businessman, Campeche, March 1990) outside investment would have to be attracted. In particular, *maquiladoras* (assembly plants) are often suggested as an appealing possibility, but in addition to Campeche's lack of industrial infrastructure, isolation is still a constraining factor as highways are narrow and poorly maintained, while the labor force has little experience with any type of manufacturing beyond the cottage level. In any event, the Campeche elite continue to be at best ambivalent about outside investment prospects, preferring the status quo to potential loss of power and influence. In particular, the city of Campeche's establishment remains adamantly opposed to increased investment by Mérida business interests, even though lack of competition gives the state capital the highest cost of living in the peninsula in many sectors. The only other options considered tend to fall back on the same old formula: the search for a new resource or monoculture export.

Meanwhile, outside the major export enclaves the bulk of the population makes a living much as it has since the conquest. In the towns and cities, Campechanos engage in primary-product processing and small manufacturing industries, petty retail and distribution businesses, provision of services, employment in the bureaucracy, and casual labor. In the countryside, the sparse population relies on subsistence agriculture, cottage handicrafts, small-scale exploitation of forest products, and extensive cattle rearing (Fig. 3.1). Fishing involves both urban and rural dwellers. Occupational structure has remained relatively stable, although the economically active population has more than doubled in most sectors over the past decade as a consequence of natural increase, in-migration, and rural-urban drift. The latter is reflected in the rapid growth of the construction industry, encouraged by a pro-union state governor (1985–1991) preoccupied with public housing projects in collaboration with the federal government. The influx of migrants and the onset of the debt crisis also prompted an expansion of the informal and underground economies, evidenced by the growing numbers of itinerant vendors, unregistered businesses, drug dealers, purveyors of contraband and traffickers in human lives, such as the *polleros* (poulterers) who smuggle Central Americans into the country through the forests of southern Campeche and Quintana Roo. Naturally, these activities are not reflected in official statistics but comprise one of the nation's most dynamic and efficient sectors because of their freedom from burdensome government regulation and the initiative and industry of the individuals attracted to them. Without these enterprises, the official state unemployment rate, estimated at 7 percent in 1990 (*Tribuna de Campeche*, 5 April 1991), would be significantly higher.

Despite the recent population explosion on the southern interior frontier, these trends underscore the coastal city bias that has been the dominant theme since the colonial era while accentuating the long-standing rivalry between Campeche, the state capital, and Ciudad del Carmen. In the eyes of many denizens of the capital "Campeche [state] is Campeche [city]—there is nothing inland," while "Carmen is full of foreigners and

88

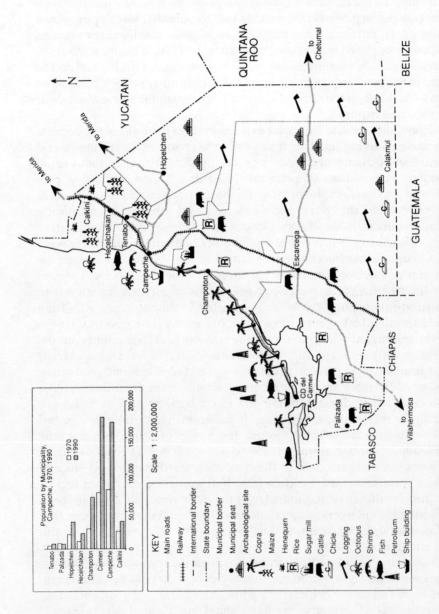

FIGURE 3.1 Campeche: Municipalities, population, and economic activities (NOTE: The municipality of Escarcega was created in 1990 after that year's census was conducted.)

upstarts" (I-135, businessman, Campeche, March 1990). The Ciudad del Carmen elite retort that "Campeche [state] is always run by the old Campeche [city] families. Those dinosaurs won't let anybody from Carmen have any power because there is some real entrepreneurship down there. That's why this state is still in the last century" (I-136, businessman and former civil servant, Campeche, December 1989). Thus, for example, Campeche denied entry to a major Mérida supermarket chain in order to protect existing businesses, while Ciudad del Carmen welcomed a branch and enjoys its discounts. Meanwhile, the ongoing modernization of urban life-styles accentuates the distinction between city and country. Most urbanites feel committed to survival in the cash economy at all costs, while rural dwellers still have the option of retreating to its margins.

Town and Country

On the surface, the city of Campeche reflects much less of the ravages of the twentieth century than most other Mexican provincial capitals. Urban growth at the beginning of this century prompted the destruction of segments of the walls around the downtown core, but enough of them still stand to provide a vivid reminder of Campeche's colorful pirate past. In addition, the core's narrow street grid, the numerous sixteenth- and seventeenth-century churches, and the gracious facades of the former homes of the mercantile elite preserve the form and feeling of a colonial city. Mangrove swamps to the north and coastal hills to the south forced the limited suburban development of the last thirty years inland and out of sight. Even the recent migrant influx that is largely responsible for more than doubling the city's population from 1980 to some 150,000 inhabitants in 1990 has been accommodated more or less discreetly on the fringes of the swamps and nestled in the rolling topography back from the coastline.

The major anachronism is immediately visible when one looks out to sea—or where the sea used to be. By the late 1950s, the combination of geographical constraints and colonial relics meant that Campeche could not build any modern facilities without destroying its past. Consequently, the state government has spent much of the last three decades extending the city seaward via landfills. The original fill immediately in front of the downtown core was promptly occupied by the governor's palace, state administrative buildings, PRI headquarters, and two four-star hotels surrounded by acres of parking lots, sports facilities, parks, and playgrounds. The contrast between "New Campeche," with its ultramodern buildings and surrealistic parks decked with abstract fountains and statues, and the aged dignity of the colonial city apparently startled the citizens so much that the new public spaces initially remained deserted.

Today, however, the annex is heavily used, particularly since the addition of Campeche's first supermarket and a shopping mall in 1985. The official motive for this new extension was to provide space for a small boat harbor and a dozen luxury hotels; it was anticipated that PEMEX would abandon its Ciudad del Carmen base for the seat of state power. This move did not materialize, however, and the lone new hotel is on the landward side of the fill. The fishing barrio of San Francisco has been cut off from sea frontage and is using a residual puddle for harborage, since the new pier's dock is three kilometers out to sea and still in shallow waters. Meanwhile, the state government has built public housing on some of the most expensive and scenic real estate in Campeche.

Despite the radical change represented by the landfill, modernization in the city of Campeche has been gradual and relatively unobtrusive overall. New and old have become grafted together more or less harmoniously in this most recent Campechano syncretism, in which tradition still plays a large part despite the "Americanized" veneer. Supermarkets, suburbs, discotheques, pizzerias, and satellite dishes epitomize the changing life-styles of Campeche's affluent classes, while public housing projects, squatter settlements, and stereos symbolize modernization for the poor, but the rhythm of daily life and the annual cycle remain much the same with a few new twists.

For the upper and middle classes, the day may now begin with a jog along the new seafront track instead of an early morning horseback ride. Leading businessmen, bureaucrats, and politicians then congregate for breakfast at the cafeteria of one of the new hotels instead of in the old cafés around the plaza to see and be seen and to keep up with the latest business, political, and social gossip which glues the system together. As the sun heats up, uniformed schoolchildren, office workers, and store clerks throng the narrow sidewalks. Cars, trucks, and buses honk their way along the increasingly congested inland arteries. Produce is disgorged at the market, where housewives and maids stoop under their daily burden. Businessmen jostle for central parking spots; decrepit pickups and Volkswagens pull up to government offices, where the minions of Mexico's still-massive bureaucracy stand around awaiting orders. Sluggish fans gasp and aging air conditioners chug and drip while secretaries peck at their typewriters and their bosses preside over meeting after meeting. Campesinos with mud still clinging to their sandals throng the lobbies of government agencies, and many are still waiting at two o'clock when the official business day begins to flag and most people head home for the main meal and siesta.

As the shadows lengthen, the stores reopen, and the pace picks up again. Middle-class mothers deliver their children to dance class, shoppers browse the new import shops, sports teams assemble, and a new wave of joggers sweeps the sea wall, including an increasing number of Campeche's matrons, who until recently eschewed all sports in public. By nine o'clock the streets are emptying, though lovers linger in the parks, and the focus shifts homeward to television soap operas, a taco or a hamburger, and so to bed. On weekends affluent teenagers cruise late in their cars, discos blare, and the hotels fill with diners and dancers. On Sundays the city sleeps except for church, sports, an occasional family outing, and the evening *paseo* (promenade), now as likely to be along the seawall as around the central plaza.

The yearly cycle follows a similar cadence. The day of the Virgin of Guadalupe, 12 December, marking the miraculous appearance of the Virgin Mary to the Indian Juan Diego in 1531, signals the beginning of nearly a month of celebration, lasting until the Three Kings bring gifts to the children on 6 January in commemoration of their visit to the newborn Christ. Government offices close for at least ten days around the Christmas–New Year peak, and attention shifts to the home, *posadas* (house-to-house processions of figures of Joseph and Mary), shopping for the festivities, and parties. The climax is Noche Buena (Christmas Eve), when late-evening mass is followed by a family feast and a round of all-night house hopping. Tradition is under assault by the plastic folding Christmas tree, which is rapidly replacing the native poinsettia, and by Santa Claus, who brings an increasing number of Campeche children expensive presents on Noche Buena, overshadowing the simple toys brought later by the Three Kings.

For many of the rich as well as for the poor, the debt crisis has combined with the increased emphasis on consumer goods to make Christmas a time of acute financial stress rather than celebration. Many of the formerly affluent have had to give up Christmas vacations abroad and even holiday visits to family members elsewhere in the Republic. Nevertheless, they still feel compelled to spend perhaps half their monthly income on toys and almost as much on Christmas decorations, new appliances, liquor, and imported delicacies, often shopping in Mérida, where prices are lower. The poor also spend far beyond their means, making tremendous sacrifices, for example, to acquire a turkey for traditional festive foods, even though the price of a family-sized bird reached $30 in December 1989 (Table 3.1). As a result:

> It takes us nearly the whole year now to recover from the *cuesta de enero* (the January hill) of bills. You borrow and sell, always falling deeper into the swamp, but you've got to do something to make Christmas for the family. You can't cut back at Christmas, even if it means no new clothes all year. (I-137, housewife, Campeche, December 1989).[8]

The somewhat-jaded aftermath of the Christmas season lasts for about a month until the festive calendar starts to wind up again for *Carnaval* (the

TABLE 3.1   "Christmas Basket" Consumer Prices, Campeche, December 1989

Product	Price	
	Pesos	*$U.S.*
Frozen turkey (1 kg)	8,000	3.00
Pork loin (1 kg)	15,000	5.64
Pork leg (1 kg)	12,000	4.51
American-type ham (1 kg)	11,000	4.14
Bacalao (dried salt cod) (1 kg)	90,000	33.80
Medium shrimp (1 kg)	20,000	7.52
Chicken (1 kg)	7,000	2.63
Grapes (1 kg)	8,000	3.00
Nuts (1 kg)	8,500	3.20
Domestic brandy (1 l)	18,500	6.95
Plastic Christmas tree (1 m high)	20,000	7.52
Tree decorations (6 balls)	5,000	1.88
Mandarin oranges (1 kg)	1,400	0.53

NOTE: U.S. $1 = $2,660 pesos; daily minimum wage = $10,000 pesos.
SOURCE: Campeche City and Ciudad del Carmen posted price lists.

Shrovetide Carnival), the last opportunity for merrymaking before the solemn season of Lent. Campeche boasts one of Mexico's three traditional Carnivals, but those of Veracruz and Mazatlán are bigger and attract more visitors. During the week-long celebration, King Ugly, his Queen and Juan Carnaval (the Lord of Misrule) preside over a succession of parades, and the citizens enjoy the attractions of the fair, sideshows, and dances. Each year, however, traditions slip farther into the background. Masks, disguises, tricks, and pranks have given way to a sequence of beauty pageants in educational institutions and social clubs, ranging from kindergarten coronations to showcase balls for the eligible sons and daughters of the elite. Few people now follow the ancient practices of Shrove Tuesday, such as parading in decorated carts and throwing blue paint to ward off evil, in part because of the current expense of the inputs.

After the burning of Juan Carnaval to signify the end of the celebration of human carnality, comes Ash Wednesday with its anointment of ashes. The following six weeks of Lent are supposed to be dedicated to reflection and abstinence from frivolous diversion and red meat (a hardship for many in these times of inflated fish prices). Then Campechanos begin to anticipate the pleasures of Easter Week, for many now more a secular than a sacred celebration, during which Mexicans from all parts of the country flock to the beach in a family escape from routine. After Easter, the long hot summer sets in. The start of the rainy season at the end of May curtails public social life to some extent. Business continues as usual, interrupted only by sundry national holidays and the fiesta of San Román in September with its pilgrimage in honor of the Black Christ, who is said to have arrived in this Campeche barrio by sea in 1565. After respect to the dead is paid on Todos Santos (All Saints' Day) and the Dia de los Muertos (All Souls' Day) on 1 and 2 November, the year winds down to the start of another cycle.

If the tempo of urban life in Campeche is still slow and measured, in the countryside the pace is even slower, more closely attuned to nature, the daily movement of the sun, the rhythm of the seasons, and the agricultural cycle. The rural population is still sparse in most areas, congregated in small towns, villages, and hamlets rather than dispersed in the fields; the innate urbanity of pre-Columbian Maya ceremonial life was reinforced by the nucleation fostered by Spanish colonial management and the federal ejidal policy of this century. "Urbanity" here is not a separation from nature—on the contrary unity with nature is the dominant theme in Maya cosmology—but a tradition of community responsibility and mutual obligations expressed in collective strategies for survival. Although many of the old expressions of community integrity, such as the *fagina* (the collective work party) are now falling into disuse, the structures are still there and are called up when the need arises, such as in the cleanup required after Hurricane Gilbert devastated the state in 1988.

On the surface, rural life-styles and landscapes appear to have altered quite rapidly in recent years. Twenty years ago the state was an empty backwater, with signs of rural modernization confined to the larger settlements along the three paved highways. The majority of the Maya inhabitants eked out a precarious living from slash-and-burn cultivation of small plots of maize, beans, and squash, employing tools and techniques probably little different from those of their pre-Columbian ancestors. Today, there is a sense of change in much of rural Campeche, at least of progress attempted if not always accomplished. New roads have been constructed, and the major highways bustle with traffic. In the southern interior, cattle barons are competing with the established producers of neighboring Tabasco on pastures recently carved out of the forest. The government has been attempting to transform both ejidos and private holdings in central Campeche and the southern deltas into the new Mexican "rice bowl," challenging the northwestern state of Sinaloa for supremacy. The Camino Real and Los Chenes districts in the north are a checkerboard of small irrigation projects for peasants. Meanwhile the frontier of forest colonization and lumber exploitation is constantly being pushed east and south toward the Guatemalan border. Schools, clinics, potable water systems, and electricity are now widespread in areas tapped by the expanding highway network. Each year more television antennas sprout from thatched huts, and the transistor radio is ubiquitous. Campesinos who used to depend solely on shanks' mare now ride buses or their ejidos' pickups. Jeans and jogging shoes are now as common as sandals and coarse white work clothes.

As in the city, however, these new elements have been grafted onto the old ways in a relatively congruous fashion, causing little perturbation of a daily life that remains centered on wresting a living from the soil. For many, the day still begins before dawn in traditional Maya huts, which most likely have changed very little in style and construction in the last nineteen hundred years (Wauchope, 1934). These houses are nearly rectangular with rounded ends and are made of poles tied together with lianas. Sometimes the spaces between the poles are filled with a mud plaster to increase weatherproofing. Usually, four upright poles support the palm-thatched roof over the single room below. The floors are bare earth, hard-packed by the constant slapping of bare feet and assiduously swept and sprinkled with water each day. The furnishings are few and simple, consisting of a bare minimum of household utensils, hammocks, and the odd bench or chair. Virtually every household, however, now exhibits some symbol of modern times in pride of place—a modest television set, a shiny stereo receiver, a refrigerator, a sofa, plastic webbed chairs. A separate structure behind the house serves as a kitchen, and in the backyard a thatched screen shields the latrine if there is one.

The day begins early because the men need to reach their milpas, perhaps five or ten kilometers or more from home, at first light to do as much work as possible before the sun gets hot. Meanwhile, the women commence the daily round of making *pozole* (maize gruel) for breakfast, preparing corn for tortillas,[9] hauling water, and doing the inevitable laundry and the marketing, if there are goods to be sold or bought and money to pay for the latter. The children are sent off to school if one is accessible and if the family considers education important and can afford the necessary shoes, clothing, supplies, and loss of household labor. The men return from the fields in early or mid-afternoon, depending on the season and the distance from home, then eat the main meal of the day and rest in their hammocks before bathing and donning clean clothes. Personal cleanliness is one of the most striking characteristics of the Maya; bathing is believed to be vital to good health, while the women's dazzling huipiles tend to make foreign visitors feel that they are using the wrong washing powder. After dinner comes relaxation with the family, now often in front of the television, or a stroll to the plaza, which even the smallest hamlet considers essential as a symbol of civilization and the dignified life. Following sports for the youths, relaxed conversation for their elders, and a couple of beers in the *cantina* (bar) or store for the more affluent men, most of the inhabitants return to their homes at dusk. Then come final chores and perhaps more television, as international politicians and personalities are fast becoming household names even in this remote region, where many people have never visited Mérida let alone Mexico City. By nine o'clock sounds of activity are dying down, and another day comes to an end in the rocking of hammocks.

The yearly round in the countryside follows the same basic pattern as in the city but with less emphasis on formal religious and secular celebrations. This is not so much because of a lack of resources for public display but because of the persistence of pre-Hispanic Maya sacred cosmology, which has a strongly pragmatic and personal dimension linked to the imperative of agricultural production in an uncertain natural order. This cosmology is laced with Spanish Catholic symbols and concepts but is structured via complementary dualities rather than Western dichotomies (Faust, 1988). Thus the spiritual and the tangible aspects of everyday life are interwoven rather than mediated. Humans as part of nature must interpret and appease the rains, the winds, and the land itself if a successful corn harvest is to be obtained. Agricultural practices in themselves are important religious rituals with immediate practical meaning as part of a strategy for survival. In this context, the dry season and the wet season become more immediately significant than Christmas or Easter, the year being read by nature's signs and the folklore surrounding their interpretation rather than by dates on a calendar. However, the major milestones of the religious cycle of Catholicism, including local events such as pilgrimages, are more widely and fervently observed than in the rapidly secularizing city.[10]

The dry season in November brings the *nortes* (northers), the "bad winds" that "dry your skin, chill your bones and make a man want to beat his wife" (I-8, ejidatario, Pomuch, December 1989). Christmas is marked by a series of posadas, and the humblest hut boasts a crèche or nativity scene. The season is also celebrated by a succession of dances demanding considerable stamina of both legs and liver. Then, according to the local saying, "January is a stew, all mixed up"; successive days exhibit the weather of the months of the year and, following the Xoc-Kin, the Maya day count, allows the prediction of auspicious planting weather. A carpet of yellow wildflowers in this month (*tajonal*, the first honey harvest) portends a good year for maize, "the body of Our Lord" or "Saint Maize." In "Febrero loco" (crazy February), which brings both Carnaval's masks and tricks and the five evil days of the old Maya calendar, one must be on guard because anything can happen. Easter brings the solemn observance of the stations of the cross. When the oak and the wild apple or breakax flower in late spring and swarms of flying ants appear, it is time to get ready to plant. If *los Duenos de los Vientos* (the gods who own the winds) are late in bringing the *Chaacs* (rain deities) to water the sprouting maize, then the h-men must perform the rainmaking ceremony. However, the summer rains can also destroy what they have created if agricultural technology fails or the moral order is violated. Many Campeche Maya believe that the destruction wrought by Hurricane Gilbert, a rare phenomenon on the Gulf side of the peninsula, was intended as punishment "because people don't live good lives anymore" (I-7, ejidatario, Pomuch, March 1990). The rains also bring sickness "and your babies die because the doctor and the shaman are profiting from inflation so you can't afford to consult them" (I-5, ejidatario, Pomuch, February 1990). So it goes, as fathers pass on the wisdom to their sons, mothers teach their daughters, and the living revere and care for the dead.

This is not to imply that traditions remain static or act as impenetrable armor against the onslaught of modernity or the Protestants, who have been steadily increasing their ranks in Campeche over the past two decades. Conversion seems to appeal in particular to families whose expenditures on alcohol are a major factor contributing to the perpetuation of their poverty. However, joining a Protestant church and giving up drinking also means shunning traditional community rituals and mutual support networks, accelerating the erosion of custom. Each year Maya cosmology and folk knowledge recede farther into the background of daily life, relegated to the consciousness of the old as younger generations expand their horizons into the national culture and lose fluency in the Maya language. Nevertheless, many of the guiding principles of the old moral order still prevail, influencing the course and direction of change and the management of crises in the Campeche countryside.

The Debt Crisis in Campeche

The national debt crisis first impinged on some Campechanos' consciousness in 1982, when the state's economy finally seemed to be entering a phase of genuine dynamism in both the export and domestic sectors. The new offshore oil wells were just coming into full production, the Americans' voracious appetite for Campeche shrimp was well established, and the expanded transportation infrastructure and new federal agricultural development policy together made it appear that at last something might be done to stimulate productivity in the stagnant countryside. In this climate of increasing confidence, the state government began to seek fresh markets for potential exports, while a few independent investors planned innovative projects in spite of capital flight and the tendency of both political and business establishments to stifle initiatives from outside the system.[11] Meanwhile, urbanites and some rural sectors stepped up consumer spending on both durables and more frivolous items, and even the ejidatarios made plans beyond supplying the day's dinner. Then came the oil glut, the subsequent plunge in barrel prices, and the end of economic optimism.

In Campeche as in the rest of the country, the crisis has meant a decline in standard of living and productivity that affects both town and country, but strips the already decapitalized agricultural sector of its last resources. In the first few years, Campeche's isolation, provincialism, and lack of economic modernization provided some degree of insulation from the national debt fallout. In some ways, in fact, the crisis seemed to reinforce the status quo; "Campechanos didn't have much to lose to begin with," and "a closed society closed in on itself even more" (I-132, businessman, Campeche, March 1991). Plans for new government development projects were, of course, immediately shelved, but people were accustomed to abrupt discontinuities in public-sector programs. Fledgling business ventures were hit hard by the devaluation of the peso, particularly if they owed money in dollars on imported equipment and other technological inputs, but such initiatives were few. Even the 100 percent inflation in 1982 did not occasion deep concern, for the most part being dismissed as "just another government screw-up—another craziness from Mexico [City]" (I-140, businessman, Campeche, March 1991). Capital flight increased, but this was already common for those with significant resources to protect. Crisis side effects such as shortages in basic commodities were felt locally but tended to be perceived as temporary inconveniences endemic to the inefficient Mexican production and distribution system.

As time passed, however, and the crisis became a way of life with no end in sight, the cumulative effects of austerity eroded the comfortable bases of Campeche life. Extensive cutbacks in civil service jobs, inflation, reduction of subsidies on foods and cooking fuel, and an increase in gasoline prices of 4,380 percent over the first six years of the crisis (*El Dia*, 17 December 1987) combined to reduce purchasing power. Acquiring a second or third job, wearing old clothes, and consuming less protein became the norm as families struggled to maintain some facsimile of their former life-styles. The wage and price control pact of 1987 resulted in some deceleration in inflation, but "people felt that they had slipped so far back they could never catch up" (I-141, professional, Campeche, December 1989). A threshold seems to have been reached about the time that Salinas assumed office in 1988, when Campechanos from all walks of life claim that: "Things really got hard," "the burden became unbearable," "the crisis really got to the countryside," and "it became obvious that something has truly got to change in Mexico." Whether the reforms initiated by the Salinas administration are comprehensive and enduring enough to resolve the crisis remains to be seen. In the interim many Campechanos have developed new strategies for survival marking, for some, a major change in old patterns and attitudes that may not be reversed if and when better times arrive.

In particular, the debt crisis seems to have shocked many of the urban elite and upper middle classes out of their complacency. Continuing capital flight is not enough to provide a comfortable hedge against inflation, and Christmas in Las Vegas, educating children in North America, summer trips to Disney World, and shopping sprees or medical appointments in San Antonio are now often only a memory. Confidence has given way to caution in the face of continuing fears of massive devaluation and a government that seems serious about tapping a neglected source of revenue, the pocketbooks of the affluent: "You put one part of your savings in jewelry, send part abroad, invest another part in houses, only one or two modest houses, or they'll get you with taxes, and another part in land but not too much or they'll expropriate you" (I-142, civil servant, Campeche, January 1990). Businessmen too are facing an end to "tax paradises" under fiscal reform. Most Campeche businesses are small and were classified as "minor contributors" under the old tax system; now they are included under a standard formula for all enterprises and must maintain one set of books, charge value-added tax, keep receipts, and be scrutinized by government accountants. This requires a major change in operating practices:

> God knows the tax system needs reform, but small business can't manage all this bookkeeping; neither can you afford to put everything down on paper. Anyway, when you look at a pen made in Mexico, who knows what percentage of the cost is materials, labor, value-added, or what? Only the Japanese know stuff like that. It's all to satisfy GATT requirements anyway, not to help businesses like mine. We will have to shut our doors soon, I am sure. (I-132, businessman, Campeche, March 1990)

The economic opening promoted by the Salinas administration is particularly threatening to Campeche businessmen, with their tradition of resisting investment from Mérida, let alone from abroad. The possibility of an American presence in Campeche is especially intimidating:

> If the American cruise ships come, or they develop a resort at Sabancuy, they'll take over the state, just like they did in Quintana Roo. The worst is that the Mexican family will be destroyed. I don't want my family to live like they show on television, with no time for each other, no traditional values, no moral basis. (I-143, professional, Campeche, November 1989)

At the same time, however, the new import shops are eagerly patronized, even in these times of austerity—diet ice cream, foreign cosmetics, and gourmet potato chips at $3 a can being seen as infinitely superior to Mexican products. All in all, Campeche businessmen want things to get better but feel that "big capital would swallow up the little fishes here" (I-132, businessman, Campeche, March 1990).

Perhaps the sector most devastated by the debt crisis in Campeche is the bureaucracy. All government dependencies have suffered budgetary retrenchment and program cutbacks, and some have been eliminated altogether. This means extensive job loss, early retirement, and hiring freezes. In Campeche, employees of the Ministry of Agriculture and Water Resources (SARH) who have been fortunate enough to hold onto their jobs no longer enjoy the privileges of the boom years. Only very senior officials now rate a chauffeur. Indeed, the massive fleets of shiny government trucks and Volkswagens have shrunk to a few decrepit vehicles, many of which have been sold to employees who are often unable to afford the gas to perform the field components of their jobs. At the same time, the government's widely publicized campaign against misuse of public-sector resources and corruption means that official vehicles are less frequently observed in obvious personal use (such as on Sundays at the beach), development agency banquets at luxury hotels are much more restrained than in the past, and denunciations of corrupt employees appear almost daily in the press. This does not mean, necessarily, that corruption and malfeasance have disappeared. On the contrary, increased workloads, deteriorating equipment, and pitiable pay compared with the private sector combine to reduce morale:

> Our main problem now is personnel. We have good engineers, the best, with fifteen, twenty years seniority or more, who take home 700,000 pesos a month, just $260. You need more than that for food alone. And if your car breaks down, well, it stays broken. So those who can, leave SARH and go to the private sector or the state government where the pay is better. And the rest, well, they will have to take on the jobs of the eliminated programs in addition, when they can't even get their own work done properly. It's dangerous to make judgments when you don't know what's going on out there [in the country]. But if they don't go out when they should, can you blame them? (I-138, civil servant, Campeche, March 1991)

> You pad your work sheets, invent a meeting, go to another office instead of out to the country, and when you do go out it has to be worth your while— you take a box of tomatoes, watermelons, a case of mangos, whatever they [the ejidatarios] have got. Wouldn't you? (I-144, civil servant, Campeche, December 1989)

In this context, the government's campaign to trim and clean up the bureaucracy in order to make it more effective in increasing productivity seems somewhat contradictory under austerity budgets. "You don't get good work out of someone who works for nothing" (1-138, civil servant,

Campeche, December 1989). Meanwhile, agriculture and the ejidatarios
in particular have borne the brunt of the reforms and cutbacks.

While the upper and middle classes in Campeche have suffered a
drastic deterioration in standard of living and morale, the urban poor
have had to struggle even more desperately simply to survive. The
"popular classes" spend most of their time and energy matching means
and ends. For many, the government wage and price controls initiated
purportedly to protect them appear to be the primary cause of their
afflictions. News of the next increase in the minimum wage is eagerly
anticipated but without any real hope of alleviating the daily struggle
to balance the family budget. Those fortunate enough to be regularly
employed in 1990 had to get by on a minimum wage of 10,000 pesos a day.
They do not have to worry about keeping a car running, but gasoline
price increments push up the price of public transit too (Table 3.2).[12] Conversation tends to be dominated by rumors of increased tortilla prices,
food shortages, or the black market in black beans. An old lady stares at
the goods in a subsidized food shop, knowing that she can afford only one
or two items in the regulated basic food basket (Table 3.3). Consumption
of "popular fish" such as jack mackerel, regarded as trash less than a
decade ago, has increased (Table 3.4). Some buy fewer tortillas, while
others buy more, compensating for less protein with additional bulk, with
the result that state nutrition levels show a noticeable decline, particularly
amongst children, as powdered milk and meat have become luxury
items.[13] Thus, paradoxically, "the crisis in Campeche has made us fatter:
an extra kilo of tortillas a day makes two on the hips" (I-145, housewife,
Campeche, November 1989).

For those without regular employment, each day is dominated by the
search for a daily wage. Bars, refreshment stands, and street corners carry
rumors of the prospects of work. Men wait at the outskirts of town for a

TABLE 3.2   Miscellaneous Service Costs, Campeche, March 1990

Service	Cost	
	Pesos	$U.S.
Hotel, 4-star double room	100,000	37.60
Hotel, 1-star double room	15,000	5.64
Restaurant meal (1st grade)	20,000	7.52
Restaurant meal (popular grade)	7,000	2.63
Dental visit (tooth filling)	15,000	5.64
Bus fare (city)	800	0.30
Bus fare to Mérida	8,700	3.27
Bus fare to Mexico City	70,800	26.62

Source: Field observations.

TABLE 3.3   "Basic Food Basket" Consumer Prices, Campeche, January 1989

	Price			
	Supermarket		"Popular" Store[a]	
Product	Pesos	$U.S.	Pesos	$U.S.
Soup pasta	373	0.14	439	0.17
Vegetable oil (1 l)	2,230	0.84	2,230	0.84
Oat cereal (1 kg)	4,493	1.89	4,086	1.54
Instant coffee (100 g)	3,258	1.22	3,158	1.19
Instant chocolate (400 g)	2,782	1.05	2,700	1.02
Boullion cubes (225 g)	3,420	1.29	3,383	1.27
Margarine (90 g)	541	0.20	522	0.20
Pasteurized milk (500 ml)	970	0.36	961	0.36
Powdered milk for children (450 g)	5,051	1.90	5,051	1.90
Detergent (560 g)	1,172	0.44	1,150	0.43
Laundry soap (400 g)	987	0.37	966	0.36
Ground beef (1st grade) (1 kg)	14,500	5.45	13,500	5.08
Beefsteak (1 kg)	14,500	5.45	13,500	5.08
Dry beans (1 kg)	2,750	1.03	1,100	0.41
Eggs (1 kg)	2,275	0.86	2,275	0.86
Toilet paper (4 rolls)	3,549	1.33	3,514	1.32

[a]"Popular" stores are operated by government agencies such as CONASUPO. Regulated prices are enforced.

Sources: Instituto Nacional del Consumidor, Delegación Campeche, 10 January 1989, and field checking.

contractor's truck which is short a man. Domestic service positions with room and board for less than minimum wage are eagerly sought for the elder daughters of families with too many mouths to feed. A regular job in construction is the almost impossible dream. If a boy can get taken on as an unpaid errand boy, then become assistant and perhaps even a master artisan, then he will be set for life because of the relatively high wages of the privileged construction workers' union and the possibilities for moonlighting. If conventional sources of employment fail, then increasingly people turn to activities beyond the law—drug dealing, burglary, hijacking a bus—as Campeche's formerly "safe" cities and towns catch up with the rest of the modern world. The increasing stress of life on the urban edge is reflected in the incidence of popular millenarian movements such as the Casa de Josué in 1982, when the eruption of the Chichonal volcano in Chiapas combined with the anxieties of the debt crisis to trigger the emergence of a sect in a Campeche barrio under a prophetess who ordered the construction of a Noah's Ark (Bojórquez Urzaiz, 1985).

TABLE 3.4   Selected Consumer Prices, Campeche, March 1990

	Price	
Product	Pesos	$U.S.
Pharmacy		
Toothpaste (125 ml)	2,300	0.86
Antidiarrheal suspension (290 ml)	3,501	1.31
Cold remedy (30 capsules)	680	0.26
Sinus spray (15 ml)	1,816	0.68
Antibiotic (28 tablets)	10,000	3.76
Appliance store		
Small refrigerator	991,760	373.00
Small kitchen stove	423,430	159.19
Pedestal fan	143,000	53.80
Blender	90,000	33.83
Public market		
Red snapper[a] (1 kg)	6,000	2.26
Small snook (1 kg)	6,000	2.26
Large seabass (1 kg)	10,000	3.76
Dogfish (1 kg)	7,000	2.63
Jack mackerel (1 kg)	2,750	1.03
Large shrimp (1 kg)	26,000	9.77
Miscellaneous		
Regular gasoline (1 l)	600	0.23
Tortillas (1 kg)	700	0.26

[a]Fish prices enforced during Lent 1990.
SOURCE: Field observations.

The impact of the debt crisis on the Campeche countryside was apparently less dramatic at first because of the subsistence production cushion and the relatively recent and still restricted nature of market integration. Wage labor was not widespread in most areas of rural Campeche in 1982; sale of surplus staple crops was sporadic and consumption of modern-sector items still embryonic. However, many households had become accustomed to depending on the cash income of at least one occasional wage earner, and in most years campesinos produced some surplus for sale. Virtually everyone bought some consumer items on a regular basis. For example, soft drinks had become a status necessity even in remote communities lacking electrification for refrigeration.[14] Thus the 31.1 percent decrease in real agricultural minimum wage between 1981 and 1983 (World Bank, 1986) and the continuing decline of official crop prices against rising production costs were a severe shock to rural household budgets, causing abrupt contraction of spending on nonessentials.

It is only in the past few years that the full impact of the debt crisis has been felt in the Campeche countryside. The main effects have been a gradual but cumulative retrenchment and recession as state intervention in peasant agriculture has focused on the few productive sectors while high interest rates, government pricing and subsidy policies, and the soaring cost of agricultural inputs have combined to create de facto deficit production. The net result is the paradox that commercial agriculture is not a business proposition, as Campeche's agricultural sector by and large has become even more entrenched at the household subsistence level. "The life of the campesino is a dance in reverse as we have gone backwards even more over the last ten years" (I-22, ejidatario, Tinún, January 1990). The countryside continues to be subordinated to the interests, decisions, and mistakes of outsiders.

In summary, the long-term roots of the agricultural and debt crises in their Campeche manifestations go back to the colonial era and the legacy of dependency first on mercantilism and then on raw-material exports, while the area now occupied by the state of Yucatán emerged as the region's administrative and economic center. These historical forces promoting external dependence and internal disparities have been compounded by the interplay between increasing integration of the region into the domestic market and the opposing forces for separatism and continuing isolation from the national mainstream. Although, until recently, the effects of the import-substitution growth model have been somewhat muted in Campeche by virtue of distance from the center, historical and economic circumstances, and the desire of its inhabitants, the state has been influenced deeply by the generalized ethos of agricultural decapitalization. Thus the national policy of promoting industry over agriculture, of sacrificing the interests of the countryside to those of the growing urban centers, and of favoring the north over the south has made the agriculture of the Yucatán Peninsula one of the least dynamic in the country, requiring large imports of staples to feed its population (Menéndez, 1981).

Campeche's general economic inertia—the legacy of a series of past booms and busts and of tensions between center and periphery on international, national, and regional levels—has been exacerbated over the past three decades by the mistaken strategies selected for exploiting the agricultural frontier. In the process, fragile and complex tropical ecosystems have been subjected to the direct transfer of inappropriate temperate technologies, causing irreversible ecological devastation as well being a failure in production terms. The net result has been a progressive erosion of the traditional bases for making a living while failing to substitute viable alternatives, as increasing reliance on state initiative became the modern variant of an ongoing external dependency cycle. From the perspective of many Campeche peasants:

The more things change, the more they stay the same, at least in the countryside. Everything they say and do in Mexico [City] only means more sweat, blood, and hunger for the campesinos. After five hundred years of oppression, while the fine folk in Campeche [City] condoned the rape of our resources, why should we believe that anything will be different now? (1-8, ejidatario, Pomuch, December 1989)

Notes

1. After the sudden and mysterious Classic Maya collapse in the Guatemalan and Mexican Petén in the ninth century A.D., the northern portions of the peninsula became the focus of Maya culture. The Putún Maya occupied southern Campeche and the east coast of the peninsula, while the Itzá established a base at Chichén Itzá and dominated the entire northern part of Yucatán under the League of Mayapan, a loose confederation of virtually autonomous cities. This alliance remained more or less stable from A.D. 987 to 1224, when an influential family of the Itzá lineage, the Cocoms, forced the Itzá to abandon Chichén. The Cocoms continued to rule northern Yucatán from the city of Mayapan until 1441, when an alliance of secondary Maya cities under the rival Xiu group undertook a successful uprising. This brought centralized Maya government to an end as the great civilization disintegrated into warring petty provinces (Morley, 1956; Nesbitt, 1980).

2. Human sacrifice does not appear to have been a dominant motif in the Yucatán Maya realm until the Postclassic, when its practice increased after the arrival of the Itzá (Morley, 1956; Nesbitt, 1980). Ah-Kin-Pech was located on the main Postclassic migration route of the Itzá and Xiu who brought with them the religion of Kukulkán (Quetzalcoatl) (Piña Chan, 1977: 9).

3. This discussion follows Wilson's (1980) delineation of the southern boundary of the peninsula from the Río Sarstún, which forms the border between Belize and Guatemala, to the Laguna de Términos and the Gulf of Mexico in southern Campeche. Other definitions locate the peninsula's southern limit somewhat to the north of this (e.g., Wadell, 1937).

4. Generally, rainfall in the peninsula decreases from the southeast (Köppen Am, tropical monsoon) to the extreme northwest (Köppen BS, semiarid). In the intermediate tropical savanna zone (Köppen Aw), annual rainfall ranges from 1,000 to 2,500 millimeters, while the driest month has less than 60 millimeters of rainfall. The mean annual temperature is always above 18° C, while humidity averages 80 percent (Messmacher, 1967).

5. The critical significance of the availability of natural water supplies in the peninsula is reflected in the range of terminology employed to denote distinct occurrences. Cenote is the term commonly used in the north for a variety of sinkhole forms containing water. In the eastern interior of Campeche, the Maya word *chen* (well) is widely applied to different types of subterranean cavities. Aguadas were often maintained as reservoirs until the recent advent of potable water systems. In the south, bajos have been of vital importance throughout the period of human settlement. True cenotes generally occur in clusters rather than in

random distribution, with the major concentrations around Chichén Itzá and west and southeast of Mérida (Wilson, 1980). Only a few true cenotes occur in Campeche.

6. Located in an uninhabited forest cenote near Chan Santa Cruz, the Cross began to "speak" through ventriloquism to reassure the Maya of their survival. The cult provided the Cruzob Maya with a cultural focus, a higher authority, a nexus of social integrity, which kept them alive as a viable military force until defeat by General Bravo of the Mexican army in 1901 after which the Cruzob area was detached from the state of Yucatán to become the Federal Territory of Quintana Roo (Reed, 1964).

7. The revolution came late to the Yucatán (1915) and did not exhibit the violent or military phase characteristic of other parts of the country (Joseph, 1980). Most of the strife came in its aftermath, particularly in connection with the land reform issue, which naturally was bitterly opposed by the hacendados. Intending to make an example of the Yucatán, Cárdenas arrived in Progreso in 1937 with a boatload of engineers, surveyors, agricultural experts, and bureaucrats and presided over the largest single episode of agrarian reform ever undertaken in Mexico (Joseph, 1980; Reed, 1964). All hacienda lands except a 150-hectare nucleus were turned over to the campesinos as ejidos. The ejidal units were too small for efficient cultivation, however, and the ejidos lacked management experience and capital and frequently could not afford to replant the fields. Meanwhile, the fiber plants remained in the hands of the former plantation owners until nationalization in 1964. State monopoly of the cordage industry and supervision of production on collective ejidos accentuated economic inefficiencies and further distorted the incentive structure, resulting in a dramatic decline in profits and the impoverishment of the ejidatarios (Baklanoff, 1980; Brannon and Baklanoff, 1987).

8. January has become the traditional time for implementing the largest increase in the prices of consumer goods and services; in January 1990, price increments on items in the basic food basket) ranged between 3.1 percent and 42 percent (*Excelsior*, 27 February 1990).

9. Preparing corn for tortillas is a time-consuming process. First the corn must be shelled, cooked in lime water until the kernels soften and left to stand overnight. Then the soft grains known as *nixtamal* are ground on a *metate* (grinding stone) to form *masa*, a coarse-grained cereal, which is patted into tortillas to be cooked on a griddle. The advent of commercial mechanized *tortillerias* to even relatively small villages over the last two decades has liberated many countrywomen from at least some of the steps in this process. The more affluent simply buy the tortillas needed for the day. Those with more limited resources buy the raw masa or just take their prepared kernels to the tortilleria for grinding.

10. In addition to the fiesta of the Black Christ of San Román, four pilgrimage festivals associated with the Virgin Mary are important in the Maya yearly calendar, two in the state of Campeche and two in Yucatán (Faust, 1988). The Campeche fiestas at Hool and Chi'uiná are associated with the miraculous appearance of the Virgin in the village aguadas. The fiesta of the Maya Virgin of Candelaria (Candlemas) at Hool beginning on 2 February has attracted both rural and urban Campechanos since colonial times (Farriss, 1984).

11. For example, in 1980 an association of businessmen from Ciudad del Carmen established a large cashew plantation for the European market. Funding had been arranged from France, when the state and federal government stalled on the necessary permits and licenses. The scheme was then caught up in the debt crisis, proving particularly vulnerable since a large segment of the debt was in dollars for imported agricultural equipment. After years of financial struggle, the plantation eventually became a casualty of Hurricane Gilbert.

12. Public transit fares in the city of Campeche rose 60 percent in January 1990, while long-distance bus rates rose 21 percent. Massive increases in the costs of utilities, telephone, telegraph, and postal services also are common.

13. Rural malnutrition in Campeche was estimated at 47 percent in 1989, while 28 percent of the state's population were considered to be living in "extreme poverty," particularly in the 35 "popular colonies" surrounding the two major cities (*Tribuna de Campeche*, 20 January 1990).

14. Consumption of soft drinks was estimated at 70 million bottles a day nationally in 1989 (*Excelsior*, 15 February 1990).

4

The Milpa Meets
the Machine

A man is his milpa. If he doesn't grow maize, then who is he? How can you make the struggle? They are taking that away from us—who we are. (I-22, ejidatario, Tinún, February 1982)

Agricultural development is a business just like any other business. You have to look after yourself, your own interests. So you can only get ahead if you know the right people, who can get things done if they owe you, or you have the right favor to trade. The campesinos, well, they will never learn the game. It wouldn't work if they did. (I-130, civil servant, Campeche, November 1981)

El agro (agriculture) is much more than a way of making a living for over a third of the work force. It is a way of life not only for the farmers but for the politicians, the agrarian bureaucracy, the purveyors of cultivation inputs, and the myriad intermediaries who feed off the land and its producers. It is also an ideology with its roots both in the pre-Columbian past and in revolutionary reform, and rhetoric about the state's eminent domain and the social function of land tends to override the practicalities of making the soil produce. In this context, agriculture has become virtually synonymous with the state, at the core of national identity, and its fortunes symbolic of the health and welfare of the country. Thus a crisis of Mexican agriculture means much more than the failure of the nation to feed itself, but implies the inability of the country to sustain its identity. In this sense agriculture takes on a dual political significance, as both the preserver of the most enduring symbols of revolutionary reform and the barometer of the nation's economic condition. If the ejido and social justice must be sacrificed to the productivity imperative, then rhetoric and reality would seem to be headed for a collision course which will shake the very foundations of Mexico's social fabric.

In Campeche, agriculture is at the center of public life. Almost two-thirds of the front-page headlines of each of the two major local newspapers are devoted to agricultural and forestry themes—the progress of the rice harvest, the amount of bank credit allocated to a crop cycle, the illegal sale of tropical wood, the late payment of crop insurance. Since the onset of the debt crisis these headlines have tended to have a desperate slant—"Three-quarters of the State's Irrigation Units Abandoned," "Agricultural Production in the Worst Chaos Ever," "The End of Illusions in the Countryside," "The Majority of Rice Equipment in Disrepair" (*Crónica*, 2 January 1990; *Novedades*, 16 March 1990; *Tribuna de Campeche*, 30 December 1989; *Tribuna de Campeche*, 25 December 1989). As in the rest of Mexico, agricultural news is announced before it happens, perhaps to offset the negative press anticipated when the desired results are not obtained. Thus the headline "Self-Sufficiency Achieved in Maize" is very likely to presage a disastrous harvest. Optimistic statements from the agricultural development agencies about plans for more investment in the most beleaguered areas, diversification options, regional stimulus programs, and organizational improvements are counterbalanced by denunciations of corruption, announcements of budget cuts, lists of bankrupt ejidos, and statistics on the decline in the hectarage dedicated to commercial production, in addition to news of the usual plagues, diseases, and storms.

This detailed attention to agriculture reflects the number of Campechanos involved in the sector directly and indirectly as producers, consumers, planners, administrators, technicians, and distributors, in addition to the politicians who must walk the populist-productivity tightrope. Agricultural news is a topic for daily discussion in both rural and urban households, cafés, banks, the market and offices to a degree that would seem inconceivable in North America. There is little other economic news to report, and there is an increasing awareness of the risks of dependence on one or two export enclaves. Agriculture is the last resort, the constant in terms of making a living from the days of the ancient Maya to the present. If it fails, how will Campechanos live?

These concerns are particularly acute because modern agricultural development in Campeche is very recent. It is only in the past two decades that it has become the object of concerted government attention. Consistent with the state's economic history, this modernization quickly focused on yet another possible single export, rice. In those areas deemed most suitable for commercial agriculture, mechanization replaced slash-and-burn methods and milperos were driven out to the geographical, social, and economic margins as traditional practices became the scapegoat for the state's agricultural underdevelopment. The outcome has been a dramatic transformation of both rural landscapes and life-styles from which some ejidatarios undoubtedly benefitted in the short run while the majority of peasants have become enmeshed in dependency relationships associated with the increasing bureaucratization of agriculture that have restricted their ability to farm productively. Some ejidatarios have been able to transcend this dependency as public sector cutbacks have released opportunities for stifled individual initiative. For others, the ethos of state tutelage is too deeply ingrained. Furthermore, the ecological devastation caused by inappropriate agricultural technologies and the cutbacks and input-cost increments associated with the debt crisis reduce formal options and compound the uncertainties inherent in any agricultural enterprise. Thus the postcrisis retreat from commercial agriculture in Campeche has rendered many producers dysfunctional even at the household subsistence level as reliance on modern inputs persists but the economic viability of such dependence declines.

In this way, the ideology of Mexican agriculture, the history of state-planned agricultural development in Campeche, the legacy of the modernization strategies employed, institutional constraints, and the evolution of national agrarian policy combine to constrain present-day opportunities. To understand the role of the state in creating the current crises in the countryside and examine possible solutions, it is necessary to establish an agricultural baseline. In particular, as the failure of the machine prompts a second look at the vitality of peasant agro-ecosystems as a point of departure for sustainable development, it is important to understand the dynamics of making milpa.

Making Milpa: The Problem or the Solution?

Throughout the Yucatán Peninsula, the landscape shows remarkable alteration at the hands of an agricultural people possessing a bare minimum of primitive tools. Everywhere one encounters the testimony of the many centuries of Maya civilization not only in the numerous ruins of great cities but also in the almost complete modification of the original vegetal cover through the agency of the *roza-tumba-quema* (clearing-felling-burning) cultivation demanded by the swidden system and the systematic exploitation of the forests for dyes, hardwood, chicle, and building materials.

For the Maya, maize was and is the key to their survival as a people and a distinctive culture. Without maize "the Maya could not have developed . . . the most brilliant aboriginal civilization of the New World" (Morley, 1946: 142). Thus it is not surprising that maize became the center of Maya cosmology. Consequently, maize is much more than the primary staple, constituting a metaphor for life and its meaning in which both the product and the process are sacred. In the natural order, human beings are but a part of the universe, insignificant creatures at the mercy of its whims unless they can interpret the will of the gods. Thus, making milpa demands propitiation of both natural and supernatural forces, requiring an intimate knowledge of nature and a detailed reading of the far-from-favorable environment.

Tropical karst means no surface water, for the most part. In addition, the winter-spring dry season can be highly erratic in length. The shallow calcareous soil is often mineral-deficient, concentrated in small solution hollows and depressions in the rough, rocky, eroded terrain. Soil fertility varies considerably, however, and the prized red and black soils rich in organic matter can prove very productive, at least during the first cultivation cycle. The water-supply problem can also be managed effectively, except in the most severe drought years, through careful selection of milpa location and perfect timing of planting based on correct interpretation of natural signs. Today as yesterday, the Maya milpa system is a highly efficient and sustainable agricultural technology given the environmental constraints as long as sufficient land per person can be held in reserve to maintain a viable rotation cycle and the will to make milpa survives.

The importance of recognizing and selecting the most appropriate soils for milpa production is reflected in the detailed typology of soil types developed by the Maya (Table 4.1). In Campeche, the best maize soils are considered (both by the Maya and by the government agronomists who have adopted local terminology) to be *kan-kab* and *k'akab*, well-drained rhoeadic yellow-red luvisols with high organic matter that collect at the foot of slopes. In addition, *yaax-hom*, a moderately drained chromic luvisol in flat areas of colluvial accumulation, is deemed to be good for milpa, particularly in dry years. *Tzek'el*, a stony lithosol, and *pust-luum*, a rendzina, both draining quite rapidly, can make good maize land also in the absence of extended droughts during the prime growing period.[1] Thus hillsides and better-drained flat areas near the slopes are the preferred milpa locations as they were at the time of the conquest: "on the earthy ground where it is to be found, no trees grow, but only grass. But where they sow over the stony parts they secure crops, and all the trees grow, some of them marvelously large and beautiful. The cause I think is that more moisture is preserved among the stones than in the earth" (Landa, 1978 [1566]: 93). The expansion of mechanization made the poorly drained bottomlands of *ak'alche*, a gley vertisol, apparently attractive for staple cultivation in government agricultural projects. These experiments have had disastrous results in the main, confirming that the Maya were right to avoid these heavy clays for maize production, although they are

TABLE 4.1   Selected Maya Terminology for Soils in Campeche

Maya Terminology	Characteristics	Crop Aptitude	Total Area (ha)
Chaltun	Pure rock	Nonagricultural	N.A.
Tzek'el	Calcareous rock with soil cap, very rapid drainage, low productivity	Maize and beans (roza-tumba-quema), citrus	1,715
Eklu'um tzek'el	Calcareous rock with soil cap and humus layer	Maize (roza-tumba-quema)	N.A.
K'akab	Humic soil with red-tinged mineralization	Maize (roza-tumba-quema)	N.A.
Chocol k'akab	Mineralized humic soil mixed with calcareous stones	Maize (roza-tumba-quema), irrigated fruits	N.A.
Kan-kab	Deep fertile soil, orange to gray, good drainage	Vegetables, maize (roza-tumba-quema), mechanized maize, sugarcane, fruit	4,200
Chaklu'um kan-kab	Deep soil, intense red	As above	N.A.
Sabana		Pasture with periodic burning	N.A.
Ak'alche	Low-lying, poorly drained seasonal wetlands, low productivity	Mechanized rice, sown pasture, sugarcane, dyewood	432,000
Yaax-hom ak'alche	Fertile soil with thick humic cap, moderately well-drained	Maize in dry years, peanuts, beans, sown pasture	101,400
Pust-lu'um	Rapid drainage, low productivity	Citrus, maize, pasture	125,300

NOTE: N.A. = Not Available.
SOURCE: FIRA, 1972; SARH-INIFAP, Edzná, 1985; field observation.

suitable on occasion for crops that like "wet feet" such as rice, sugarcane, and pasture. Since prime maize soils comprise less than 20 percent of those available for agriculture in Campeche, these lands are increasingly hard to find.

The Campeche Maya who still make milpa according to the "old ways" employ agricultural practices and technologies probably little changed since Classic times and even before. The seasons progress in an orderly pattern, mainly differentiated by the alternation of wet and dry seasons that dominates the agricultural cycle. Each man plants from two to four hectares, often in two or more fields in order to hedge against crop failure by covering for possible microclimatic variations in rainfall patterns, localized attacks of pests and diseases, and so forth. The mundane activities of making a living are entwined with the spiritual realm which makes this possible, as each stage in the cultivation process is accompanied by the appropriate ceremonies to appease the deities who own the natural forces that must be harnessed.

The first operation in making milpa takes place at the beginning of the dry season, sometime between October and January, with the selection of new field locations based on the proximity of a water supply if possible and on the height and density of the brush, which indicate both the quality of the soil and the recency of prior cultivation. Second-growth forest fifteen to twenty feet in height, reflecting an optimal fallow period of fifteen to twenty years, is preferred for milpa because it is relatively easy to fell. The boundaries of the field are then delineated (with piles of stones marking each corner in alignment with the path of the sun), and the area is paced out in *mecates* (twenty-by-twenty-meter squares). The next step is to cut down the vegetation with ax and machete, preferably very early in the dry season, when the trees are still saturated. Everything is cleared except the tallest trees and a few palms to provide thatch for houses and outbuildings. The brush is then dragged into piles and allowed to dry for at least three months before burning. In the case of milpa that produced a crop the previous year, clearing is left to a few weeks before the burn. One man can clear two or three mecates a day of new milpa, meaning that about thirty man-days of labor is required in total for the average three hectares (Table 4.2). With the assistance of family members or fellow milperos the actual time required for this operation can be reduced to about two weeks. The milpa will be cultivated for two or three years, until returns are no longer worth the labor investment, and then fallowed.

The burning of the piled-up vegetation and stumps takes place in April and early May, before the rains begin. During this period the whole countryside is enveloped in a mysterious haze, in sharp contrast to the glaring clarity of the normal Campeche dry-season daylight, while the smell of wood-smoke is all-pervasive. This is a critical time for the milpero. If he burns too early, the brush may not be dry enough, an extra weeding may be necessary, or the fertile ashes may be dispersed by the winds before planting time. At the same time, there is the risk of being caught by an unseasonable rain with the field not yet fired. When the reading of the

TABLE 4.2   Average Labor Days in the Annual Milpa Cycle for 75
Mecates (3 ha)

Operation	Number of Labor Days
Felling brush	30
Burning brush	2
Shelling corn for seed	1
Planting	9
Weeding	28
Doubling corn stalks	5
Harvesting corn	15
Shelling corn (on rack or by primitive degrainer)	7
Transporting harvest (2 round trips a day)	35
Other activities (selecting fields, measuring milpa, constructing field shelters and corn cribs, inspecting for pests and diseases, etc.)	48
Total	180

SOURCE: Field observations.

natural signs for optimal burning or planting times is ambiguous, the
h-men (shaman) may be requested to consult his day count to interpret
the future from the past. For example, in the January *cabañuelas*, a complex
system of weather prognostication in which each day represents a month,
a dry 4 January followed by a rainy day means that April will be a dry
month, good for burning, and May a rainy one safe for an early planting.
If all goes well, the milpa is torched on a day when the wind is blowing
strongly and steadily in order to ensure a "good burn," one in which com-
bustion of the brush is complete.[2]

Planting takes place in late May and early June with the beginning of
the rains, when the appearance of certain birds, frogs, or flying ants and
the flowering of trees in the brush such as the oak herald the approach of
the season. One mecate is planted at a time at a rate of about eight mecates
a day, requiring on the average some nine days' work. The pointed wooden
digging stick used for this was once fire-hardened but now has an iron
point. With this stick, small holes about four inches deep are dug, one for
each hill of maize, aligned in rows running both parallel to the edge of the
mecate and diagonally to its corners. Four to six kernels of seed saved
from the previous year's harvest are dropped in each hole, generally
including at least two varieties of yellow and white corn planted in separate areas to avoid cross-pollination. After planting, the milpero may step
on the holes to cover them up, although if the burn has been hot enough
the soil will fall in of its own accord. Sometimes bean or squash seeds are
dropped into the same holes as the maize. Alternatively, a separate part of

the milpa may be set aside for a vegetable garden. The planting starts with the mecate in the northeast corner, and follows a squared-off spiral pattern said to attract the rains as well as to facilitate the correct alignment of each hole (Faust, 1988). Then the milpero waits to see if he has read the signs correctly, followed preparation procedures meticulously, and complied with the necessary ceremonial offerings to the gods who own the winds so that the rains will fall at the proper time and in the right amount. In some years there is a margin for error, as a second planting may be possible if the rains are delayed and a rain-making ceremony has proved of no avail. In other years, both plantings may shrivel before the rains settle into a regular regime. Conversely, the new maize may be washed away or rot because of excessive moisture. In addition, crops may fail or be attacked by plagues as a result of some offense against the *aluxes* (the pixie-like sacred beings of the milpa) generally involving failure to comply with the sacred obligation to reward the gods of nature with food and prayers (Faust, 1988).

Care of the milpa after sowing is often somewhat haphazard. Milperos in the Camino Real and Los Chenes say that a first-year milpa must be weeded at least once and a second-year milpa twice if reasonably high yields are to be obtained. In practice, this recommendation is not adhered to strictly, especially if the milpero obtains some other employment during the growing season. Weeding is critical in second-year milpa, however, to minimize the rapid decline in productivity, which can amount to 20–50 percent of the previous year's yield. When the ears are ripe in the early fall, the stalks are bent over to keep rain from getting inside the ears, causing mold, and also to protect them from predatory birds. Then the maize is left to dry and harden on the stalks until November, when it may be harvested after the first ears have been offered to the gods who own the winds in thanks.

Most campesinos in fact leave the ears on the stalks throughout the dry season, as late as the end of March, going to the milpa from time to time to bring home enough for short-term household needs or to sell to get money for a specific purpose. A few milperos remove their harvest from the field on the cob in early winter and carry it home to store where they can protect it better from rodents and fungus. Others harvest the ears and store them in thatched shelters in the field until their families can husk and shell the maize and carry it in sacks to the village. A man can harvest about four or five mecates a day, depending on the yield and the amount of weed growth. Maize is shelled by hand, by clubbing a hammock filled with ears, by spreading out the ears on a rack and beating them with long poles, or with a simple degraining machine.

Yields vary with soil quality, attention to weeding, and the weather. In good years, milperos expect about 80 kilograms per mecate or 2 tons per hectare from the very best fields under the traditional system and perhaps

3 tons if chemical fertilizers are applied. Production may fall by as much as 50 percent in the second year, depending on the care given to cultivation.[3] In normal years, the average new milpa yields 0.75–1 ton per hectare, and 0.50 ton is not uncommon in a drought cycle. These production figures are considerably less than estimates for the Classic period. Morley (1941) and others suggest that change in weeding technology rather than soil exhaustion has been the major cause of diminishing yields and shortened cultivation cycles in the Yucatán Peninsula—that weeding by machete, which disperses the seeds, as opposed to the hand weeding likely practiced in ancient times increased vegetal competition to the point that two-year milpas rather than up to five-year cultivation cycles became the norm.

Milpa production in Campeche seems to have been declining steadily in recent years, even in the less densely populated regions, suggesting that the system is indeed under increasing stress from factors additional to soil exhaustion:

> Twenty years ago a man would have been ashamed to get less than a *carga* [42 kilograms] per mecate [1 ton per hectare]. Only those with vices or who had offended God would attract such luck. Today, two-thirds of a carga, half a carga, is the norm and even less when the bad years come as they do more frequently now. God is castigating us with severity here for our sins as [Hurricane] Gilbert reminded us. (I-51, ejidatario, Nilchi, January 1990)

It is also indicative that the amount of milpa planted per farmer appears to have dropped in much of the Maya zone of northern Campeche, from four hectares in 1970 to two or three hectares or even less in 1990: "My father planted at least a hundred mecates. I always planted a hundred mecates. But now it's not worth it, it doesn't give [enough]. Why? Well, who knows? The government disturbed the rhythm of life too much, I think" (I-52, ejidatario, Nilchi, December 1989).[4] The system does, however, appear to be continuing to function more or less in balance in terms of the man/land equation, partly because of the emergence of other alternatives for making a living: "Our sons would rather work in construction in Campeche or be a waiter in a restaurant in Cancún than sweat in the sun. Life is not *alegre* [lively] enough for them here any more" (I-24, ejidatario, Tinún, March 1990). Although many milperos regret this exodus, some admit that it does take the pressure off the land and get rid of the malcontents. Others are attempting to dissuade their sons from continuing in traditional agriculture by encouraging education that will offer "an escape from the country and all its uncertainties" (I-117, ejidatario, Poc-Boc, March 1990). At the very least, education is perceived as providing members of the next generation with "a better chance for defending themselves against the government and all the other exploiters of the campesino" (I-118, ejidatario, Hecelchakán, February 1990).

As making milpa retreats from its central position in life for all Maya, so does adherence to its attendant ritual. Redfield (1941: 230, 269) noted a significant decline in the regularity and completeness of performance of agricultural ritual in the more modernized towns and villages of Yucatán that attributed to "the relatively more secular character of life," suggesting that "even for those who continue faithful, religion has lost most of its connection with the rest of life and is to a considerable degree a separate and specialized division of behavior." The expansion of Protestantism has made the syncretized Catholic religion identifiable as a separate category for the first time, and this increasing compartmentalization of religiosity is reflected in the secularization of agricultural activities. The process appears to have operated much more gradually in Campeche than in Yucatán, either because of the slower pace of social change or because traditional ritual still proves functional as a hedge against the uncertainties generated by arbitrary state intervention in addition to nature's unknowns.

Faust's (1988) ethnographic study of a Maya village in central Campeche confirms that agricultural ritual was alive and well in the mid-1980s, even in a community relatively close to the state capital. In the northern Camino Real and Los Chenes regions, however, it had already lost considerable ground by 1970:

> I do not like to bring my father to the fields. I have respect for him because he is my father, but he does not know anything about modern ways of farming . . . Well, some of the old people still believe in the old gods and the rituals and things like that, sacrifices they make, so they think they can make it rain that way . . . But do the Chaacs know how to operate a sprinkler system? (I-119, ejidatario, Hopelchén, July 1970)

As the failure of agricultural development projects has sent many campesinos back to the milpa, some apparently abandoned rituals have been resurrected. Campeche campesinos today tend to refer to them as things that "some say" and "others believe," expecting ridicule if they admit to sharing them. Nevertheless, the extent of knowledge about the details of the ceremonies that still persists suggests that these are not discarded beliefs but still central to agricultural practice, likely to persist as long as Maya make milpa. Increasingly, however, the imperative of earning cash income from agriculture, the necessity for acquiring new skills in order to do so, continuing faith in modern technology despite its failures, and the desire for a better life for the children make this ancient knowledge essentially something to fall back on rather than the core of Maya existence. Thus one of the principal reasons why milpa is perceived no longer to yield enough is that it has ceased to be a "respectable" occupation in the eyes of the milperos themselves.

Other reasons cited by Campeche campesinos for the decline in interest in making milpa include climatic change over the past two decades and deforestation. Dry years are said to come every three years now instead of in eight-to-ten-year cycles, and the rains are increasingly unpredictable "not so much in quantity as in terms of raining when it shouldn't" (I-99, ejidatario, Monclova, February 1990). If the climate is changing, it may be because of the rapid rate of deforestation, vast areas of the southern and eastern interior having been logged out for migrant colonization and cattle ranching, and to global alterations in the ozone layer, the carbon dioxide cycle, and so forth. The decline in areas of virgin forest is of concern to milperos even though they prefer to locate their fields in secondary growth, because it represents the loss of important reserve land for future swidden as well as useful terrain for hunting and gathering medicinal plants.

While Maya milperos feel that they help to preserve the forest by respecting it, the government agricultural development agencies tend to regard traditional subsistence strategies as the most ecologically destructive of human activities, citing forest fires from slash-and-burn, followed by illegal hunting, wood-cutting, and chicle gathering, as the main causes of devastation. Forest fires resulting from an uncontrollable milpa burn appear to be quite rare, however,[5] and damage is usually relatively minor compared with that occasioned by the wholesale cattle-ization of southern Campeche and commercial logging operations. That shifting agriculture is not inherently destructive of forest land in itself is apparent from the evidence of slash-and-burn cultivation by the Classic Maya in the mature jungles of the Petén ten centuries after the high culture's collapse (Lundell, 1937). It only becomes so when population increase or encroachment of other economic activities squeezes the forest reserve and shortens fallow periods below the regeneration threshold or where immigrant settlers are unfamiliar with local conditions (Gradwohl and Greenberg, 1988).

The official antagonism toward traditional agricultural practices has had other repercussions. BANRURAL and SARH have compelled credit recipients, even those practicing slash-and-burn cultivation, to use hybrid seed, considering it more reliably productive. This has proven to be not necessarily the case, as hybrids are dependent on commercial fertilizers (also included in the credit package) and are not adapted to local conditions as is the indigenous maize (now recognized as being more drought-tolerant) (I-146, civil servant, Edzná, January 1990). Attempts are being made to derive crossbreeds specifically adapted to Campeche conditions, but in the interim many milperos have lost their carefully selected horde of native seed varieties and have become dependent on standard hybrids and fertilizer to sustain yields that are generally little higher than under the traditional system. Moreover, hybrid seed reserved from the previous year's harvest does not breed true and declining yields are common.

Traditional tools and techniques and are also denigrated, by implication if not directly. BANRURAL and SARH tend to prefer large-scale single plantings to small-patch interplanting, permanent cultivation to rotation, the use of pesticides to hand weeding, mechanized sowing to digging stick planting, combine harvesting to hand picking, and so forth. If campesinos resist this degree of dependence on new technology they are considered "backward", especially if they opt for more diarios (credit advances for labor days) for hand work over the increased profits presumed to be concomitant with mechanization. These introduced technologies have, however, proved not only to be largely ineffective in Campeche but also to cause more degradation to the land in a short period than the Maya have occasioned in thousands of years of careful management. Imposition of these outside practices also often creates a counterproductive psychological climate: "You feel that you are worthless, that they know everything and you know nothing. They think they have to tell us how to farm and in truth, these are not our ways. Nature is not a machine to be driven" (I-83, ejidatario, Yohaltún, March 1990). Furthermore, an agricultural development strategy that discounts or ignores traditional expertise is likely to run into serious problems: "Agriculture has to follow nature's timetable, not the bank's. Everybody knows that it's no use planting until the oak blooms and it's no use planting maize in ak'alche. But the bank doesn't listen. It's as if we didn't exist except as a debt on paper" (I-38, ejidatario, Nilchi, December 1989).

Many Campeche agricultural agents have been fully aware from the beginning of the imperative of incorporating traditional knowledge into planned development strategies: "In a region such as the Yucatán Peninsula, where the soils exhibit characteristics which are so special and different from those of other regions of the Republic, it is to be hoped that the empirical knowledge of the Maya farmer will be considered to be important and, in fact, it cannot be discarded lightly" (Fondo de Garantía y Fomento para la Agricultura, Ganadería y Avicultura [FIRA], 1972: 12, my translation). Despite this recognition by individuals, the agricultural bureaucracy has been unwilling or unable to incorporate campesino input beyond a token level. This is not, of course, to say that the milpa system as practiced in Campeche today is necessarily the most effective use of the land. On the southeastern frontier, immigrant colonists often make milpa indiscriminately, intent only on maximizing short-term profit, and in other regions milpa yields are declining noticeable as a result of increasing competition for the better soils and the lack of attention to weeding: "If you know that you are not going to make anything, then why bother to weed?" (I-23, ejidatario, Tinún, March 1990).

All these reasons for the decreasing interest in making milpa tend to be come down to one central factor: the declining market value of maize as opposed to the rising costs of production, particularly on marginal land. Over the past twenty years or so, virtually all Campeche campesinos have become dependent to a greater or lesser extent on the sale of maize. No one is completely self-sufficient; everyone needs to make some cash purchases, however modest. At the same time, the majority of milperos have become increasingly dependent on some modern agricultural inputs, such as hybrid seed, fertilizer, and pesticide and even hired labor, as competing family obligations deplete the household labor pool: "If you can only sell a third of your harvest and you make 300,000 pesos from the sale, but it cost you 260,000 pesos to grow it, not counting your labor, then why bother with the extra beyond the needs of your family and the livestock? It's better to look for some other way [of making a living]" (I-39, ejidatario, Nilchi, January 1990). Thus the low official guaranteed price of maize is seen as indicative of the government's lack of esteem for the campesino and, in particular, for the milpero. Making milpa may provide the security of knowing that probably the family will be fed, but it also underscores the milperos' economic and psychosocial marginality: "The milpa provides a refuge from inflation, if you keep strictly to the old ways of cultivation. But, at the same time, it's a kind of prison, or rather, a brand like they put on a cow, which shows everybody that Campeche campesinos can't make it in the modern world" (I-100, ejidatario, Monclova, March 1990).

The government agricultural development programs initiated in Campeche after 1970 attempted to improve the economic viability of ejidos through the introduction of mechanization, irrigation, technical assistance, and credit. It was hoped that these measures would stimulate diversification into more lucrative crops than maize and other traditional staples, thus increasing Campeche campesinos' subsistence security and reducing the likelihood of out-migration in areas where the milpa system appeared to be under the most stress. Unfortunately, as a result of these programs most campesinos are still essentially making milpa, that is, growing maize at marginal production levels, using a combination of traditional and modern technologies. Under this new agricultural syncretism, many maize growers have become dependent on modern inputs and on the development agencies that dispense them. The reasons for the failures and qualified successes amount to a bias toward the export sector and the interests of the urban consumer. Thus modern milperos have been made marginal to the national economic sphere instead of forming an integral part of a natural universe as in the past. The struggle to grow maize continues, but its traditional significance is eroding. Consequently, it is not surprising that without the substitution of a modern meaning in terms of adequate remuneration for their efforts, many Campeche campesinos express a desire for a fate better than making milpa.

The ultimate paradox is that the agricultural crisis is essentially a crisis of food production—specifically the nation's inability to produce the basic staples required to feed its growing population. Traditional cultivators have always been an important source of such staples, albeit on a minimal scale individually. To agricultural agencies, however, at least until very recently, the milpa system has represented one of the main causes of the food problem, in that the extensive land reserve is wasteful and production is strictly limited by primitive technology, indigenous seeds, and so forth. This attitude may be changing since the onset of the debt crisis and the crippling expense of massive food imports to a devastated national economy, particularly since attempts to promote commercial staple cultivation by ejidatarios under state management have accumulated such a poor record.

PRONASOL may imply a new appreciation of traditional agriculture or at least a renewed respect for peasant staple producers' ability to farm productively when left to do so with a minimum of state interference. In advancing interest-free credit for up to four hectares of crops to individual campesinos, requiring no guarantees other than the word of the producer, it marks a radical departure in agrarian policy. In this context, making milpa, in a modified, modernized form, may become more than a fading metaphor for Maya cosmology—a part of the solution, in the short-run at least, rather than a part of the problem. Alternatively, PRONASOL may serve only to reinforce the distinction between cultivators with the potential to grow high-value crops and those relegated permanently to subsistence production. This would continue to preserve maize primarily as an peasant crop for autoconsumption and perpetuate poverty as the lot of the staple producer, in an attempt to turn the clock back and repeasantize those who have failed to perform under previous misguided state agricultural development strategies.

Agriculture Before State Intervention

State intervention in Campeche agriculture first appeared on a significant scale with the agrarian reform of the Cárdenas administration in 1937, which created collective ejidos on more than half of the land of the henequen zone. Only the northern portions of the Camino Real and Los Chenes districts were affected by this collectivization. The change was a mixed blessing for the new ejidatarios, many of whom were at a loss when bereft suddenly of the stability and sometimes-benevolent paternalism of the old order. In Campeche, the majority of the ex-peons immediately converted most of the henequen lands to maize and other staples or abandoned the collectives to make milpa where they could. Individual ejidos were established at this time in the more populated rural areas, mainly in the center and north of the state, although often formal title was not acquired until decades later. Tracts of national lands were also set aside in this period.

The mere fact of land reform did not constitute a significant state presence in Campeche. The Maya continued to make milpa as always and had little contact with government agencies except for negotiating the creation of new ejidos or the granting of *ampliaciones* (extensions) in the forests of the southeast. Maize cultivation remained almost an exclusively Maya activity, separated from the production of commercial crops by tradition as well as the lack of alternatives. This surface distinction between commercial and subsistence agriculture, however, masked an underlying systemic unity that has become increasingly apparent as peasant production has been subsumed to the expanding national economy, with the state as the new patron.

State-directed planned agricultural intervention in its contemporary form began in Campeche in 1963 with an ambitious colonization scheme along the Candelaria River, but a concerted effort to modernize peasant agriculture was launched only after 1970. At that time, the profile of agricultural activities in Campeche differed little, in essence, from that of the colonial era. The state was still a sparsely populated backwater where the majority of the mainly Maya rural inhabitants were slash-and-burn milperos. The only significant commercial agriculture consisted of small enclaves of sugarcane and copra along the central and southwestern coast and the vestiges of henequen estates in the extreme north. Cattle ranching was beginning to expand on new pastures created by accelerating colonization of the interior forested frontier. These operations, however, were generally rudimentary, on unimproved grasses, with skinny, disease-ridden stock poorly adapted to the tropical milieu. Small-scale logging operations and chicle collection in the dense southeastern forests constituted the only other options for making a living from the land, but these sectors were experiencing grave problems as a result of overexploitation and the absence of effective forest management. Despite its relatively favored situation vis-à-vis the other peninsular states in terms of agricultural soils, Campeche was handicapped by their dispersion in small areas, its dependence on rain-fed agriculture (except in the case of sugarcane), its small local markets, and its restricted interior communications and isolation from central Mexico. Thus agricultural production was confined essentially to relict plantation culture and milpa.

It was estimated that in 1970, 34 percent of Campeche's population, some seventy-nine thousand persons, was economically active (FIRA,

1972). The majority were classified as urban dwellers (69 percent), although primary activities in agriculture, cattle raising, forestry, and fishing remained the dominant occupational category. Per capita income was approximately 7,000 pesos ($560),[6] an increase of over 100 percent from 1960 largely due to the flourishing shrimp industry. Income was concentrated in the hands of the small urban elite. Ejidatarios formed 38.75 percent of the population occupying 46 percent of the land, with the remainder being devoted to private properties and national lands. Because there were more private properties over five hectares in size than under, meaning that low population density had allowed the avoidance of fragmentation of holdings, the prospects for agricultural development seemed good provided that the fragile tropical soils were exploited with care.

More than half the state was estimated to be forested, almost two-thirds of this forest being exploited to some degree for cattle or milpa (Fig. 4.1). Only some eighty-eight thousand hectares or 1.6 percent of the state's land was devoted to agricultural activities, while extensive cattle ranching occupied almost 1 million hectares or 14 percent. Consequently, it is not surprising that the value of agricultural production amounted to only 109,084,000 pesos, about two-and-a-half times the revenue generated by the mainly small-scale forestry activities (Figs. 4.2 and 4.3). In agriculture, 80 percent of the value was derived from four main crops—maize, sugarcane, copra, and rice. The latter constituted a new endeavor as an experimental, state-directed mechanized activity on ejidos, although the crop had been cultivated on a small scale since the beginning of the nine-

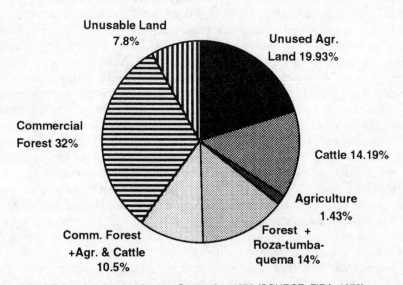

Unusable Land 7.8%

Unused Agr. Land 19.93%

Commercial Forest 32%

Cattle 14.19%

Agriculture 1.43%

Comm. Forest +Agr. & Cattle 10.5%

Forest + Roza-tumba-quema 14%

FIGURE 4.1   Land use estimates, Campeche, 1970 (SOURCE: FIRA, 1972)

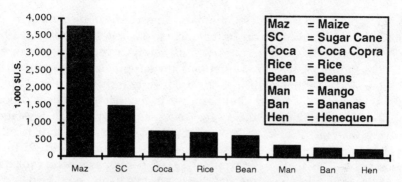

FIGURE 4.2   Agriculture production, Campeche, 1970 (SOURCE: FIRA, 1972)

teenth century. The traditional Maya occupation of beekeeping was also a significant generator of revenues through exports to the United States and Europe. Expansion was hampered, however, by widely fluctuating yields of 3,000–6,000 tons from year to year as a result of irregular rainfall and infrastructural constraints.

Meanwhile, some 75 percent of the rural work force, fifteen thousand individuals, depended on the milpa system occupying sixty thousand hectares (FIRA, 1972). Average yields were estimated at 900 kilograms per hectare, and given that each rural family consumed some 4 kilograms a

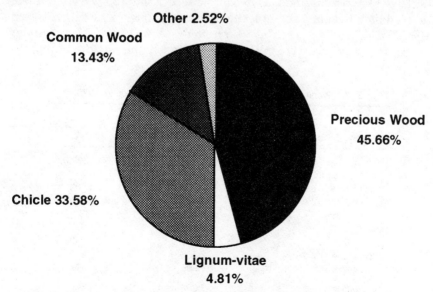

FIGURE 4.3   Value of forest production, Campeche, 1970 (SOURCE: FIRA, 1972)

day including feed for domestic animals, almost two-thirds of the harvest could be sold, resulting in an annual income of some 1,605 pesos at 1970 prices (Table 4.3).[7] This amount would barely cover the needs of an average family of five or six persons for supplementary foodstuffs, clothing, and essential medicines.[8] Consequently, many subsistence cultivators went to collect chicle in the forests in the dry season in addition, earning a further 2,000–3,000 pesos, or searched for casual day-labor clearing the bush (FIRA, 1972; Vogeler, 1976). Dry-season labor for the small logging companies was also available on occasion, yielding 25 to 30 pesos a day plus food, approximately 3,000 pesos per season (Vogeler, 1976). Some ancillary revenue and dietary supplements could be derived from small livestock, bees, and a few fruit trees and vegetables raised around the house or close to home, such activities being more common in the Maya north. Full-time beekeepers could earn an average of 8,867 pesos, two-thirds of the honey being exported at a price over a third higher than the domestic rate (FIRA, 1972).

The majority of the owners of the larger private agricultural properties and ranches were essentially absentee landlords, maintaining their primary domiciles in Campeche or Ciudad del Carmen and hiring families to live on the properties as farmworkers and caretakers. Coco plantations were not large, averaging about sixty hectares per family, but produced a comfortable gross income of about 300,000 pesos per year. Ranchers owned large landholdings (by Campeche standards), ranging from five hundred hectares to two thousand hectares or more, and some 50 percent of them derived their livelihood completely from their estates, obtaining between 100,000 and 3,150,000 pesos per year from the sale of cattle. The remainder of the large ranchers were involved in other activities in addition, parti-

TABLE 4.3   Income Estimates for Rural Producers, Campeche, 1970

Category of Producer	Annual Income	
	Pesos	$U.S.
Large rancher (500–2,000 ha)	100,000–3,150,000	8,000–252,000
Coco plantation owner	300,000	24,000
Medium-sized rancher (40–500 ha)	20,000	1,600
Beekeeper	8,867	693
Logging laborer	3,000	240
Chicle gatherer	2,500	200
Maize milpero	1,605	128
Per capita income	7,000	560

Sources: FIRA, 1972; Vogeler, 1976.

cularly shrimping—the only economic sector in Campeche in 1970 which generated sufficient surplus for diversified investment. In the south, the numbers of medium-sized residential cattle ranchers were growing rapidly, particular in the river zone and around Escárcega. These new ranches ranged between forty and three hundred hectares in size, of which an average sixty hectares was sustained in pastures, supporting about thirty head of cattle. This hectarage was extended each year via additional forest clearings used initially for maize or rice. It was estimated that a typical ranch could generate income of around 20,000 pesos a year, sufficient to cover family necessities, worker wages, and operating costs with a little left over for reinvestment in the holding.

In this context, it is important to note the direct connection between the coming of the first migrant colonists to the forested frontier and the appearance of the ranchers close on their heels. This sequence has become the norm in the tropical forests of Central and South America as the supposedly "underutilized" rain forests are "opened up" for agriculture by landless migrants from more densely populated areas either on a spontaneous individual basis or under planned government resettlement schemes. Once the forests have been breached by the sweat of the colonists or by heavy machine contractors with lucrative government contracts, the ranchers flock in to take advantage of the new clearings for pastures, hiring the first migrants to push back the treeline. As the sequence continues, the migrants tend to be squeezed out economically if not literally back to the retreating frontier; there is no place for slash-and-burn in a treeless landscape, and if the colonists attempt cattle rearing themselves, the small scale of their activities competes unfavorably that of the large ranchers who dominate the market. In 1970 this process was still incipient in southern Campeche but advancing very rapidly, in some places bypassing the milpero-colonizer stage completely by going straight to pasture. Overall, the process clearly benefited the ranchers, the clearing contractors, and their government patrons more than the pioneer colonists: "the cattle eat up both the milpa and the *monte* (forests), but spit out the campesino" (I-120, ejidatario, Escárcega, August 1970).

Thus, by 1970 embryonic forces for change were becoming apparent in Campeche, including both economic and demographic processes. Whereas in 1960 Campeche had been one of the three least populous states, with scarcely 3 inhabitants per square kilometer and a total population of 168,219, by 1970 the density had reached 4.46 inhabitants per square kilometer or a total of 250,391 persons (FIRA, 1972). The principal reason for this population increase was, as in the rest of Mexico, the dramatic drop in mortality rates since 1950, as opposed to only a slight decline in the birth rate, in response to improved health care services and disease eradication programs as well as urbanization. Population growth was also due increasingly to the influx of landless migrants, both from the neighboring states of Tabasco and Veracruz and from more densely settled areas of northern and central Mexico. The growth of Escárcega from 3,000 inhabitants in 1960 to 6,000 in 1968 is indicative of the impact of these pioneers, and the ranchers who followed in their wake, in beginning to reorient the demographic map of the state away from the historical emphasis on the coast and the northern interior.

The predominantly Maya zones of the Camino Real and Los Chenes have been the area of greatest rural population density in Campeche since the colonial era, despite limited agricultural opportunities, because of their relatively accessible water supplies. In the Camino Real, the water table is relatively close to the surface by virtue of the region's location between the edge of the coastal plain and a low ridge of hills. Los Chenes means "the wells" in Maya, referring to the occurrence of perched water tables. Both regions participated in the henequen boom at the turn of this century and cultivation continued on a significant scale until the 1950s. Consequently, relatively good communications by road and rail were developed much earlier than in the rest of the state, facilitating interaction with both Campeche City and Mérida. As henequen production declined, the Camino Real and Los Chenes returned to dependence on milpa and small-scale forestry. By 1970 these regions were beginning to feel noticeable stress of increasing population pressure on the milpa system, reflected in shortened rotation cycles, decreased yields, and incipient rural-urban migration (Gates, 1972).

Both agriculture and forestry were regarded as the "weak links in the Campeche economy," with only incipient cattle ranching showing some promise and even this admittedly often representing less than optimal use of the land (FIRA, 1972: 48). While expansion of mechanized rice cultivation seemed an attractive option, doubts were expressed about its potential given the lack of good drainage and soil leveling and "innumerable details which indicate to us that this is not really a strong program" (FIRA, 1972: 68). As far as basic food supplies were concerned, with the exception of maize, sugar, and beef, extensive imports from other states were required to satisfy the inhabitants' needs. The state's economy was totally dependent on shrimping as a virtual "monoculture." Something had to be done to diversify the economy and, in particular, to stimulate agriculture in order to provide Campeche campesinos with a more secure livelihood if the threat of rural-urban migration was to be reduced. Furthermore, the state government was concerned about the haphazard development of the frontier, where spontaneous colonization and the rapid expansion of cattle rearing had begun to give it an anarchic "Wild West" profile. Most significant was the growing imperative of transforming traditional ejidos to satisfy Mexico's basic-foods deficit and accommodate increasing demands for concrete improvements in rural social welfare. All in all, it appeared to be time for a concerted effort on the part of both the federal and state government to promote and rationalize agricultural development in Campeche, focused on the ejido but intended to maximize expansion possibilities for private initiative and, implicitly, for the development agencies themselves.

The Institutional Web

By 1970 there were already numerous official players in the incipient agricultural development game in Campeche. The Secretaría de Recursos Hidráulicos (the Ministry of Water Resources—SRH) had emerged as the most influential development agency after 1940 because of the national priority given to heavy public-sector investment in rural infrastructure, particularly dams and irrigation works, in order to foster large-scale, commercial agriculture in central and northern Mexico. It remained well-funded and continued to focus on infrastructure, although it had become increasingly involved in integrated rural development projects such as the ambitious Papaloapan and Grijalva river basin programs. Since the majority of its professional employees were hydraulic engineers, SRH was more comfortable with the finite and predictable tangibilities of dams and drains than with the more subtle but critical social processes involved in the modernization of peasant agriculture. Consequently, big plans with big budgets for physical artifacts were preferred to small works for rural development.

The Secretaría de Agricultura y Ganadería (the Ministry of Agriculture and Livestock—SAG) was concerned with the overall planning and articulation of national agricultural priorities and production targets as well as with research and the promotion of specific programs and projects. Agricultural extension activities were becoming increasingly significant at the local level as modernization programs for peasants expanded. Here as in SRH, there was often a huge culture and credibility gap between engineers and ejidatarios. Although SAG's engineers were agronomists rather than dam builders, their métier was still technology rather than society, with a bias toward modern cultivation practices developed in temperate rather than tropical zones. Furthermore, specific training in agricultural extension was very limited and emphasized social work rather than technical communication. The outcome when engineers or extensionists met with peasants to "discuss" a new development tended to be the antithesis of communication, with the former resorting to standard speeches about progress in the countryside and the latter listening with silent suspicion. Proponents of the machine and practitioners of the milpa seemed to have little in common but the soil and the tradition of appropriation of it by outsiders.

The Departamento de Asuntos Agrarios y Colonización (the Department of Agrarian Affairs and Colonization—DAAC) was particularly influential because the state's sparse population and presumed agricultural potential made it a prime destination for both spontaneous and planned colonization. It had escaped earlier waves of migration from the densely populated uplands, which began in the 1930s with Cárdenas's promotion of private colonization in Quintana Roo and the Tuxtla mountain region of Veracruz. This movement had continued in the Gulf lowland states throughout the 1940s and 1950s, gradually filling in the "underutilized" national lands under the Federal Colonization Law proclaimed in 1946 to regulate the creation of colonies of small landowners. This law had been replaced in 1962 by legislation creating a new variant of the ejido, the *Nuevo Centro de Población Ejidal* (New Center of Ejidal Population— NCPE), which had opened the way for government resettlement of peasants displaced by commercial agriculture in central and northern Mexico. Sparsely populated states such as Campeche seemed to offer a safety valve for social tensions in areas where the pressure of increasing population on the land had become acute. In addition to promoting colonization, DAAC was responsible for the mechanics of agrarian reform—the cumbersome procedure of issuing legal titles to ejidos—and tended to be submerged in paperwork to the detriment of the critical process of resettlement.

The Banco Nacional de Crédito Ejidal (the National Ejidal Credit Bank—BANJIDAL) controlled and channeled federal funding destined for ejidal modernization efforts. This involved not only financial transactions but also organization and supervision of all the agricultural inputs and labor dispositions in each ejido as well as, in collaboration with the other key agricultural agencies, determining the crops and hectarages to be planted. Thus BANJIDAL was not just a lending institution but a bank that farmed. Obviously, this placed it, together with the parallel agricultural insurance agency ANAGSA, in a very powerful position and one that could readily be abused by those more interested in personal advancement than in the progress of the peasantry. The communication gap between the bank and its new clients, the ejidatarios, was even greater than that between the latter and the development agency engineers. Campeche campesinos were undergoing their first contact with official bank credit. Their only previous encounters in this area had been with traditional merchant usury or some preliminary ventures into instalment purchasing of modern consumer goods such as bicycles, and these experiences had often been unpleasant. The bank credit system and the institution's officials were even more of a shock, as was the shift from agricultural practice that traditionally had no cash costs to one in which every input was purchased and each activity had a peso value. Largely illiterate and innumerate, the ejidatarios found the various charges and interest rates a complete mystery, even if, as was rarely the case, they were allowed to see their accounts. The bank officials, who seldom ventured out of their air-conditioned offices and vehicles, were unwilling or unable to explain the mechanics of credit in terms the ejidatarios could understand. Thus, from the beginning, the outlook in terms of efficient production and prompt debt repayment by the modernizing ejidal sector was inauspicious.

These four agencies were surrounded by a host of other entities and dependencies involved to a greater or lesser degree in rural development. In the credit sphere, the Banco Interamericano de Desarrollo (the Inter-American Development Bank—BID) was active at the international level in collaboration with the government and the Fondo de Garantía y Fomento para la Agricultura, Ganadería, y Avicultura (Fund for Guaranteeing and Promoting Agriculture, Livestock, and Poultry), later the Fideicomiso Instituido en Relación a la Agricultura (the Fiduciary Trust Instituted with Relation to Agriculture—FIRA), a specialized agency of the Banco de México that financed long-term credit, often in tandem with the World Bank. In addition, two other national agricultural banks were active in Campeche. In the area of basic infrastructure—an important component given the agricultural development strategies selected—the Secretaría de Obras Publicas (the Ministry of Public Works—SOP) and the Comisión Federal de Electricidad (the Federal Electricity Commission—CFE) were charged with road construction and electrification respectively. In 1971, the core colonization component passed from DAAC to the new Comisión Intersecretarial de Nuevos Centros de Población Ejidal (the Interministerial Commission for New Centers of Ejidal Population—COINCE), which was set up specifically to establish "colonization basins" in the southeast and the north of Mexico. Other key agencies included CONASUPO to which the ejidatarios were required to sell their production at nationally established prices.

These agencies were eventually joined by myriad new institutions and programs, as each presidential term contributed its own priorities and projects. In addition, although the rural development scene in Campeche was dominated initially by federal institutions, state agencies became increasingly significant. Meanwhile, few offices were eliminated, although DAAC was elevated to the ministerial level as the Secretaría de Reforma Agraria (the Ministry of Agrarian Reform—SRA), and SRH and SAG amalgamated as the Ministry of Agriculture and Water Resources (SARH) to form the titan of the agrarian bureaucracy, still retaining a bias toward physical infrastructure. In addition, BANJIDAL was fused with another agricultural credit bank to form BANRURAL, making the institution even more monolithic with over 450 branches all over the country by the late 1970s (*Excelsior*, 6 June 1990). This proliferation of agencies and burgeoning of bureaucracies meant that communication, coordination, overlap, omission, and negligence were often major problems, compounded by the abrupt sexennial discontinuities in policies and programs and the associated turnover of politically appointed senior officials. For the ejidatarios, the institutional complexity of the agrarian bureaucracy was overwhelming, especially in the initial phases of the rural modernization thrust, as the maze of acronyms for the various agencies and programs now part of their economic horizon seemed to emphasize their increasing loss of production autonomy: "It's like they are talking in some kind of secret language or code. They say 'The BID says you can't do this and it doesn't come under FIRA, and ANAGSA won't insure it unless PRONASE (the Promotora Nacional de Semillas—the National Seed Agency) supplies the seeds'. What that means is 'No! You have to do it our way', I think" (I-121, ejidatario, Hopelchén, July 1970).

These government institutions were joined in the development business by key elements from the private sector, such as the purveyors of farm machinery, fertilizers, pesticides, pharmaceuticals, and other agricultural inputs, merchant middlemen, processing industries and the heavy-equipment contractors who undertook the extensive forest clearings that spearheaded the rural modernization strategy. Large landowners also participated in the ejidal development boom, benefiting from the infrastructural improvements and often deriving more advantage from the programs intended to stimulate peasant agriculture than did the peasants themselves. Indeed, the main beneficiaries of planned agricultural modernization of Campeche ejidos are outside the peasant sector, in the ranks of the private interests and public servants who are in a prime position to benefit in both the formal and the underground economies from rural developments on this scale.

Planned agricultural development for ejidos, irrespective of its results, became the new boom that the state needed. The rapid expansion of the rural development industry not only created thousands of jobs and contracts, stimulated the supply and service sectors, and channeled resources to the countryside but created a spirit of dynamism and a sense of progress which involved the ejidal beneficiaries at least as much as the developers. Consequently, the collapse of this boom in 1982 was demoralizing to town and country alike, particularly because it represented the ruin of an ideal rather than a reality. Thus the roots of the agricultural crisis in Campeche lie not only in the historical legacy of political-economic forces but also in the very recent record of state rural development strategies, as two decades of government intervention in the peasant sector have resulted in a crisis by planning as well as by conjuncture:

In the old days we were the peones of the hacendado, now we are the peones of the bank. It's just another form of slavery isn't it? There is nothing new in this world. We campesinos will never really be masters of our own land as long as the government has the rights to the maize from our milpa. (I-8, ejidatario, Pomuch, December 1989)

Notes

1. Under the soil classification scheme now used in the United States, terms such as "rendzina," "laterite," and "terra rossa" are no longer employed, but more detailed studies are necessary before the new categories can be assigned exact peninsular equivalents (Wilson, 1980).

2. A "bad burn" results in a milpa still strewn with piles of debris and reduced ash deposits, diminishing both productive area and soil fertility as well as increasing the likelihood of plagues and pests. In addition to being a consequence of early rains, a bad burn can occur when freak winds make the fires jump the breaks cut around the milpa, prematurely consuming the surrounding bush in reserve for planting in future years.

3. In the frontier areas of southern Campeche, maize yields on new milpa are considerably higher than the state average, and second-year yields often exceed those of the first (see, e.g., Vogeler, 1976).

4. Estimates of the amount of milpa planted per capita and average maize yields in northern Campeche in 1970 (Gates, 1972) were roughly consistent with those noted by Morley (1946), Redfield and Villa Rojas (1934), and Steggerda (1941) for the state of Yucatán, indicating little significant change in the system in the interim.

5. Maya milperos are extremely careful about the construction of firebreaks and the avoidance of burning on days of strong, gusty winds. The Quintana Roo fire of 1989, which consumed many thousands of hectares of forest, cannot be blamed on slash-and-burn per se, its spread having been encouraged by the damage to the brush caused by Hurricane Gilbert the year before as well as by the inefficient firefighting strategies employed.

6. The exchange rate was 12.50 pesos to U.S. $1 in 1970.

7. In the late 1960s, there was considerable variation in maize yields in Campeche between the more densely populated north and the newly settled south. FIRA (1972) estimated 800 kilograms per hectare in the north and 1.2 tons per hectare in the south (FIRA, 1972). Vogeler (1976) reported good-year yields as 750 kilograms per hectare and 1.7 tons per hectare respectively. My own estimate (Gates, 1972) for the Camino Real ranged from 700 kilograms per hectare in an average year to 1.2 tons per hectare in a good year.

8. Vogeler estimated surplus corn for sale ranging from 836 kilograms to 5,830 kilograms per household, which would net from 627 to 4,372 pesos at an average .75 pesos a kilo. He calculated the average weekly food budget as 69.8 pesos, U.S. $290 per annum (Vogeler, 1976).

5

The Industry of Disasters

This was new land, good land, but the government sucked up all the juices and left a desert. (I-81, ejidatario, Yohaltún, March 1990)

If BANRURAL had behaved like a bank, if the Ministry [of Agriculture and Water Resources] had restricted itself to technical matters and the campesinos had been left alone to farm as they know how, maybe we could have survived the crisis. If we had treated agriculture like economics, not like politics, then perhaps it would not be finished here. (I-131, civil servant, Campeche, February 1990)

Nations with frontiers are doubly fortunate. In addition to space to grow beyond the "edge of civilization," a frontier can provide a symbol of the future, a reconfirmation of national identity, even a panacea for social ills. Frontiers are also, by definition, fragile and ephemeral, as Mexico has found out to its cost.[1]

Since the articulation of the agrarian reform framework in the 1917 Constitution, Mexico has been preoccupied with claiming "underutilized" and idle lands for agriculture. It is natural that the sparsely populated tropical forests of Mexico's southeastern lowlands were regarded as vacant territory, a virtual vacuum waiting to be filled with the overflow from the congested uplands. It was not so logical to assume, however, purely on the basis of the exuberant tropical vegetation, that the frontier could be converted with dispatch into fertile fields, particularly via the large-scale mechanized technology of temperate latitudes. Furthermore, the lowland forests were neither unoccupied nor underused but essential to the swidden system of traditional agriculturalists as well the source of other invaluable natural resources. This land-use profile, though not necessarily the optimum for all times and contexts, represents a sophisticated and sustainable adaptation, evolved over many centuries, to a highly complex ecosystem.

For more than two decades after the first official recognition of the tropical frontier as a safety valve in 1941, the only systematic development of it was associated with the grandiose and ill-conceived Papaloapan Project initiated in 1947 in the state of Veracruz. This integrated river-basin development, modeled on the Tennessee Valley Authority, embraced both agricultural and social goals via disease control, drainage, land reclamation, improved communication, and planned colonies for Mazatec displaced by the construction of the Aleman Dam and peasants relocated from the uplands. Inadequate planning, poor institutional coordination, excessive paternalism, and, above all, lack of knowledge about tropical soils and agricultural systems made most of these colonies short-lived (Ewell and Poleman, 1980; Poleman, 1964).

Over the past twenty-five years, because of continuing demographic pressures in the uplands and associated rural unrest in conjunction with the deepening agricultural crisis, the tropics have received renewed attention. The aridity of most of the country and the prior development of all the prime irrigated areas have made the desirability of expanding rain-fed agriculture seem obvious. With some eight million hectares potentially available for new agricultural developments in Veracruz, Campeche, Yucatán, Chiapas, and Quintana Roo, it was hoped that the area could cover a significant portion of the domestic food deficit as well as provide land and labor to appease peasant demands (Restrepo Fernández, 1978; Szekely and Restrepo, 1988).

The first phase of Plan Chontalpa in Tabasco's Grijalva River basin was launched in 1966, aiming initially at benefiting some eleven thousand primarily local families on 139,000 hectares by 1976, with further expansion projected in a second step (Comisión del Grijalva, 1966). The plan attempted to remedy some of the defects of its precursor in the Papaloapan through a self-help approach to the construction of resettlement facilities and increased emphasis on agricultural experimentation, especially research on soils and physiographic conditions. In 1974 work commenced in the Uxpanapa resettlement zone on 260,000 hectares of tropical rain forest in the Isthmus of Tehuántepec to relocate three thousand Chinantec families displaced by the Cerro de Oro Dam in northern Oaxaca. Both projects encountered serious difficulties in establishing viable cropping systems adapted to the humid tropical conditions in addition to a variety of social problems associated with the relocation of often unenthusiastic "beneficiaries" and the compulsory collectivization of production. Uxpanapa, in particular, has been the center of both social and ecological controversies; biologists in Mexico and abroad criticized the planned destruction of one of the nation's last remaining areas of virgin forest while some anthropologists were outraged at the "ethnocide" represented by the displacement of indigenous populations (Barabas and Bartolomé, 1973; Ewell and Poleman, 1980; Partridge and Brown, 1983).

Problems encountered during these experiments with large-scale mechanized agriculture confirmed that, contrary to initial expectations, tapping the potential of the humid tropics was by no means an easy task. Tropical ecosystems are among the most diverse and complex in the world, home to more than half the known species of flora and fauna, and are still the least studied and understood. One hectare of forest may contain as many as two hundred different species of trees and innumerable smaller plants, animals, and insects, each adapted to a very specific ecological niche. Once large areas have been cleared for agriculture and settlement and the delicate natural equilibrium has been upset, many of these species are unable to survive and reproduce (Gliessman, García, and Amador, 1981). In particular, direct transfer of agricultural technologies from temperate zones has done incalculable damage ecologically and has failed to achieve production goals. Attempts to turn the tropical lowlands into a granary have proven especially destructive in that unnecessary expanses of land have been clear-cut, heavy machinery, fertilizers, and monocultures have destroyed delicate tropical soils, and the introduction of crops unsuited to the climate, soils, and terrains has had disastrous results.

Agricultural research institutes have been set up to investigate new strategies for rational exploitation of these difficult environments so that production can be increased without destroying the fragile balance of tropical ecosystems. Increasingly, researchers are looking at traditional agricultural systems as a starting point, since they are almost by definition well adapted to local ecological conditions and take advantage of a wide variety of resources rather than depending on monoculture (Gliessman, García, and Amador, 1981). Additional crops and techniques could be imported from other parts of the tropics with comparable ecological conditions rather than from temperate zones and, after careful experimentation, could be integrated into mixed systems of small-scale multiple resource exploitation in patchwork clearings instead of large clear-cuts (Ewell and Poleman, 1980; Gradwohl and Greenberg, 1988). Unfortunately, research funding has dwindled under austerity, and progress has been slow, particularly in communicating to project planners in a hurry that tropical environments should be adapted gradually to changing human needs. Devastation of the forests continues in response to short-term economic imperatives, with peasants the guinea pigs in the experiments.

The mechanized granary model of tropical lowland exploitation was introduced to Campeche a few years later than to its neighbors by federal development agencies apparently oblivious to the problems encountered in previous experiments. State-planned agricultural development aimed to transform Campeche's tropical forests and the ejidal sector within the span of a few years into highly productive, efficient farms on the model of a Mexican Iowa. Thus it is not surprising that, on balance, the battle was lost, as expensive projects have become expensive failures with the assistance of the agrarian bureaucracy which has a tendency to work against its proclaimed goals. The constraints on state initiative are intensified by the structure and modus operandi of the bureaucracy, with the result that the inherent risks and uncertainties of the development planning exercise are compounded by the institutional infrastructure itself, as well as by the unforeseen complexities of initiating capital-intensive commercial agriculture on the humid tropical frontier (Gates and Gates, 1972). Unfortunately, the environment and the ejidatarios have been the ultimate losers in the industry of disasters.

The specific models of state intervention in ejidal agriculture employed in Campeche over the past three decades represent the various agrarian horizons or development strategies dominant in agricultural policy at different points in time. Ambitious frontier colonization schemes were the style of the 1960s—the adventure of pioneering new lands reflecting the lingering confidence generated by the fading "Mexican miracle." Modest irrigation projects were characteristic of the early 1970s, part of the new emphasis of the international aid community on integrated development and the transfer of intermediate- and small-scale technology to the rural poor. Capital- and technology-intensive agricultural development zones, initially with a colonization component, surfaced in the mid-1970s. These large-scale projects were reminiscent of the Papaloapan and Grijalva programs in their grand design but focused on only one or two crops and on production more than social development.

Since 1982 agricultural development projects on the drawing board have come to an abrupt halt and existing programs have been sharply curtailed. After several years of caretaking operations, a new concentration on "rehabilitation"—allocating the now-scarce, public-sector resources to the more salvageable of the previous partial successes and failures—is emerging. Nevertheless, the predominant solution for projects where deficit production has become the norm has been "cattle-ization," by design or by default. Thus the planned-development cycle in Campeche encompasses pioneer colonization, small- and large-scale mechanized agriculture, and marginal cattle operations—a sequence common for tropical frontiers. The federal government, which in many senses created the national agricultural crisis through its interventionist strategy is now attempting to plan its way out of it. It remains to be seen whether the processes that have decapitalized the countryside to the point of dysfunctionality can be reversed or if both the ejidal system and the quality of the agricultural environment have been damaged irretrievably.

The gap between goals and results that is intrinsic to the industry of disasters in Campeche can be examined in terms of four case studies, each representing a different development model in the chronological cycle of state intervention in the ejidal sector: frontier colonization along the Candelaria River, small irrigation projects in the Camino Real and Los Chenes, and two projects in the Valley of Edzná agricultural zone—the Bonfil resettlement scheme and the Yohaltún "state farm."

Frontier Colonization Along the Candelaria

The Candelaria colonization scheme predates the main effort to modernize agriculture in Campeche's ejidal sector. Nevertheless, it is important because, despite obvious flaws, it became the model for subsequent colonization and agricultural development efforts in terms of the spirit and purpose of transforming the tropical frontier.

State-directed colonization along the Candelaria River in southern Campeche near the Guatemalan border was initiated in 1963, shortly after New Centers of Ejidal Population (NCPE) had been made the only permitted colonization form. Six new settlements were laid out in the tropical forest on 33,800 hectares of national lands reconstituted as ejidos. The Department of Agrarian Affairs and Colonization (DAAC) confidently promoted the scheme in glowing terms as a lush, fertile paradise with unlimited potential for the balanced commercial production of foods, cattle, and lumber, all with the aid of extensive mechanization and technical assistance, where the colonists would live comfortably in model towns provided with full community services (Siemens, 1966).

The seven hundred families who were the initial settlers were selected primarily from the overcrowded, drought-prone Laguna region of the central upland states of Coahuila and Durango, where there was no shortage of eligible landless candidates entitled to ejidal plots under the agrarian reform law. The new colonists arrived enthusiastic about the potential of the frontier and familiar with collective farming (their homeland having been the site of Mexico's first experiments with the collective ejido in the 1930s). In addition, many had considerable experience with modern agriculture as braceros in the United States. This relatively high degree of cosmopolitanism and technical sophistication seems, however, only to have made adjustment to life in the colonies harder. Accustomed to the arid uplands, with comparatively dense settlement in the prime agrarian pockets and access to modern urban amenities, many new colonists were discouraged when they saw the impenetrable humid tropical forest that had to be cleared, dismayed by the oppressive climate, and depressed by their isolation from city life.

All-weather road access had been promised by the government but did not extend to the majority of the colonies until 1975. For twelve years the river provided the only access to the railhead town of Candelaria, only a few kilometers away by land but many hours by launch. Physical remoteness, cultural isolation, dietary change, the stress of coping with unfamiliar diseases, snakes, insects, and so forth and the constant battle against forest reencroachment combined to induce massive culture shock in many colonists, who perceived the struggle to tame the tropical environment as hopeless and the government's promises as lies. More than 50 percent of the initial immigrants left within the first two years of arrival, and, though they were replaced by recruitment, high turnover has been an ongoing problem. As one colonist recalled the experience:

> It was a complete change of life. We were all homesick, but many lacked the fare to leave. The forest here suffocates you. You can't breathe, and you get sick. In case of a snake bite, you probably would die in the launch. And worst of all, back home there were machinery, cars, movies, ice cream—you could amuse yourself. Here there was nothing—no road, no light, no movement, just the endless struggle against nature that continues to this day. We have just grown old, struggling to survive. (I-107, ejidatario, Estado de México, March 1982)

Meanwhile, the costs of the initial settlement phase had risen to more than double the original estimates (Siemens, 1966).

Even more significant than isolation in inducing anomie was the poor economic performance of the scheme from the beginning. Although initial mechanized clearings had been made, the equipment did not last long in the harsh tropical environment. The colonists lacked maintenance skills, and parts were unavailable. Tractors and bulldozers were soon rusting in the bush, while water pumps and electrical generators often remained out of service for weeks awaiting repair.

Initiation of collective credit groups for cattle, maize, and rice in the late 1960s resulted only in minimal gains because of technical and administrative problems—scarcity of equipment, delays in fertilizer shipments, an infestation of Johnson grass in the government-issued rice seed, and lack of effective agricultural extension—as well as factionalism within the collectives. In addition, the colonies' isolation compounded the usual problems of marketing peasant crops. Cattle had to be driven overland to Tenosique some seventy-five kilometers away. Maize and beans were transported to Candelaria by launch for sale to CONASUPO, which frequently rejected the consignments for quality reasons—leaving the colonists with no alternative but to sell to the local *coyotes* (merchant middle-men), who bought low and sold high. Many colonists abandoned any attempt at market production and adopted slash-and-burn staple culti-vation with digging stick and machete, a far cry from the mechanized cotton of their homeland or their experience in the United States. The majority of the families barely managed to subsist and were heavily in debt, occasionally requiring government emergency aid (Siemens, 1979).

If agricultural prospects were dismal, life in the new towns was equally so. The concrete block houses were built according to one basic plan and looked sterile despite homemaking efforts. The town sites were laid out identically in a spacious grid pattern, with broad residential avenues and large central plazas complete with circular concrete bandstands, the ultimate symbol of Latin American urbanity. Some attempts were made at community beautification through ornamental plantings, statues, side-walks, and so forth, but within a few years the plazas were overgrown and the avenues had shrunk to rutted paths in the bush. The overall aspect by the early 1970s was one of increasing dereliction and decay, a far cry from the ambience of modern urbanity advertized in a DAAC recruit-ment brochure in 1964, where unworried parents would enjoy swimming, dancing, and reading to their children after a productive day's work (Siemens, 1979).

Life in the Candelaria colonies has changed surprisingly little to this day. Fewer than a quarter of the original colonists remain. The rest are later recruits or children of the first settlers, now of age and eligible for ejidal rights. The towns still seem in imminent danger of being swallowed up by the jungle. The number of abandoned houses is witness to the fact that, despite continuing demands for land elsewhere in Mexico, there is no waiting list for admission here. The occasional home now boasts a television, cookstove, or store-bought furniture, indicating that some colonists at least have found a way to profit from the still-limited oppor-tunities for advancement in the Candelaria through small businesses, ejidal office, or outside patronage.

One would have expected the completion of the road to have triggered dramatic change, but it is "all-weather" only to four-wheel-drive vehicles and the sturdiest trucks, and the more distant colonies are not uncom-monly cut off for months at a time in the rainy season. Several bus lines run by the colonists in the late 1970s are now defunct because of the high cost of maintenance and the dissension that plagues many peasant cooperative ventures. The inhabitants are thus dependent on infrequent private vehicle traffic for visits to Candelaria, although each colony has an ejidal truck for official use. This means that they are vulnerable in the event of a medical emergency. Secondary-school children have to board in Candelaria, an expensive proposition for most families. Consequently, a sense of cultural and mental isolation still prevails. For many colonists the social highlight is an outing to Candelaria's cantinas, which the majority can ill afford. Meanwhile, members of the younger generation are increasingly unwilling to put up with the colonies' remoteness and the hard life of a subsistence farmer, and many leave for extended periods or permanently—the army or migrant labor in the United States constituting the most popular avenues of escape.

Much of the initial mechanized clearing has reverted to brush or has been sown with African grasses for pasture, now deteriorated through lack of weeding and reseeding. Cattle rearing has proven the most lucrative economic operation, especially in the colony of Estado de México, which may be able to benefit from a new milk-processing plant at the peninsular highway–Candelaria junction if local roads are improved substantially (Table 5.1). Only a small percentage of the colonists have benefited from this enterprise, however, because of the limited manpower required and the widespread mistrust of such collective ventures. In fact, in most colonies today the collective herds have been divided up and are run on an individual-family basis, further reducing economies of scale and bargaining power vis-à-vis the Candelaria cattle brokers. Meanwhile, most labor in the cattle sector consists of clearing the forest and maintaining pasture and fences for the private investors promoting this activity in the zone, often involving the (until recently illegal) renting of ejidal plots. Thus many colonists have become essentially laborers on their own lands.

TABLE 5.1   Credit Production, Selected Candelaria Colonies, Campeche, 1988 and 1989

	Colony					
	Venustiano Carranza		Monclova		Estado de México	
Crop	1988	1989	1988	1989	1988	1989
Sown (ha)						
Rice	10	10	0	25	0	0
Maize	200	80	80	55	90	40
Harvested (ha)						
Rice	10	0	0	0	0	0
Maize	200	80	80	55	90	40
Production (tons)						
Rice	12	0	0	0	0	0
Maize	170	40	45	22	50	16
Cattle						
Pasture (ha)	–	550	–	867	–	1,808
Number of head	–	430	–	432	–	2,546

SOURCE: SARH, Candelaria, 1990.

Lumber is exploited on a small scale but mainly by outside entrepreneurs, and little valuable timber remains except in the most remote areas.

With respect to commercial agriculture, the main problem is lack of machinery. Equipment is "rented" by the colonists as part of the credit package, but it often fails to arrive in time or breaks down at critical points because of the problems associated with the operation of heavy machinery in a high-rainfall zone. Other critical agricultural inputs such as fertilizer and pesticides are also frequently delayed. Agricultural extension and other technical services are available only on a limited basis. As a result, the colonies' ejidal leaders are devoting an ever-increasing amount of their time and scarce financial resources to traveling to meetings in Candelaria, Escárcega, and Campeche, often being absent for days on end.

Mechanized rice has been the most successful crop in three of the colonies. Only relatively small hectarages are involved, however, and initial high yields have not been sustained because of declining soil fertility and the Johnson-grass problem as well as the input supply constraints (Table 5.1). Total crop failures on significant percentages of the rice lands are frequent. Beans and maize are generally grown without credit under the milpa system, as they are highly prone to plagues as a result of the humid conditions. Yields of mechanized maize averaged only 600 kilograms per hectare over the 1988 and 1989 agricultural cycles because of floods and erratic rains.[2] Yields have also been reduced on occasion by problems within the collectives, mainly related to schisms between procollective ejidatarios and advocates of agriculture on an individual basis. Recently the trend, in response to the poor performance of agriculture in general, has been toward individualization or at least breaking down the units into smaller working groups.

Although a new bridge link to adjacent recently developed frontier areas has been constructed, field access roads have seriously deteriorated. Much of the terrain requires extensive drainage before production can be expanded, and the dry-season irrigation initially planned has not materialized because of problems with land leveling. The original optimistic expectations of large-scale mechanized agriculture and diversified resource exploitation have evaporated, and the colonies are limping along economically with only minimal returns from small credit ventures. The main beneficiaries are the wealthy Candelaria merchants and cattle barons who control the local economy, along with the traders in drugs, contraband timber from Guatemala, and illegal immigrants from Central America, who profit from the region's relative isolation and a continuing frontier mentality concerning contraventions of the law.

One major change has occurred on a regional scale. The Candelaria colonies are no longer isolated pockets of "civilization" on a remote jungle frontier. The surrounding national lands have been filled in by more recent allocation of tracts to NCPE and ejidal extensions for peasants from the more densely settled areas of northern and central Campeche as well as for settlers from upland Mexico. These ejidos compete favorably with

TABLE 5.2   Evaluation, Candelaria Colonization Scheme, Campeche

Development Model and Year of Initiation	Tropical frontier colonization via N.C.P.E. 1963
No. Beneficiaries and Region of Origin	700 landless families from central uplands (La Laguna—Durango, Torreón, Coahuila).
Settlement and Land Tenure	6 colonies with townsites. 5000 hectares *ejidal* land/colony. 20 hectares individual plot/family plus collective agricultural operations.
Development Goals	Balanced commercial production of foods, cattle and lumber, with extensive mechanization, technical assistance, irrigation, and agricultural extension.
	"Showcase" urban centers and project infrastructure.
Project Outcome	1. High % abandonment of colonies due to generalized anomie, poor economic performance, tropical milieu, and physical isolation.
	2. Little mechanization and extension. No irrigation.
	3. Minimal returns from small collective agriculture operations due to input supply constraints, soil degradation, technical, administrative, and social organization problems.
	4. Reliance on subsistence staple cultivation and cattle.
	5. Deteriorating project infrastructure.
	6. Local merchants, cattlemen, and underground economy outside project are main beneficiaries.
Diagnosis	Overly ambitious goals due to political expediency and inadequate knowledge of humid tropics led to abrupt reduction in state support after initial construction, and settlement phase.
	Marginal surviving operations facilitated assumption of economic control by outside entrepreneurs as part of overall "cattle-ization" of frontier.
	Result: low cost, extensive cattle ranches at high opportunity cost.

the Candelaria colonies for the limited resources of the credit bank, while government enthusiasm has turned to new, apparently more promising ventures elsewhere.

The Candelaria colonization scheme was proclaimed in a fanfare of overly ambitious goals, based only on the unfounded assumption of the ease of tapping the potential of the humid tropics and the political expediency of accommodating the landless from more congested zones (Table 5.2). The harsh reality of the obstacles to survival on the frontier caused immediate dismay in colonists and development agencies alike, both equally inexperienced in this milieu. This disillusionment, along with insufficient funds for infrastructure and basic social services and changing national and regional priorities, resulted in an abrupt reduction in government support immediately after the initial settlement. The colonists have been left to fend for themselves, receiving only token attention under the various small-scale federal programs for ejidal development. This neglect and the marginality of surviving credit operations have facilitated the expansion of economic control by local entrepreneurs from outside the project, who monopolize transportation, manipulate prices, and extend high interest loans. In particular, they are intent on exploiting the colonies to obtain cheap cattle. Consequently, the colonies are becoming extensive cattle ranches at high opportunity cost in terms of returns to land, labor, and initial investment capital, while the majority of colonists eke out a precarious living from rudimentary shifting cultivation. One colonist summed up the Candelaria experience as follows:

> Life here is now only half sad. A few with ambition can improve themselves, but only by standing on the shoulders of the rest . . . But the majority here lack the acumen to carve our own road like that. We are still innocent, at the mercy of the whims of those with big ideas. And the government is the worst of all. That's our Mexico. The government promises the campesinos everything to tranquilize us. Then they bury us here to rot in the jungle. (I-123, ejidatario, Monclova, March 1982)

Small Irrigation Projects in the Camino Real and Los Chenes

As the Candelaria scheme receded into obscurity, government attention turned to the establishment of more modest colonies in somewhat less remote areas. It became clear that some kind of overall strategy for regional rural development was necessary if the state was to continue to receive large consignments of peasant immigrants from northern and central Mexico. Furthermore, new settlements would have to be coordinated and rationalized with planned agricultural development for native

Campechanos, particularly in the more densely populated northern Maya zone. However, apart from acknowledging the need for more systematic planning and more careful attention to infrastructure and mechanization, other concrete lessons from the Candelaria experience seem to have been overlooked.

In the mid-1960s, three new centers of ejidal population for northern colonists were established in the Escárcega frontier boom area—Conquista Campesina, Adolfo López Mateos, and División del Norte. Two other such settlements were established on the Champotón River, close to Champotón but with access initially only by launch. Of these new settlements, Ulumal and Moquel, along with Venustiano Carranza, one of the Candelaria colonies, were to receive small irrigation units under the auspices of a new federal program to stimulate ejidal agriculture, which would concentrate its attention, however, in the Maya zone. Although predating the official "rediscovery of the peasantry" in 1970, this program reflected the growing awareness of the incipient national agricultural crisis. Most significant was the determination to reorganize ejidal relations of production by encouraging collectivization in commercial agricultural undertakings. This reorientation was proclaimed officially in new agricultural legislation in 1971 but had emerged de facto with the expansion of directed agricultural credit societies several years earlier. The focus on collectives, credit, mechanization, modern cultivation inputs, and key innovations such as irrigation as a package marked an important departure from the improvisational and contingent nature of previous planned agricultural development in Campeche.

The Plan Nacional de Obras de Pequeña Irrigación (National Plan for Small Irrigation Works)[3] began in 1967 under the auspices of the Ministry of Water Resources, partially financed by the Inter-American Development Bank. The goal was to provide peasants with a more secure livelihood through the introduction of mechanized commercial agriculture, technical assistance, and credit, with irrigation as the central innovation. It was hoped that these measures would reduce out-migration by providing steady employment in areas where economic conditions were precarious and there were few apparent possibilities for spontaneous growth (SRH, 1967).

By 1970 there were fourteen new small irrigation projects in Campeche and an additional project involving the rehabilitation of an earlier abandoned scheme. Of these projects, twelve were located in drought-prone Camino Real and Los Chenes. Traditional agricultural systems were under particular stress in these districts in the late 1960s as a result of population growth and several successive years of highly irregular precipitation, bringing alternating droughts and floods. Attempts had been made to alleviate this situation by granting some afflicted ejidos extensions in the southeastern forests, but this could not be regarded as a long-term solution. It seemed as if the small-scale transfer of intermediate technology might promote regional revitalization as well as incorporate the peasantry into the national economy. By December 1974 the number of projects had increased three times, with a fivefold increment in annual expenditure over 1970. By 1985 there were more than sixty projects in the Camino Real alone.

A typical irrigation project consisted of thirty to a hundred hectares of irrigated land benefiting twenty to thirty ejidatarios, with provisions for future expansion by means of additional wells. Much work was done by hand after the initial clearing and plowing with heavy machinery. Portable aluminum pipes with overhead sprinklers were to be operated by the peasants. Some in-field extension assistance was available, particularly in the initial stages. Agricultural equipment was obtained through the credit bank and other ejidal supply agencies. As in the Candelaria, all credit-based production was done collectively.

The small-irrigation-project format was clearly intended to promote intensive use per capita, involving high-value crops requiring capital-intensive production methods. The innovations involved were relatively simple and inexpensive. This, together with the gradual approach to the diffusion of modern technology, seemed to offer a distinct advantage over previous experiments with large-scale rapid comprehensive modernization by minimizing "technical shock" and avoiding the contracting of huge debts by the beneficiaries before the enterprises were really viable. It was intended that eventually the ejidatarios would manage the projects independently with a minimum of government and bank supervision, an improvement over the paternalism that had been the norm (see Gates, 1981, for details).

Unfortunately, these projects failed to live up to their initial promise. During the early years, many of them were barely viable since the bank and SRH decided to devote them primarily to low-value staples such as maize and beans. Generally, crop yields were substantially higher than under the milpa system, but after repayment of debt obligations little if anything was left over for the ejidatarios who subsisted on their diarios.

Experiments with more lucrative vegetable crops proved impossible to sustain on a significant scale because of the failure of the development agencies to locate reliable markets. Small orchard plantations got off to a slow start, hampered by disease and malfunctioning irrigation systems. In particular, the ejidatarios had problems with the overhead sprinklers, being unwilling or unable to follow the schedule for moving the pipes in part because the projects tended to be at some distance (ten kilometers or more) from their villages according to the availability of appropriate soils. Technical problems with other equipment and shortage of machinery contributed to frequent crop losses, leaving the peasants in debt to the bank at the end of the cycle. As a result, many projects experienced high dropout rates and some folded altogether. To protect themselves against likely project crop failures, the majority of the remaining peasants hedged by continuing to make milpa on the side, consequently not devoting their full time and energy to the irrigation units. The net result was aptly summed up by one ejidatario as "million peso milpas" (I-8, Pomuch, December 1975), in that all the program had achieved by the mid-1970s was increased staple production at high investment cost, with the bulk of the risk and debt burden falling on the "beneficiaries" (Gates, 1981; Gates and Gates, 1972).

By 1975 little official enthusiasm for the projects remained. Instead, attention had turned to a new large-scale billion peso resettlement scheme at Edzná. The development agencies felt, however, that the small irrigation projects were "getting by" on the whole, blaming the limited progress on members' inability to work harmoniously together in collectives and their failure to take credit obligations seriously (I-154, civil servant, Campeche, December 1975). In particular, the bank officials exhibited little sympathy for peasants experiencing their first contact with the credit system. If the peasants were in debt at harvest time, having spent their advances and regarding other production credits as wages, the bank refused them credit the following year rather than recognizing the need for agricultural extension (I-155, civil servant, Campeche, December 1975). Meanwhile, the peasants complained about the loss of production autonomy, the bank officials' authoritarianism and malfeasance, and the inadequacy of technical backup, particularly the ministry's failure to solve recurring problems such as pipe specification errors resulting in low water pressure, faulty pumps, deteriorating equipment, and lack of spare parts—all of which greatly increased the debt burden of the afflicted projects.

Today, of the 350 irrigation units constructed in the state of Campeche, only 90 have functioning irrigation systems, and half of these had fallen into disuse until recent rehabilitation efforts. This represents an investment loss of more than 41 billion pesos over two decades (I-138, civil servant, Campeche, January 1990). Of the units that are still operational, with or without irrigation, the majority are still barely viable, though a few are thriving, in relative terms at least. The key to "success" appears to have been the initiative and adaptability of specific groups of ejidatarios rather than any particular change in official economic or administrative strategy. The leaders of these units have been able to break the stranglehold of blanket official selection of project crops and marketing strategies through their awareness of potential options and alternative ejidal support services and their willingness to take their own risks. They have opted for diversified production, with various combinations of staple crops, orchards, vegetable gardens, and cattle and small livestock rearing. Mangos, in particular, have flourished in the region, though merchant intermediaries from central and northern Mexico have skimmed off much of the profit. Irrigated tomato production is regarded as promising despite vulnerability to plagues in view of the potential for capturing the early national market and is now being promoted on a regional scale along with orchards in those projects with functioning irrigation systems.

Perhaps most important, members of the more successful projects have recognized the negative effects of internal dissension within the collective, of co-optation or corruption of peasant leadership, and factionalism. To some extent they have solved these problems in their own way, either by expelling corrupt, troublemaking, or lazy members or by reorganizing the collective into smaller credit groups or working parties along kin and other factional lines. For example, in the Pomuch project, one group now specializes in mangos and small livestock, another in vegetables, and a third in watermelons, each controlling different wells although credit was until recently administered to the unit as a whole. This subdivision of the terrain between the three dominant families and their followers has greatly improved project viability through a marked reduction in the long-standing friction between the factions. The mangos are sold mainly to merchants from central and northern Mexico under arrangements made by the development agencies, while the vegetables and melons are sold locally in Pomuch and Campeche, a market promoted by the peasants themselves. A definite advantage also goes to those projects whose members have learned to cope effectively with the bureaucracy through increased ability to understand the paper work, better understanding of the credit mechanism, awareness of current agrarian policy and new ejidal programs, and familiarity with the "rules of the game" in dealing with officials and politicians. In this sense, the small irrigation program has been a positive learning experience for the more literate, innovative, and self-motivated minority, but most project members continue to passively accept government direction and tend to be suspicious of initiatives from their peers (see Gates, 1976).

The fact remains that not even the most dynamic small irrigation projects are making profits fully justifying the high investment costs. Production is far from efficient, hampered by insufficient market planning and technical assistance, delays in allocating key machinery, endless red tape and meetings, malfunctioning irrigation systems, obsolete or deteriorating equipment, and inflexibilities and inadequacies in the credit and crop insurance programs. In the most marginal projects, members are unable to afford their irrigation systems or fix broken tractors and there-

TABLE 5.3   Credit Production, Pomuch Irrigation Project 1, Well 1, Camino Real, Campeche, 1985–1989

Crop	Year	Sown (ha)	Harvested (ha)	Production (tons)
Maize	1985	30	29	61
	1986	17	0	Total loss
	1987	24	24	52
	1989	28	N.A.	N.A.
Zapote[a]	1985	20	0	0
	1986	20	0	0
	1987	5	0	0
	1988	5	5	1.5
	1989	5	N.A.	N.A.
Tomatoes[b]	1989	10	5	36

NOTE: N.A. = Not Available.
[a]In the case of tree crops, "sown" means planted or previously planted.
[b]Irrigated.
SOURCE: SARH, 1990.

fore cultivate milpa on the project land—thus making barely enough to live on. The net result has been an epidemic of defaults on bank loans, making many projects ineligible for credit.

A number of projects have problems with "peso millionaires"— members who have become relatively wealthy as a result of individual manipulation of the system at the expense of their peers. Perceiving themselves to be landlords, they hire nonproject peasants as day laborers at subminimum wage to work in their stead. In some projects the majority of work is done by hired labor of this type. In others the members perform their project tasks, cultivate milpa on the side, and in addition hire out as day laborers when the opportunity presents itself. The end result is a complicated network of obligations and informal labor contracts, and it thus becomes difficult to maintain membership continuity and increase agricultural skill levels systematically as well as to attribute responsibility for production.

Of four projects monitored in depth since their initiation in 1969, one had been defunct for fifteen years prior to rehabilitation in 1990, one is devoted to nonirrigated staple cultivation and a small orchard, one has a hand-watered mango plantation, and one has developed a variety of small livestock and agricultural specializations (Tables 5.3–5.5). In all of them malfunctioning irrigation systems and lack of reliable markets limit the scale and scope of operations and therefore traditional cultivation of staples remains the core activity, with maize yielding 2–5 tons per hectare in good years but incurring significant losses about half of the time. Only about a quarter of the membership shows up for work on a regular basis, but members of this active minority can earn enough to sustain their families from diarios and their share of any profits as long as credit is extended.

Initial expectations of highly productive, capital-intensive agriculture have evaporated, and with the debt crisis and the failure of Campeche's oil boom to generate any spillover into rural areas other than to further inflation many peasants are experiencing a progressive decline in levels of consumption. Most of the Campeche small irrigation projects are too marginal to stem this tide. The majority of the beneficiaries view the program as just one more example of misleading government promises and thus devote to the projects the minimal attention they feel is merited.

The experience indicates that although the small-scale transfer of a limited number of innovations would seem to involve less risk and dislocation than megaprojects of the "modernize-everything-in-sight" variety, this is not necessarily the case if intensive use per capita under high-value crops cannot be sustained (Table 5.6). Given the small scale and limited scope of activities, there is little margin for error: a broken pump, a plague, a market glut, or heavy rains can result in no profit and the withdrawal of credit for the next cycle. While diversification would seem the best way of hedging, the concomitant reduction in size of operations further increases marginality. The level of uncertainty is high, and the debts on paper are astronomical in proportion to the benefits accrued. Essentially, the projects now serve as just another subsistence-level option in the range of peasant strate-

TABLE 5.4   Credit Production, Pomuch Irrigation Project 1, Wells 2 and 3, Camino Real, Campeche, 1985–1989

Crop	Year	Sown (ha)	Harvested (ha)	Production (tons)
Maize	1985	35	35	35
	1986	25	0	Total loss
	1987	14	14	35
	1988	34	0	Total loss
	1989	50	N.A.	N.A.
Mango[a][b]	1985	50	50	200
	1986	50	50	250
	1987	50	50	300
	1988	50	50	200
	1989	50	50	480

NOTE: N.A. = Not Available.
[a]In the case of tree crops, "sown" means planted or previously planted.
[b]Irrigated.
SOURCE: SARH, 1990.

gies for survival—one that scarcely justifies the anxiety, frustration, and loss of production autonomy it entails. As one project member put it:

> We still owe them for the broken-down tractor, and it will be twelve years before we have paid for the new one. And there's the bill for the generator and the number-two pump. The degrainer doesn't work, and they are going to discount for moisture in the beans. I often feel that we are employees on the bank's farm, paid to labor on our own land, on the debt treadmill until we die. Is it worth it? (I-8, ejidatario, Pomuch, November 1985)

TABLE 5.5   Credit Production, Pomuch Irrigation Project 1, Wells 4 and 5, Camino Real, Campeche, 1985–1989

Crop	Year	Sown (ha)	Harvested (ha)	Production (tons)
Maize	1985	113	101	80
	1986	101	0	Total loss
	1987	101	95	276
	1988	81	0	Total loss
	1989	101	N.A.	N.A.
Maize[a]	1985	3	3	12
	1988	10	0	Total loss
Watermelon[a]	1985	2	2	16
	1986	2	2	12
Mango[b]	1985	6	3	9
	1986	6	3	9
	1987	6	3	6
	1988	3	3	2
	1989	3	3	2
Zapote[b]	1985	6	3	9
	1986	6	3	9
	1987	6	3	7
	1988	3	3	2
	1989	3	3	2
Chile[a]	1986	4	4	21
	1987	25	9	33
Squash[a]	1986	12	4	11
Tomato[a]	1986	2	2	2
	1987	6	0	Total loss
	1988	19	19	132
Mixed vegetables	1986	2	2	9

NOTE: N.A. = Not Available.
[a]Irrigated.
[b]In the case of tree crops, "sown" means planted or previously planted.
SOURCE: SARH, 1990.

TABLE 5.6   Evaluation, Small Irrigation Projects, Camino Real and Los Chenes, Campeche

Development Model and Year of Initiation	National Plan For Small Irrigation Projects. Small-scale transfer of intermediate technology. 1969
No. Beneficiaries and Region of Origin	20-30 local Maya *ejidatarios*/project
Settlement and Land Tenure	12 projects in 1970 (over 200 in 1985), each with 60-100 irrigated hectares in collective production.
Development Goals	To provide peasants with more secure livelihood through intensive agriculture via irrigated, high-value crops. To reduce rural-urban migration.
Project Outcome	1. Concentration on low-value staples, small orchards and horticulture because of failure to locate reliable markets, malfunctioning irrigation systems, and input supply constraints. 2. Initial high membership turnover because of perceived lack of project viability and large debts, together with poor credit bank relations. 3. Discord in collectives except where labor organization restructured by *ejidatarios* along kin and factional lines. 4. Most peasants only part-time members, relying on traditional subsistence strategies and hiring surrogate labor for project obligations. 5. Widespread loan default under debt crisis due to high credit costs and low value of production. 6. Recent limited success with mangos and vegetable production.
Diagnosis	Unless intensive use per capita under high value crops can be sustained, small-scale transfer of limited innovations involves as much risk and dislocation as mega-projects. *Result:* "million peso *milpas*;" (high risk and uncertainty for project members dependent on staple crops).

The Valley of Edzná Agricultural and Resettlement Zone

In 1971, the newly created Comisión Intersecretarial de Nuevos Centros de Población Ejidal (COINCE) decided, on the basis of preliminary studies by the Ministry of Water Resources (SRH), the Department of

Agrarian Affairs and Colonization (DAAC), and other agencies, that some thirty thousand landless families from other parts of Mexico could be accommodated on a million hectares in the center of the state over the course of the 1970s at a cost of over a billion pesos. These families were to open up the new lands for commercial agriculture, in particular rice and orchards, as well as for modern intensive cattle rearing and managed forestry. At a later stage, a further million hectares was to be developed in areas of the northern Maya Camino Real and Los Chenes regions. The Valley of Edzná, fifty kilometers southeast of the city of Campeche, along with a large area south of Champotón, was selected as the first target in this massive directed colonization effort. The valley was designated a development zone for mechanized agriculture for thirty-five hundred resettled ejidatario families, involving some 120 wells, 52 drains, and thousand of kilometers of roads on over two hundred thousand hectares (Fig. 5.1). Existing population was sparse, confined to seasonal logging operations and a handful of Maya settlements whose inhabitants practiced slash-and-burn milpa cultivation, plagued by alternating droughts and floods. The ancient Maya had developed an important civilization in the area, however, as evidenced by the Classic ruins of Edzná at the entrance to the valley, reservoirs, a canal network, and the thirty-five kilometer Dren Maya (Maya Drain) traversing the zone. Evidently, intensive agriculture had been feasible in the past, and now the valley was to be "reborn" through injections of modern technology under the guidance of COINCE, which embraced 15 ministries and government dependencies with SRH (later SARH) as the lead agency (SRH, 1974).

The "Millionaire Ejido"

Six New Centers of Ejidal Population (NCPE) were to be constructed initially in the northern portion of the valley, primarily benefiting colonists from central and northern Mexico. The first of these, Alfredo Vladimir Bonfil, was created by presidential decree in December 1973, allocating twenty thousand hectares to five hundred heads of families. Unlike the Candelaria project, which had recruited largely from one district in the central uplands, Bonfil drew colonists initially from three main areas, Guanajuato, Tamaulipas, and Veracruz, and this set the stage for the intense political factionalism that has marked the history of the settlement. The majority of the new colonists were young and landless but had considerable familiarity with modern agriculture, having been forced to migrate widely through Mexico and the United States as day laborers, braceros, and smallholding colonists in their struggle to earn a living. None had been ejidatarios before.

Diversified agriculture was to occupy half the land, with sown pasture

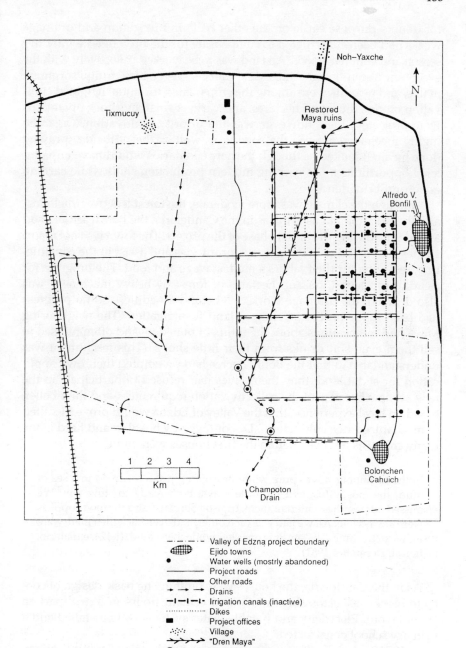

FIGURE 5.1   Edzná development zone, Bonfil, Campeche (SOURCE: SARH, 1975)

for double-purpose cattle on the other half after irrigation and drainage works had been constructed to compensate for the prolonged winter dry season and summer floods. All land was to be worked collectively, with the exception of ten-hectare individual parcels. Vegetables, fruits, sorghum, maize, and peanuts were among the crops slated for initial irrigated cultivation on five thousand hectares, and various small livestock operations were projected. Rice, however, was the priority. Cultivation was to be highly mechanized, with the sowing as well as the pesticide spraying done by air. It looked as though the new ejidatarios would have unparalleled opportunities for learning modern production skills while earning good profit dividends.

Although the climate was more moderate, the forest less overwhelming, and the isolation not as acute as in the Candelaria, the Bonfil settlers had a hard time during the initial phase of the project. The town was not ready, so they had to lodge in temporary dormitories and assist in the construction, receiving for their labors a modest wage and food. The program for clearing fourteen thousand hectares of forest by heavy machinery was also delayed, the drainage works fell behind schedule, and no progress had been made on the leveling of land for irrigation. The neighboring Maya had reservations about the influx of outsiders and often refused to sell them even soft drinks from their little shops. (This resentment was understandable in that the Bonfil decree had preempted their own application for ejidal land; they themselves had refused to participate in the new scheme because of the collectivization requirement and their belief, based on local experience, that the Valley of Edzná would prove ill-suited to mechanized rice cultivation.) Discouraged by hostility and hard labor, many colonists left even before the first houses were built:

> In the beginning it was pure wilderness here—just a dirt road in a sea of mud, the mosquitos, and the little Maya, both ready to sting you! We missed our families, entertainment, tripe on Sundays, and the food supplies were always late. All we had was each other, and even back then there were fights all the time. The sensible ones left while they could. (I-124, ejidatario, Bonfil, December 1981)

As in the Candelaria, the houses were built in one basic design of concrete blocks, asbestos sheet roofs, and cement floors in a grid-pattern street layout. Electricity and potable water systems were installed and a primary school constructed.

In 1974 and 1975, the first two years of full-scale agricultural operations, the rice harvests were spectacular, as might be expected on new land. This advantage was enhanced by the disciplined effort of many Bonfil ejidatarios, already highly motivated toward mechanized production and determined to play a significant role in the agricultural decision-making process. Some, in particular, were dedicated to promotion of the collective ideal whereby "union makes strength" if members adhere to its tenets, organize carefully, and work hard (I-93, ejidatario, Bonfil, November 1981). As a result of these efforts, rice harvests yielded 11 million tons from four thousand hectares in 1975. This provided the ejidatarios with very good dividends after credit repayment, part of which were redistributed in kind as furniture and domestic appliances on the initiative of the ejidal president. News of this unheard-of arrangement quickly spread through Campeche's ejidal sector, exacerbating the resentment of preferential treatment to outsiders, and Bonfil became known as the "millionaire ejido" where, thanks to the government, colonists reclined on sofas watching television. On a wider scale, Bonfil gained fame as a "model project," visited by hundreds of national and foreign agricultural, development, and technical experts, as well as by groups from other new centers and local ejidos hoping to learn from this experiment.

In the next few years, however, extended droughts followed by heavy rains caused crop failures and equipment problems, tractors and harvesters with conventional tires proving incapable of maneuvering in the mud. Soils in much of the rice zone were poorly drained heavy gleys, the ak'alche of the bottomlands avoided by the Maya for milpa. These soils deteriorated rapidly with the use of heavy machinery in the initial clearcutting, mechanized cultivation, and the absence of crop rotation, resulting in progressive leaching, desiccation, and acidification. Furthermore, Johnson grass brought in with the government rice seed in 1977 greatly reduced yields, and the harvesters contracted from the official ejidal equipment service often arrived late and in disrepair.

Discontent among the ejidatarios grew as dividends disappeared, irrigation was delayed, the promised ten-hectare individual parcels were reduced to two hectares to conform with the 1971 legislative reform, dissension plagued the collective, the level of consultation in decision making did not meet the ejidatarios' demands, and relations with SARH in particular deteriorated. The ministry was constrained by technical problems with the wells, difficulties in land leveling and drainage, objections by the ejidal leaders, and the shift in federal agricultural policy. The ejidatarios were outraged by "more government lies" and drove the SARH extension agents out of town for undertaking promotional campaigns without informing the ejidal authorities, for "arrogance," and for "talking to dissident individuals secretly at night" (meeting between SARH and Bonfil ejidatarios, Campeche, December 1975).

By 1978 Bonfil's collective operations were in chaos. The ejido was in default for 46 million pesos in rice credit and had incurred a huge debt for agricultural machinery. General assemblies of the ejidatarios were "bear gardens," with the members disputing the debt balance and denouncing the development agencies. Increasingly the ejidatarios attacked their own directorate for making arbitrary decisions without consulting the membership, in particular for irregularities in the management of ejidal funds, claiming outright fraud on occasion by leaders acting alone or in collusion with outside interests.

The ejidal leaders had grown extremely powerful by virtue of the scale and scope of the activities to be managed, which placed large funds at their discretion, and their unusual business and technical acumen. They maintained that some decisions were not readily communicable to the membership at large, especially when prompt action was required. Furthermore, they defended their shifting of credit resources from sector to sector regardless of the official designation as necessary to cover shortfalls caused by delays in bank funding and to provide the ejidatarios with as many diarios as possible. Whatever the case, this made accounting difficult and engendered suspicion: "Who knows where the money goes? One thing is certain, the smart ones in the ejidal commissariat don't finish their term poor! Like [you-know-who] with his rice ranch down there in Palizada. And how did [so-and-so] get his private cows?" (I-125, ejidatario Bonfil, November 1981). These various disputes increasingly became reduced to a schism between procollective and individualist factions, which tended to alternate in leadership positions, each incoming administration vociferously denouncing the actions of its predecessors. Meanwhile, outside agitators and confidence men took advantage of the discontent to promote schemes such as the sale of "legal" titles to individual parcels.

In this climate, some Bonfil members became full-time peasant politicians, with lawyers and briefcases, dedicated to presenting the ejido's demands in government offices. These confrontational tactics were unusual in the mid-1970s, when the normal interaction between ejidatarios and officials involved for the former a long wait outside an agency in the hope of admittance, hat in hand, to make a respectful request that was likely to be ignored. As well as being audacious, this strategy was often surprisingly successful in terms of winning an unprecedented degree of autonomy from the development agencies in a number of critical areas. Most likely these concessions were awarded because of the high profile of the Valley of Edzná project at the national level, in addition to the ejido's connections with influential procollective elements of the leadership of the CNC. Other ejidatarios reacted against both the politicization of agriculture and its disappointing economic performance, becoming absentees living in the city of Campeche or withdrawing completely from collective activities and advocating total privatization of the project.

Meanwhile, the majority of the ejidatarios had reorganized into groups of twenty-five members, each responsible for a designated hectarage under the direction of Bonfil's elected leaders. It was hoped that this would facilitate organization of production, in particular the provision of labor assignments for each ejidatario, which had grown to be a complicated matter given the large proportion of the work that was mechanized. Some members resisted this breakdown into minicollectives, preferring to work in one larger unit under the literal terms of the presidential decree, but most of the machinery was divided up among the smaller groups. Over the years, a number of these groups requested that credit be extended to them directly, but BANRURAL continued to allocate resources to the ejido as a whole—a source of continuing friction and abuse of funds within the community (I-140, civil servant, Bonfil, July 1985).

Bonfil today looks relatively prosperous on the surface. A Catholic church, a kindergarten, secondary and preparatory schools, an ejidal meeting hall, a post office, a cinema, and a CONASUPO market have been constructed, several of these with ejidal funds. A significant number of the ejidatarios (almost one-third) can afford pickup trucks or motorbikes as well as televisions and other modern appliances and furnishings. Outbuildings have been constructed in the house yards, which are filled with fruit trees and vegetable plots. The roads bustle with young cowboys, each herding half a dozen animals in a cloud of dust or through a sea of mud, depending on the season. Within the project, however, underemployment is an ongoing problem except for the few with specialist skills and the relatives and cronies of the ejidal leadership, who are assigned the ever-fewer year-round jobs. Many of the men obtain employment elsewhere in the state, often using skills acquired in the project experience such as heavy-machine and tractor operation or repair, working for government agencies, private contractors, or other ejidos. Others roam seasonally as agricultural laborers in various parts of Mexico or the United States as they did before coming to Bonfil. A sizable contingent has abandoned agriculture for construction work in Campeche. Meanwhile, shops and other small businesses have proliferated, numbering over fifty enterprises in 1990, reflecting both the entrepreneurial bent of many Bonfil residents in putting past dividends to work and the increasing inability of the project to support its members in the style to which they have become accustomed.[4]

Cattle rearing has flourished, covering investment costs and paying sizable dividends, and dairying looks promising even though expansion possibilities are limited by the failure to construct the promised milk-processing plant. Little full-time manpower has been required in these sectors, however, especially since 1983 when half of the collective herd was sold to pay off the bank debt and the remainder distributed among interested members, who received an average of five head per capita. The recipients were mainly individuals with past experience of cattle rearing in their northern homeland and sons to assist with the herding and eventually inherit the stock. A third of the ejidatarios opted for a cash settlement instead, including "the old, the infirm, the childless, and those terrified of cows" (I-64, ejidatario, Bonfil, February 1990). Considerable resentment has been generated by this cattle redistribution, from which some individuals emerged with both more stock than others and greater access to pasture. A further substantial step away from collectivization was taken when the developed lands were divided up shortly thereafter, each ejidatario receiving ten hectares of seasonal crop land, four hectares of "irrigated" land, and five hectares of "improved" pasture. Because "irrigated" land tends to mean a field located near a nonfunctioning well—only three of the project's twenty wells being in partial operation for agriculture supplying only 30 hectares in 1990—ejidatarios with cattle normally use these plots for pasture as well as "renting" extra grassland from those who opted out of the cattle business. "Improved" pasture refers to five hundred hectares of Johnson grass in the abandoned rice zone and thirty-five hundred hectares planted with African grass over a decade ago and now degenerated. In 1990 Bonfil possessed a total of 4,410 cattle, owned by 330 ejidatarios operating herds averaging 13 head per family (Table 5.7). The cattle are mainly zebu-Swiss crosses, which generate significant income from sales of steers and milk. Meanwhile, collectives are not totally defunct; one group continues to operate a steer-rearing enterprise with bank credit on five hundred hectares.

Agriculture has incurred huge debts and provides minimal dividends beyond diarios, as rice yields which had averaged 2.75 tons per hectare in 1975 (reaching 13 tons in some areas) dropped sharply after just a few years of cultivation to a 1.16 ton average from 1984 through 1989 (Table 5.8). Because of the high degree of mechanization involved, rice work is available on any scale only in July and August, when intensive

TABLE 5.7   Livestock Holdings, Bonfil, Campeche, 1989

Livestock	Total Animals	Total Owners
Double-purpose cattle	4,410[a]	330
Young bulls (with credit)	500	10
Horses	470	320
Sheep	80	8
Goats	90	2
Beehives	100	4
Mules	10	8

[a]Including 2,496 breeding cattle.
SOURCE: SARH, 1990.

TABLE 5.8   Credit Production, Bonfil, Campeche, 1984–1989

Crop	Year	Sown (ha)	Harvested (ha)	Production (tons)	Yield (tons/ha)	Value (1,000 pesos)
Rice	1984	1,035	417	592	0.57	20,187
	1985	3,455	3,181	7,761	2.25	413,142
	1986	3,228	75	57	0.02	5,518
	1987	3,809	3,442	9,570	2.51	2,277,660
	1988	3,703	2,747	4,569	1.23	1,087,422
	1989	3,810	750	1,832	0.48	428,876
Maize	1984	317	300	600	1.9	20,070
	1985	250	112	87	0.35	4,691
	1986	79	50	60	0.76	5,760
	1987	322	191	219	0.68	53,655
	1988	1,958	0	0	0	Total loss
	1989	220	50	150	0.68	51,750
Beans	1984	2	2	0.5	0.25	26
Cotton	1984	45	45	18	0.39	1,829
Sorghum	1986	122	122	256	2.1	12,544

Source: SARH, 1990.

hand weeding is required. Consequently, many project members continue to work elsewhere, sending their wives in their stead or hiring the local Maya and Guatemalan refugees from the nearby camp to perform their collective labor obligations.

SARH has realized belatedly that the Valley of Edzná is not well suited to rice cultivation, though production continues inefficiently at high cost in terms of mechanization and disease and weed control. A third or more of the harvest is lost most years due to drought, floods, Johnson grass,[5] and progressive soil deterioration, as well as continued input supply delays and shortages. After 1983, the Bonfil rice area was cut from over six thousand hectares to around thirty-five hundred hectares. In 1990 only a few hundred hectares of the best land were projected to be sown. Paradoxically, Hurricane Gilbert may have been the last straw for rice production in Bonfil because of its failure to damage the harvest appreciably. While it flattened and drowned Bonfil's maize crop in September 1988, the still-young rice plants were not harmed by the heavy rains and therefore the insurance company did not declare the crop a total loss. At 1.2 tons per hectare, yields were insufficient to repay credit costs and the whole project fell into default.

This is the essence of the problem with marginal ejidal agricultural projects: investment costs can only be covered by having a portion or all of the crop designated as a loss. Thus it has become the practice in Bonfil, as in many other ejidos, to persuade ANAGSA to declare a crop a *siniestro total*

(total loss). The ejidatarios then harvest and sell the crop, pocketing the proceeds, while credit repayment is covered by insurance and default avoided. This is the only way a marginal ejido can come out a little ahead on the year's operation overall, with funds available to support the members' families and cover new labor costs. Thus, agrarian policy and practice have promoted a wholesale industry of disasters that operates on two levels—the formal layer of official statistics on crop losses and the underlying network of underground agreements, payoffs, and trading of favors representing the real strategy for survival within the system.

Little progress has been made in other crops, partly because of the lack of irrigation. Limited trials with vegetables and fruits at a test well had good results, but the wells and many of the project's field access roads are now in a state of extreme disrepair. Sorghum also looks promising on the basis of investigations conducted by the adjacent government agricultural research station. Maize has done poorly except in the limited area of kan-kab on the edge of the bottomlands, with yields averaging less than half a ton per hectare over the last five agricultural cycles. However, experiments with raised bed maize cultivation have been very successful.[6] The only new agricultural operations are a few independent initiatives, such as small mango and citrus plantations and a society of twelve ejidatarios who planted irrigated tomatoes and watermelons on four hectares without credit, hampered by lack of capital and the water shortage. Many Bonfil ejidatarios would like to grow sugarcane and cotton, but the only sugar mill in Campeche is at full capacity, and a cotton experiment in Bonfil in 1984 had poor results. A piggery proved unable to compete in the regional market with animals from the Yucatán, where balanced feed is also produced. An experimental fish farm run by the wives of ejidatarios was abandoned because of the inability to control algae buildup. Bonfil has become a viable cattle ranch, which is satisfactory to the credit bank but an embarrassment to SARH, whose expensive investments in capital infrastructure are redundant in an extensive operation, and a disappointment to the ejidatarios who had expected to participate in diversified, efficient modern agricultural production.

The "bad politics" that have plagued Bonfil since its inception are less visible today, but ejidal leaders are often under public attack, and tensions between collectivists and privatizers are not far from the surface. Whereas political power has tended to shift between the two camps, in recent years the balance seems to have shifted irreversibly toward the individualists. The irony is that, on the whole, it appears to have been the most able individuals who both embraced the collective ideal most fervently and were able to derive the greatest personal profit from the process. This process is reflected in the widening gap between the new rich, middle, and poor classes. Those who have prospered are clearly either former ejidal politicians or those with initiative or special aptitudes. At the bottom are the majority of simple farmers who rely solely on the project to survive; no trucks are parked outside their houses.

For its part, SARH has recognized the fallacy of attempting to convert the humid tropics indiscriminately into a granary, but in view of this agency's past record of inefficient proyectismo it is debatable whether this lesson will deter future efforts along similar lines. As a senior civil servant remarked, "In Campeche, we spent fifteen years on the wrong crop in the wrong place. Now we have a cattle ranch with the best nonworking irrigation system in Mexico, and it will happen again as long as we think that development is for the technician, that pretty wells matter more than people" (I-136, civil servant, Campeche, November 1985).

The Valley of Edzná project was originally intended to be "the dorsal fin of the whole state's development" (I-136, civil servant, Campeche, November 1985). Today, the Bonfil component is clearly marginal in relation to the massive capital and technology inputs as a result of the misguided rice concentration, the expanded cattle emphasis, and the lack of viable alternatives, while wholesale clear-cutting and mechanized cultivation have caused largely irreversible ecological damage (Table 5.9). Bonfil is also a failure as a collective experiment, pushed to the breaking point primarily by the failure of the rice monoculture, the consequent imperative of compromised crop reports, and the concomitant search for individual strategies of survival. A significant number of the Bonfil migrants are able to live fairly comfortably, but mainly from investment of past dividends and outside activities rather than from current returns to the project itself. These more adaptable, ambitious, skilled, or corrupt individuals have been able to benefit from the relocation experience and from side effects such as the acquisition of marketable skills or the development of client relations with outside power brokers. Most are essentially no longer peasants but private ranchers, nonagricultural entrepreneurs, or laborers, often in violation of the agrarian code and technically no longer eligible for ejidal rights and project membership. Meanwhile, the majority of the members of this "millionaire ejido" scour the countryside in search of low-paid casual labor opportunities as they did before coming to Campeche, subsist from milpa, or sit on their porches hoping that profit dividends will materialize while the local Maya and Guatemalan refugees increasingly perform the limited project tasks. In this respect, the most noticeable consequence of the Edzná project has been the acceleration of partial proletarianization, reflected in the accentuation of economic differentiation, as the migrants have responded in different ways to the various opportunities and constraints offered by a rural development of this scale.

One Bonfil ejidatario summed up the situation as follows: "Here, if you have initiative, there is real opportunity to do well for yourself and your

TABLE 5.9   Evaluation, Edzná Agricultural and Resettlement Zone, Ejido Alfredo V. Bonfil, Campeche

Development Model and Year of Initiation	Large-scale agricultural and resettlement project emphasizing cereals. 1973
No. Beneficiaries and Region of Origin	500 landless families from central and northern Mexico.
Settlement and Land Tenure	*Ejido* (N.C.P.E.) and townsite on 20,000 hectares as part of 200,000 hectares agricultural zone. Initially 10 hectares individual plot/family plus collective lands. After 1977, 2 hectares individual plot, remainder in collective.
Development Goals	Intensive, heavily mechanized, diversified agriculture with irrigation planned for 50% land (rice emphasis), 50% pasture for cattle. A model agricultural zone with state-of-the-art technology.
Project Outcome	1. Immediate shift from diversified agriculture to rice monoculture.
	2. Sharp decline in rice yields after first two years as a result of equipment input supply problems, droughts, Johnson grass, lack of rotation, and rapid soil deterioration.
	3. Increasing cattle emphasis. No irrigation or diversified annual production. Collapse of small livestock experiments.
	4. Deteriorating relations between *ejidatarios* and development agents.
	5. Dysfunctional collectives due to graft, corruption, lack of production autonomy, underemployment, and generalized anomie. Privatization of herds and 50% of land after 1983.
	6. Increased internal socio-economic differentiation associated with partial proletarianization and demise of collectives.
	7. Irreversible environmental damage.
Diagnosis	Misguided rice concentration in unsuitable zone led to increasing dependence on cattle, prompting absenteeism and employment of local Maya and Guatemalan refugees as surrogate labor.
	Result: viable cattle ranch with marginal secondary rice operation.

family and to screw the government and your compañeros in the process" (I-61, ejidatario, Bonfil, October 1985). Another project member provided a less opportunistic appraisal: "The failure of rice was the main cause of the erosion of the collective idea in Bonfil. As it exhausted the soil, it consumed the spirit of the ejido. The fundamental optimism of the collective is incompatible with the cynicism of the industry of disasters" (I-65, ejidatario, Bonfil, February 1990).

A State Farm

The second phase of the Edzná project got under way in 1978 in the region of Yohaltún in the southern portion of the valley, involving seventy-five thousand hectares. As in the northern section, population was sparse, consisting of a few settlements of spontaneous colonists and a handful of ejidos dating back to the late 1930s. Some of these ejidos had been abandoned around 1950 because of the region's remoteness and lack of water and reoccupied by different ejidatarios some fifteen years later. As in the area around Bonfil, Yohaltún's soils consisted mainly of poorly drained heavy gleys in bottomlands, subject to similar problems with winter droughts and summer floods but with even more irregular precipitation and an extended dry season. In addition, the topsoil was very shallow, overlying a particularly thick bed of caliche, which absorbs all surface moisture immediately. Consequently, preliminary drainage and irrigation works were even more critical for sustaining reliable agricultural production. The original plan was to involve the construction of five New Centers of Ejidal Population for landless families from central and northern Mexico and a sugar mill, but this plan was scrapped as a result of the Bonfil experience and changing national agricultural priorities.

By the late 1970s, increasing staple production had become the overriding imperative and efficiency the watchword. Thus the productivity drive would be on ejidal land, but ejidatarios would not be entrusted with the actual farming—the record of planned agricultural development having shown that depending on peasants only complicated the process and increased the likelihood of failure. This sentiment was implicit in the organization of agricultural activities in Yohaltún, which, from the beginning was operated essentially as a state farm on which government agencies would produce rice before eventually turning over the land to the beneficiaries. In this way, the government could recover the high costs of infrastructural investment in short order without having to incur additional expenses in the form of de facto subsidies to privileged ejidatarios or to contend with the political maneuverings of colonists who were a far cry from the stereotypical passive peasant.

The 1980 law for promoting agricultural and livestock production was designed to increase production and promote self-sufficiency in basic foods through the formation of "production units"—associations of ejidos or between ejidos and private interests or the state for commercial agricultural activities, with favored access to credit, mechanization, and other modern technical inputs under the direction of SARH. For the Yohaltún project this meant the elimination of plans for a sugar mill in favor of a total concentration on rice, which would be produced directly by the Promotora Nacional de Granos Alimentícios (the National Foodgrain Promotion Company—PRONAGRA) on existing ejidal lands or on national lands that would later be granted to ejidos. It also meant the de facto elimination of the colonization component, at least as far as the construction of new settlements for additional out-of-state migrants was concerned. (One more NCPE settlement, Melchor Ocampo, was constructed near Bonfil in 1981.) Instead, Yohaltún was to benefit existing ejidos in and around the project zone, which included more than 500 Maya from northern Campeche as well as 122 spontaneous colonists from northern and central Mexico and from Tabasco and Yucatán (Sandoval Palacios, 1982). These would be supplemented later on by ejidal migrants, primarily from within Campeche, who would be responsible for constructing their own settlements. Thus, the focus in Yohaltún was explicitly on production; the ejidatarios were almost incidental.

Even without the necessity for building settlements, the costs of infrastructure for Yohaltún were high, reaching 538 million pesos as opposed to 475 million for Bonfil. In addition to extensive drainage works and a hundred irrigation wells and forest clearings, an eighty-kilometer (unpaved) road had to be constructed from near Champotón on the coast to the development zone, in addition to more than two hundred kilometers of project roads. Preliminary studies had indicated that Yohaltún had more serious soil and climatic drawbacks for agriculture than the northern portion of the valley, and therefore SARH projected a land use scenario of about five years of full-scale rice cultivation followed by a cattle-rearing emphasis as crop yields decreased (SARH, 1979). In the interim, Yohaltún was to constitute the largest rice project in the Western Hemisphere (Sandoval Palacios, 1982). Production was to be totally mechanized; the ejidatarios would be involved in this state agribusiness empire only as unskilled labor.

After a 300-hectare trial in 1978, full-scale rice production commenced in 1979 on 5,138 hectares of cleared land, expanded to 14,500 hectares in 1980. Yields were considerably lower than the 3 tons per hectare anticipated, however, averaging only 1.5–2 tons in the early years, because of problems with maneuvering equipment in the mud, droughts, delays in the completion of communication, irrigation, and drainage infrastructure, mistakes in land preparation and the application of agrochemicals, insufficient harvesting machinery, and poor coordination among the various government agencies and private companies involved (Sandoval Palacios, 1982).

Meanwhile, the majority of the ejidatarios labored in forest clearing, weeding, and the construction of roads, drains, and wells, mainly for PRONAGRA and the private companies, receiving the official minimum wage, although some continued to cultivate milpa on the well-drained slopes surrounding the project. The switch from subsistence agriculture to cash wages resulted in an immediate increase in consumer spending among the ejidatarios, and refrigerators, televisions, tape recorders, and bicycles proliferated. A number of ejidatarios also opened small shops and restaurants to accommodate the increasing demand of the local population, as well as to serve the influx of hundreds of temporary workers employed in construction and forest clearance (Sandoval Palacios, 1982).

As the first phase of the Yohaltún project drew to a close, the seven ejidos in the zone began to be directly involved in rice production, operating as collective enterprises with direct bank credit as in the case of Bonfil, while PRONAGRA moved on to the new lands to be opened up in the second phase of the scheme. In the first few years of ejidal operations, most collectives managed to repay their debts for rice and small mechanized maize hectarages, with money left over to purchase agricultural equipment and pickup trucks. By the mid-1980s, however, rice yields had dropped appreciably as initial fertility was exhausted, Johnson grass spread, the soil hardened so that the rains ran off unabsorbed, and plans for irrigation wells were curtailed by the debt crisis after only a couple had been drilled. From record harvests of 10 tons per hectare in some areas in the early years, Yohaltún averaged less than I.5 tons per hectare over the last five cycles, returns that were too marginal for most ejidos to avoid default (Table 5.10). At the end of the 1989 rice cycle, the Union of

TABLE 5.10   Credit Production, Rice, Yohaltún, Campeche, 1985–1989

Year	Sown (ha)	Harvested (ha)	Production (tons)
1985	8,003	6,894	19,406
1986	5,645	1,632	2,542
1987	8,756	7,907	21,939
1988	9,019	7,249	14,178
1989	6,352	361	1,391

SOURCE: SARH, 1990.

Ejidos of Yohaltún owed 343 million pesos to BANRURAL. The rice extension projected for 1990 was cut drastically to a little over three thousand hectares of the best lands and was likely to be reduced still further.

Yohaltún today looks like a desert. "Who told you this was a rice zone? Which government agency told that lie? There used to be rice, but you missed it," says an old man clearing land for milpa on a hillside at the edge of the bottomlands (I-83, ejidatario, Yohaltún, March 1990). Rusting rice equipment lies abandoned by the roadside at the entrance to the project zone. The bulk of the population has left to find work in the city of Campeche. In the ejido of Yohaltún, houses are boarded up and all the shops have closed except for the CONASUPO store, whose manager apologizes for not stocking potato chips as the inhabitants no longer have the money for such luxuries. Since snack foods and soft drinks are ubiquitous today all over rural Mexico, even in the most remote and impoverished regions, and are sold at relatively low prices, this indicates that Yohaltún indeed now perceives itself to be a very poor ejido. Those who remain subsist from milpa cultivated on the slopes around the project as they did before the machines arrived. The road was paved four years ago, but few ejidatarios can afford to take advantage of it, as the round-trip bus fare to Champotón costs almost a day's pay. There is resentment of the government for wearing out the land and leaving the ejidatarios alone to cope with the aftermath:

> When they saw that agriculture was finished here, they abandoned us, with no help, no prospects. Goodbye, boys! There is no life left here now. When they cleared, they burned the valuable timber and fried the wildlife so there is no more game. They gave us a forestry extension near Xpujil, but nobody wants to go there now because we are afraid of the weed [marijuana] growers. They don't want to plant rice here any more. Almost nobody has cattle. We don't know how, and there is no water for cattle. The milpa doesn't deliver enough because of plagues of rats, centipedes, and slugs, but anyway nobody wants to make it any more now that we are accustomed to another way of life. So off we go. Goodbye, Yohaltún! (I-81, ejidatario, Yohaltún, March 1990)

SARH has announced that rice production is virtually over in Yohaltún and alternative forms of land use are under study. Experiments conducted in 1989 with mechanized maize production in raised beds were promising for both dry-season and summer crops, even though yields were reduced by an extended drought to 2.5 tons per hectare. Some ejidos have also achieved good results with sorghum, but are unable to continue because of loan default. Cattle rearing was built into the initial development plan, but Yohaltún is not Bonfil, and the ejidatarios lack both the experience with cattle raising and the motivation to become ranchers or dairymen:

> We are not the favored sons of the government, like those millionaires, the northerners in Bonfil. If you are a campesino from Campeche you are expendable, like a beer can, like our land here. Use it once and throw it away for cattle. But we are not ranchers here. We are not enchanted by cattle. We don't want to be cowboys. (I-84, ejidatario, Yohaltún, March 1990)

Meanwhile, the demise of rice cultivation has not deterred large numbers of new migrants from moving into Yohaltún over the last five years, mainly from the Maya region of northern Campeche, eager to make milpa on the hillsides and try their luck with mechanized agriculture if they can obtain credit from the bank. "There we had no hope. Here there is land and a chance" (I-126, colonist, Kim Pech, Yohaltún, March 1990). Colonists from central and northern Mexico are also beginning to move into the zone, eager for land however degraded. The veterans of the Yohaltún project experience are skeptical: "The newcomers will learn very soon that when the government abandons something, there is nothing left" (I-83, ejidatario, Yohaltún, March 1990).

In Yohaltún the government set out from the start to increase rice production at all costs via a state agribusiness enterprise, unencumbered by costly economic, social, and political accommodations to ejidatarios (Table 5.11). A degree of success was achieved in this respect until the debt crisis made both state farming and ejidal enterprises in rice production deficit operations. Yohaltún was a calculated risk that proved more or less acceptable in terms of production logic until outside forces intervened. If the project had been written off at this point, both the soil and the ejidatarios might have been salvaged. Instead, large-scale mechanized rice production was continued for more than five years after both soil fertility and profits had appreciably declined, turning Yohaltún into a wasteland where only those ejidatarios with no options remain to continue the struggle. As a result, the Yohaltún experiment has gained the reputation of an exercise in deliberate environmental destruction, a premeditated sacrifice of social justice to production quotas:

> Yohaltún is our disgrace. We knew we should have diversified, rotated, irrigated right from the beginning. It's a tragedy. The campesiños are disgusted, and this time you can't blame them. The rice was so pretty at the beginning, a sea of green, it made you proud. Now it makes you sick to see that desert, not even good for maize, so it's no good for the campesino. It wasn't an accident. SARH really engineered that disaster, and we knew

TABLE 5.11   Evaluation, Edzná Agricultural and Resettlement Zone, Yohaltún, Campeche

Development Model and Year of Initiation	State rice agribusiness enterprise. 1978
No. Beneficiaries and Region of Origin	500 Maya and 122 colonists from northern Mexico and neighboring states already settled in the zone, plus subsequent spontaneous settlement from within Campeche.
Settlement and Land Tenure	Existing nuclei and new spontaneous settlements organized in 7 *ejidos* on 75,000 hectares in 2 phases, operating as "production units."
Development Goals	Rice production on *ejidal* lands, without directly involving the *ejidatarios*.
Project Outcome	1. Reduced rice yields due to technical errors, input supply problems, Johnson grass, poor soils, and drought. 2. Partial proletarianization of *ejidatarios* as wage laborers on their own lands, with increased consumer spending. 3. Marginal production led to loan default under debt crisis as *ejidatarios* assumed cultivation responsibility. 4. Rural-urban migration of many original *ejidatarios*. 5. In-migration by new Maya settlers and colonists from neighboring states. 6. Irreversible environmental damage.
Diagnosis	A calculated economic risk to achieve rice production at all costs in the short term. An exercise in deliberate environmental destruction sacrificing social welfare to productivity goals.
	Result: an exhausted wasteland, with future possibilities limited to cattle, cane, and possibly raised-bed maize.

what we were doing, but they wanted tons, tons, and more tons. (I-131, civil servant, Campeche, February 1990)

The Record of State Intervention

In the early 1980s, planned agricultural development in Campeche continued the rice production effort in large mechanized agricultural zones in the Palizada area, with a secondary focus on maize and beans in the northern Camino Real and Los Chenes ejidos. Attempts to make

Campeche the nation's rice bowl continued in 1981 with the Chunchintok project on frontier land southeast of Hopelchén, where the planting of three thousand bottomland hectares of dry rice indicated that little had been learned from the Bonfil and Yohaltún experience, and five years later the land was exhausted. In the south, between Champotón, Escárcega, and Palizada in the river zone, rice lands expanded rapidly by means the newly legal "production units" involving both ejidos and private properties, generating opportunities for deviation of funds that made the program nationally notorious. In 1989 a 7-billion-peso fraud was discovered involving members of the Tumbo de la Montaña rural production society and functionaries of BANRURAL, ANAGSA, and other federal and state development agencies, who had made a number of insurance claims for fictitious and real crops declared a total loss and then sold as contraband to CONASUPO (*Excelsior*, 31 December, 1989, *Tribuna de Campeche*, 30 December 1989, 5 January 1990).[7]

At the same time, although northern Campeche was acknowledged to be ill-suited to staple crop cultivation, plans were drawn up for the development of more than four hundred thousand hectares of mechanized maize and beans, beginning with the clearing of twenty-five hundred hectares in 1981 to benefit ejidatarios in this most densely populated and increasingly impoverished area of the state. These ejidos also were organized as "production units." The program was expanded from 1982 to 1985 under the impetus of a FIRA-funded scheme for intensive maize production involving a total of thirty thousand hectares in the state of Campeche, including nine hundred hectares of new land east of Hecelchakán in the Camino Real. This latter project achieved impressive results—yields of 6 tons per hectare—but once the program was terminated and SARH was managing the projects alone production dropped to average Camino Real levels for mechanized maize of 1.5–2 tons per hectare on the better lands in normal years. With production levels only slightly above those of the milpa system and significant crop losses every third year or so due to inclement weather, these mechanized maize projects increasingly fell into default.

Meanwhile, new agricultural projects succumbed to the financial exigencies of the debt crisis, and the development agencies were confined essentially to caretaking activities in the few still viable operations. These have deteriorated rapidly over the past decade, and by 1987 over 80 percent of the 350 irrigation installations in the state were not functioning because of lack of maintenance and the cost of replacement parts. At the same time, technical support was reduced essentially to visits from BANRURAL and ANAGSA field inspectors, whose activities were restricted to crop appraisal and arranging frauds. In the last three years some effort has been made by agencies at the state level in conjunction with SARH, to rehabilitate some of these irrigation units, mainly in the Camino Real, for the production of mangos, tomatoes, citrus, zapote, and watermelons. It remains to be seen whether the reforms and new stimuli contained in this program will be able to circumvent the systemic constraints that have operated against efficient production in ejidal programs in the past.

Despite more than two decades of concerted government effort to transform ejidal agriculture and expand private-sector commercial farming, the prospects today are bleak (Fig. 5.2). In comparison with 1970, 72,610 additional hectares had been brought under cultivation by 1987, but this was largely attributable to the expansion of rice by 52,905 hectares, at least half of which were unsuited to the crop. Only 14,512 hectares of maize had been added to the 1970 area, while the hectarage under beans had been reduced by almost 90 percent, creating a severe shortage of the black beans preferred by the local population. For maize, yields per hectare had shown a slight increase over the period, but this meant little given the annual variation in harvests due to plagues and erratic rainfall.

The hectarages devoted to traditional plantation cash crops such as sugarcane and copra have increased, but cane is now at the level of capacity of the sole sugar mill, and copra production is threatened by the "lethal yellowing disease" that has already eradicated production in Quintana Roo and is in the process of decimating Yucatán's plantations. Mangos, citrus, sorghum, tomatoes, and cashews are increasing in importance, but these remain relatively small-scale operations. Although the value of agricultural production has almost tripled, most of this increment is attributable to rice. Moreover, given inflation beyond the level reflected in the peso exchange rate, the real value of production had increased only slightly. Thus the rice production effort has done little more than enable the state to maintain its 1970 position.

Pasture had increased from 1970 to 1988 only by sixty-eight thousand

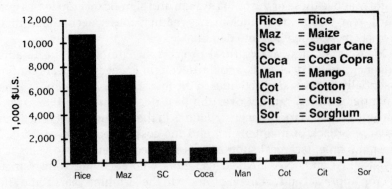

FIGURE 5.2   Agricultural production, Campeche, 1987 (SOURCE: FIRA, 1972)

hectares officially, but this figure excludes large areas in transition from rice to cattle as well as new colonization zones still in the frontier agriculture stage. The number of head had tripled while the value of production quadrupled, indicating some improvement in management technology, though production remained extensive, with only half the pastures "improved" and little of these maintained (Gobierno Constitucional del Estado de Campeche, 1989).

In summary, there is not much to show for these two decades of effort except an increasing area of exhausted soils and treeless former frontier zones in conversion to rudimentary cattle rearing. The mistaken focus on rice as a virtual monoculture through extensive, mechanized production of the upland or dry variety compounded the risks inherent to both large-scale tropical farming and planned agricultural development. The debt crisis merely provided the last nail in the coffin of an undertaking that was already doomed because marginal soil and unfavorable climatic conditions offset the initial fertility of new lands. The weakness in the proposed rice program had been foreseen twenty years ago (FIRA, 1972), and numerous warning signs had been visible from the early stages, but these were ignored in the face of the national production imperative. On a smaller scale, attempts to promote mechanized maize and bean production foundered for similar reasons, natural conditions in Campeche being far from conducive to the cultivation of cereals and legumes. In this case, the increase in agricultural input costs triggered by the debt crisis resulted in more immediate and direct repercussions as already marginal enterprises quickly became deficit operations.

Plans for developing fruit and vegetables in small areas of capital-intensive irrigated production have a long way to go before achieving momentum, and the record of similar undertakings in the past is not encouraging. The only significant possibility on the immediate horizon appears to be the proposed Lower Usumacinta Project, on the drawing board for nearly a decade but now a planning priority again as the agricultural options for Campeche contract. This project would convert a vast section of the lower Usumacinta River and its tributaries into an irrigated rice zone to be cultivated by associations of private property owners and ejidatarios. Development has been held up by the federal water law's land-tenure requirements for private holdings in irrigation zones. Given the political and economic implications of this project, however, in addition to the apparent determination of the Salinas administration to modify agrarian structure to conform to optimal production conditions, new development in some form is likely to materialize in this region in the near future.

As far as Campeche's ejidatarios, the ostensible "beneficiaries" of the agricultural development effort, are concerned, both the record and the prospects are grim, at least with respect to reliance on state initiative. Despite differences in scope and development strategy, the four models of state intervention in peasant agriculture employed in Campeche over the past two-and-a-half decades—frontier colonization, small irrigation projects, large-scale, production-oriented resettlement, and de facto state farming—have had remarkably similar outcomes. At best, small increases in production have been achieved at high cost, while the developmental risks are borne by the ejidatarios. In the process, invaluable natural resources have been destroyed without coming close to realizing the stated project goals, except for some partial success in keeping at least some peasants down on the farm.

Under each model of state-planned agricultural development, virtually the same sad story of recurrent patterns of project design, management, and implementation errors is replicated. Initial official confidence and enthusiasm expressed in overly ambitious goals and indiscriminate spending soon bog down in a morass of technical errors, misguided crop selections, red tape, deteriorating infrastructure, inadequate agricultural experimentation, extension, and market research, shortage of key inputs, environmental degradation, and eventual agency indifference. This scenario results in disappointing yields or program failures as plans devised in a Mexico City office prove unworkable, the blame for this being ascribed primarily to the "human element," the peasants. The latter are treated as just another resource to be managed, and inefficiently at that; overcontrolled collectives have meant loss of productive autonomy, manipulation by the credit mechanism, exploitation by corrupt interests, and disruptive factionalism. Wells, drains, and tractors are merely the surface layer of the network of institutionalized dependency and debt. Some Campeche project members have obviously benefitted materially from state-directed modernization but largely because of the expansion of personal horizons rather than from the projects per se. In the Bonfil resettlement scheme, especially, the combination of a more cosmopolitan peasantry and the large scale and scope of project operations offered more opportunities to *los mas listos*—those with an eye to the main chance. Even these more ambitious and adaptable individuals are likely to be limited, however, by their relative lack of skills and experience in the broader sphere beyond the project. The main beneficiaries from planned agricultural modernization remain outside the peasant sector—the agribusinesses, brokers, bureaucrats, landowners, and politicians who thrive on rural developments on this scale.

The reasons the Campeche projects have achieved very little lie in a combination of technical, economic, political, and institutional constraints. One of the most significant is the extreme centralization of public-sector decision making, responsive more to national and international

priorities than to the possibilities and impossibilities of target development regions. This, combined with the high level of bureaucratization of
the state apparatus, the dominant technocratic engineering mentality
of many agricultural development agencies, and the insufficient emphasis
on research and experimentation on tropical agriculture and ecosystems,
results in expensive projects with unrealistic goals and overbuilt infrastructure, designed for the developers rather than for the peasant in
the field. Furthermore, the paternalistic authoritarianism inherent in the
state-ejido relationship has resulted in such tight control over field operations that there is little opportunity for peasants to exercise the on-the-
ground responsiveness requisite for efficient farming, while the top-down
hierarchical structure of the bureaucratic pyramid means that the voice of
peasant experience is rarely heard. Lastly, the structure of the political
system tends to encourage abrupt discontinuities in policies and programs
and to limit accountability for poor project performance, creating a climate
that is not conducive to the sustained attention essential for realizing
long-term project goals.

At this juncture, the ongoing agricultural crisis and the continuing
need for firm restraint in public-sector spending would seem to require a
reevaluation of planning priorities and procedures and the incorporation
of lessons learned from the past. On the basis of the Campeche experience,
it would seem that key elements of a more viable agricultural modernization
program might include more contingent and locally responsive planning,
a deemphasis of physical infrastructure, a smaller scale of operations
in better-selected locations, less wide-ranging but more flexible pro-
gramming, improved agricultural extension and marketing strategies,
increased agricultural research (particularly on the potential of traditional
farming systems), and, above all, more leeway for peasant initiative and
input into the decision-making process.

A number of these elements are contained in Salinas's Programa Nacional
de Modernización del Campo (National Program for the Modernization
of the Countryside), which explicitly addresses the recapitalization of the
agricultural sector by eliminating the policies and procedures that have
most directly contributed to the production crisis. This program requires
extensive reforms throughout the agricultural development apparatus.
Some significant steps in this direction have already been taken, for example,
the restructuring of BANRURAL via the elimination of field inspectors
and the return to rural credit banking as a business proposition instead of
an exercise in deficit farming. The eradication of ANAGSA is also a positive
step. In addition, visible attempts are being made to improve both the performance and the image of SARH, which is still the dominant force in planned
agricultural development despite the recent decentralization trend.

These measures are just the beginning of the long process of getting agriculture back on its feet, however, and they do not directly address the critical issue of reversing the long-term processes that have impoverished the peasantry. PRONASOL, for example, extends interest-free credit to individual campesinos, but it is a drop in the bucket, and there is simply not enough money available to the public sector to redeem past mistakes though capital handouts. Meanwhile, although private investment in the countryside is being encouraged, investors have not exhibited much eagerness to venture additional capital. In essence, the Salinas administration appears to be relying on the free market to stimulate production. It is difficult, however, to see how market competition and comparative advantage will benefit Campeche, with its history of vulnerability to boom-and-bust cycles and a contemporary agriculture in which virtually nothing is economically viable.

As far as Campeche's ejidatarios are concerned, it will be a long time before their encounters with the industry of disasters are forgotten. This is particularly the case in that the experience has become internalized as part of the ejidos' own modus operandi; compromise and corruption have become an essential part of the current strategy for survival, and an ethos of failure has been created and perpetuated. Thus it will take a radical change in policy in favor of the small producer and a significant number of agricultural programs predicated on success instead of disaster and default for the Campeche ejidatarios to abandon their skepticism about any state initiative in agriculture. PRONASOL seems unlikely to alter this attitude in that it is perceived as at best a populist palliative—a way of disposing of the losers in the agricultural development game by sending them back to the milpa:

> PRONASOL, no, it's PRINASOL. It's just another way for the party to pacify the campesinos. The National Modernization Program will just mean more debt, more poverty, in the countryside, wait and see! They may change the name of the program, but you know the results will be the same. PRONASOL just means that they want us to be quiet and go back to scratching the rock like dogs for a few ears of corn now that they have ruined the land for agriculture. (I-3, ejidatario, Pomuch, March 1990)

From the point of view of many members of the Campeche agricultural development bureaucracy, the ejidal modernization exercise has been worthwhile despite its failures as the first serious effort to transform rather than simply exploit the state's resource base: "At least we were trying to do something, even if we failed. Campeche was actually trying to change, to make something—that in itself is a miracle" (I-136, businessman and former civil servant, Campeche, January 1990). The less altruistic members of the bureaucracy continue to blame planned development failures

on the campesinos, maintaining that they acquired both invaluable experience with modern farming and material gain and, having squandered
both, deserve to be left to their own resources:

> Would the campesinos have been better off without our help? No way. They
> were wealthy. They had more money than they had ever seen in their lives for
> a couple of years. Besides, they got some experience, some education about
> agriculture. It was all given to them, and they wasted it. Let them go back to
> the milpa. (I-155, civil servant, Campeche, March 1990)

These cynics may be correct at least in emphasizing the significance of the
learning process associated with the state-directed agricultural modernization experience. Many ejidatarios are no longer content to toil in the
fields every day with machete and digging stick just to cover minimal
household subsistence needs. Furthermore, skepticism about government
promises has prompted a significant number of Campeche campesinos
seek more rewarding strategies for making a living independent of the
dwindling state presence in the countryside:

> We have learned one thing from all this—not only how to defend ourselves
> against the government and its cohorts but how to take advantage of
> their weaknesses and follow our own best interests. They will be surprised
> what we can do for ourselves without the state meddling in our milpa (I-12,
> ejidatario, Pomuch, February 1990).

Notes

1. Part of this chapter originally appeared in somewhat different form in
Gates, 1988a, included by permission of the *Journal of Developing Areas*.

2. The normal average yield for maize in the Candelaria region is 1.7 tons per
hectare for mechanized cultivation and 900 kilograms for milpa (I-74, civil
servant, Candelaria, March 1990).

3. This program was later renamed the Plan Nacional de Obras de Riego para
el Desarrollo Rural, increasing in scale and emphasizing rural development over
strictly technical aspects of irrigation.

4. Bonfil businesses range from sizable operations to very small-scale activities, including a bakery, a pool hall, appliance, electronic, shoe, auto and bicycle
repair establishments, trucking firms, dressmakers, grocery stores, refreshment
stands, a popsicle manufacturer, a ready-made clothing outlet, a meat market,
households advertizing chicken or eggs for sale, and a tavern now that restrictions
on the sale of alcohol in NCPE have been lifted. The tavern, the pool hall, and a
restaurant are particularly well-patronized.

5. Control of Johnson grass with herbicides is expensive and often not very
effective. Rotation and planting in flooded lands via the Asiatic technique
of *fangueo*, which drowns the Johnson seed, rather than the dry cultivation

attempted in Campeche can reduce the problem. However, wet-rice cultivation requires skillful management of borders and drainage, and it is difficult for the agricultural machinery to manoeuver in the mud. Cattle can tolerate Johnson grass until new seeds are produced, after which it becomes poisonous (I-36, professional, Bonfil, February 1990).

6. Cultivation in raised beds (*cama melonera*) drains excess water via a system of borders and canals similar to those for wet rice. While the technology is not complicated, mechanized raised-bed cultivation is somewhat tricky for inexperienced operators in that care must be taken not to compact the topsoil. Field trials will continue in 1991 on several hundred hectares in the Valley of Edzná and Los Chenes. Experiments to date have produced two crops a year even without supplementary irrigation for the dry-season crop, with yields of between 2 and 3 tons per hectare (I-67, civil servant, Edzná, January 1990). This modern raised-bed system is probably not very different in essence from the agricultural technology used in the Valley of Edzná by the Classic Maya, whose hydraulic works were followed in many cases by the engineers building the infrastructure for the Bonfil project.

7. Apparently the fraud had been going on since 1985, when the original members of the society were replaced by other individuals. The leaders located and rented suitable tracts of forest land and approached BANRURAL for credit and ANAGSA for insurance for a specified hectarage to be cleared and cultivated with rice. Manipulations included obtaining credit for ten thousand hectares and cultivating only two thousand and raising "paper crops" that ANAGSA's field inspectors declared a total loss. The Tumbo de la Montaña fraud is not an isolated incident. This discussion is based on interviews with a number of informants in the Campeche rural development business.

6

In Default:
Campesinos and
the Debt Crisis

There has always been a crisis in Mexican agriculture, but nobody noticed it until they couldn't afford their tortillas. This fiscal crisis is just the result of neglecting the campesinos for so many years. The government forgot the promises made in the revolution and spent all its money on factories and plantations instead. Then when they spent money here [on ejidal agriculture] they failed. Now they don't have money or food. That's their problem. This is not our crisis. We can feed our families from the milpa. (I-53, ejidatario, Nilchi, January 1990)

It doesn't make sense. How can we be in debt to the government when it's their fault that we didn't produce anything? Everything the government touches turns out badly. But will we be better off without them? Can we make our own way now that the land is ruined? Certainly, the government owes us some recompense for the failure of agriculture. (I-30, ejidatario, Tinún, March 1990)

Cartera vencida translates literally as "a portfolio or account that has fallen due or expired." In 1990, one-third of the ejidos in Campeche were in default on loans from BANRURAL as a result of the marginal nature of most agricultural activities exacerbated by debt crisis inflation. From the perspective of many ejidatarios, however, it is not they who have failed to meet their obligations. Rather, it is the government that has defaulted on its constitutional contract with the peasantry to provide social justice in the countryside. The mere distribution of ejidal lands is no longer enough; two decades ago the government promised to stimulate commercial agriculture on ejidos, and ejidatarios maintain that any credits received under this initiative constitute only a small part of what is "owed" them in the long term. If the government has failed to comply with its pledge, the ejidatarios see no reason that they should have to repay a subsidy to which they feel entitled, even under deficit production. Thus, in the eyes of many ejidatarios, the government, and the whole agricultural apparatus it created, is in default to Mexican peasants by virtue of the continuing failure to keep the revolution's promises.

To a degree this perspective has been shared by the government; the spending of billions of pesos on the modernization of ejidal agriculture was considered a social investment—a way to reduce the danger of rural conflict and out-migration—as much as an economic one. Thus failures in economic terms could be justified by the social function of the exercise even though rural tensions were often created or exacerbated by the very programs intended to alleviate them. The debt crisis has forced a new economic realism in agricultural undertakings. If the peasants have proven unable to produce satisfactorily in the commercial sector, then they will receive no more bank credit, and other, less expensive routes will have to be found to tranquilize the countryside. Thus paternalistic authoritarianism is dwindling as economic costs and benefits have eclipsed social interests until such time as agriculture gets back on its feet, the neoliberal experiment makes such patronage unnecessary, or peasant unrest renders rural welfare a new priority.

There is another sense in which "the portfolio has expired" for agriculture in Campeche, in terms of the condition of the environmental context within which crops can be grown. Twenty years ago almost two-thirds of the state was forested. At least half a million hectares have been cleared in the interim for frontier colonization, mechanized agriculture, or pasture, often in that order with cattle as the end phase in the cycle of destruction now typical of the tropical forests of Central and South America. At the same time, the absence of effective and enforceable forest management practices has allowed much wastage of common species and decimated the precious tropical hardwoods, for example through sales of ejidal timber without permits, often with official collusion. Meanwhile fragile soils have been stripped by the use of heavy machinery in clearing and cultivation and massive applications of agrochemicals have turned the earth into an exhausted wasteland. Clear-cutting has caused changes in microclimate the extent of which is still unknown. Further environmental degradation has resulted from the oil boom in southern Campeche, where pollution has affected fruit and vegetable crops in the municipality of Carmen and has contributed to the decline of fisheries in the Gulf. Campeche today is far from possessing the natural resource potential it claimed only twenty years ago. Thus time is running out for its agricultural account in much more than strictly economic terms.

Environmental degradation can be arrested and even to a degree reversed through restoration, rehabilitation, and a shift to sustainable agriculture and forestry. In 1989, over eight hundred thousand hectares of forest in southern Campeche in the region of the ruins at Calakmul were designated a biosphere reserve by presidential decree.[1] The creation of this vast reserve would seem to buy time for environmental rescue by setting aside areas for the protection of habitat and preservation of traditional knowledge while ecologically sound management practices are developed. Such research takes time, however, and funds are still in short supply despite ongoing local studies.[2] Furthermore, despite some innovative approaches to environmental problems,[3] the gap between ecological ideals and their implementation is often vast, environmental consciousness being very recent and largely confined to the intelligentsia and the asphyxiated denizens of the capital city. Thus in many areas environmental policy continues to be mainly symbolic or a mask for political and business interests that see opportunities for a new boom. This distance between principles and practice compounds the already significant objective difficulties of enforcing reserve land-use regulations, particularly where options for making a living are extremely limited:

In principle, biosphere reserves are a good idea, but research takes time, and often it is not being conducted by those who know this region. In the meantime, who is to say that a hungry man should not make his milpa, cut a tree, shoot a deer? And who will enforce it—the military, the police, public servants like me, who should not have to be guards? Anyway, it's really for ecotourism, which is also a good idea in principle as it raises consciousness. If people see the animals and the trees, they can understand why they are worth keeping. But who will want to spend their vacations at Calakmul? Mainly foreigners, because Mexicans don't want to get too close to nature. So who will benefit? Rich tourists and those who make money out of them, those in high places. (I-142, civil servant, Campeche, January 1990)

Attempts to arrest environmental destruction through the creation of reserves and research programs to investigate more rational and sustainable economic options for the humid tropics are undoubtedly a step in the right direction. Given the extent and severity of the damage to Campeche's traditional agro-ecosystems, however, in many areas of the state there is no longer much left to "sustain." If one adds to this environmental degradation the social deterioration caused by continuing rural poverty, intensified by the debt crisis, and the generalized demoralization resulting from the repeated failures of policies and programs for the ejido, Campeche's agricultural potential is even more limited. Nevertheless, Campeche campesinos are remarkably resilient under stress as can be seen from their responses to the debt crisis—the latest phase in the ongoing agricultural crisis.

The Causes and Consequences of the Crises

Campeche's Maya campesinos tend to take a very long view of history, which is natural given their more than two-thousand-year occupancy of the region. Despite a tradition of resistance to domination, they tend also to be pacific and fatalistic as a consequence of their harmony with nature and their vulnerability both to its whims and to those of powerful outside interests intent on exploiting the resources of the Maya realm. At the same time, the Maya are highly analytical; everything has a reason, even acts of God and the government. In addition, they exhibit a keen wit that can be critical and caustic or gentle and self-deprecating, depending on the individual, the circumstance, and how much of themselves they want to reveal to others. These characteristics are highly adaptive in muting the effects of externally induced stress, with the result that any particular episode tends to be interpreted as merely another perturbation in the historical scheme of things—just what one would expect given the nature of the universe and the non-Maya. Thus Maya campesinos are capable of distancing themselves from events mentally just as, in the past, they were able to withdraw physically from unwanted contact with the outside world by retreating into the forests to make milpa (Gates, 1972).

When asked about the causes of the current national debt crisis, Campeche Maya maintain that it is merely the latest phase in an ongoing agricultural crisis (Table 6.1)—a chronic imbalance dating from the export production bias developed under the Spanish conquerors that is accentuated by the national economic growth model adopted in this century:

> This crisis is just part of the same process that has been going on in Mexico since the conquest, the rape of our forests, henequen, and now rice and petroleum. They let the foreigners take the best products out of the country, while we are supposed to be forever the laborers on somebody else's hacienda. That's the curse of *malinchismo* [complicity][4]—they sell Mexico out to whoever wants to buy. Then there is nothing left for us. That's the way it has always been. (I-3, ejidatario, Pomuch, December 1989)

It is significant that 40 percent of the Maya respondents had not heard of the debt crisis at all, while 15 percent of those who recognized its existence maintained that it was a crisis of the government or "the Mexicans"— "nothing to do with us."

Campeche's non-Maya campesinos, in the main recent migrants from other regions, are more cosmopolitan. They tend to be more literate in

TABLE 6.1   Identification and Perceived Causes of the Debt Crisis,
Campeche Peasants, 1990

Identification	Number of Respondents		
	Maya	Non-Maya	Total
Aware of debt crisis[a]	35	48	83
Debt crisis is part of agricultural crisis	17	6	23
Debt crisis is "nothing to do with us"	5	0	5
Unaware of debt crisis	25	7	32

Cause	Number of Responses		
	Maya	Non-Maya	Total
Historical factors			
Spanish Conquest	19	0	19
Díaz dictatorship	2	0	2
Incomplete revolution	7	3	10
Economic factors			
Agricultural policy	4	13	17
Industrialization	3	12	15
Export priority	2	7	9
Petrolization	6	15	21
External dependency	6	12	18
Agents			
President Echeverría	6	10	16
President López Portillo	10	21	31
President de la Madrid	1	6	7
PRI, or "the Party"	12	15	27
BANRURAL	6	2	8
Americans	3	15	18
Arabs	0	3	3
International financial agencies	2	7	9
Other			
(e.g., God's will, nature)	3	0	3
Don't know	3	1	4
Total	95	142	237

[a]The 83 respondents aware of the debt crisis identified 1 to 4 causes
per person.
Source: Field interviews.

functional terms and to possess higher levels of modern technical skills
as a result of their exposure to mechanized agriculture in their travels.
Because they came to Campeche in search of a better life, they appear to
be more frustrated by the debt crisis, which has placed new obstacles in

the way of realizing their ambitions. These campesinos are more likely to name recent events or specific agents and policies as responsible for the crisis and to draw on a broader context in attributing blame:

> The crisis began with Echeverría's ambitions to be the leader of the United Nations. So he borrowed a lot of money to spend on big programs to get the world's attention. Then came López Portillo, who filled his pockets with the revenues from our petroleum while borrowing more and more. Then the Arabs, who are scoundrels too, produced too much petroleum and bang! there goes the price, and "Mexico, pay your bills." But the strong boxes are empty, as the thieves took all the money. Ultimately, the crisis was the fault of the Americans who got too greedy for Mexican oil. (I-70, ejidatario, Bonfil, March 1990)

Both Maya and non-Maya are well aware that the debt crisis is a logical outcome of national policies and programs that made Mexico's economy both vulnerable in the world market and dysfunctional domestically. While the Maya tend to see external economic dependency as a legacy of the conquest, however, the migrants attribute it directly to the industry and agricultural export priorities of the post-World War II era. López Portillo's strategy of dependence on oil exports receives much of the specific blame, while "the party" is seen to bear the ultimate responsibility for allowing this to happen.

When asked to identify the causes of the current agricultural crisis, Maya and non-Maya campesinos tended to reply in similar vein with respect to the particular government policies and programs responsible (see Table 6.2). The long-term causes are seen to be an incomplete revolution unable to legislate social justice in the countryside, the consolidation of the PRI in absolute power, and the perpetuation of the ejido as a panacea for the people rather than a capitalized economic enterprise, reflected in the neglect of staple crop production. The crisis trigger is perceived to be the very policies and programs that purported to remedy the stagnation of traditional agriculture but instead drained the last resources out of the sector. In addition to post-1970 presidents of Mexico, the key agents responsible for this final "rape" are identified as BANRURAL and ANAGSA and, secondarily, CONASUPO and SARH:

> The crisis in the ejido today would not have happened without the intervention of the government. We were poor, but we had our own resources. Now we are poor, but we have lost our resources. We are in debt to the bank, and the soil is ruined unless you use fertilizer, but we can no longer afford it, because we can't get credit since we are in default. The government has extended its own debt trap to catch us here. (I-127, ejidatario, Poc-Boc, March 1990)

TABLE 6.2   Identification and Perceived Causes of the Agricultural Crisis, Campeche Peasants, 1990

Identification	Number of Respondents		
	Maya	Non-Maya	Total
Aware of agricultural crisis[a]	53	55	108
Unaware of agricultural crisis	7	0	7

Cause	Number of Responses		
	Maya	Non-Maya	Total
Historical factors			
Spanish Conquest	10	0	10
Henequen haciendas	7	0	7
Incomplete revolution	8	2	10
State intervention in agriculture			
Agrarian reform and the ejido	2	10	12
Crop prices	32	37	69
Credit	26	17	43
Development project errors	8	32	40
Corruption	5	19	24
Favoritism toward "outside"			
colonists	13	0	13
Deforestation	13	4	17
Milpa decline	24	5	29
Other economic factors			
Industrialization	5	13	18
Export priority	3	7	10
External dependency	7	12	19
Yucatán dominance	11	0	11
Agents			
President Echeverría	6	12	18
President López Portillo	12	23	35
President de la Madrid	6	20	26
President Salinas	4	6	10
PRI, or "the Party"	10	18	28
BANRURAL	9	17	26
ANAGSA	7	23	30
CONASUPO	14	9	23
SARH	2	13	15
State government (Campeche)	11	1	12
Americans	4	13	17
Social factors			
Demographic increase	12	3	13
Dietary change	2	0	2
Out-migration	9	0	11
Total	282	316	598

[a]The 108 respondents aware of the agricultural crisis identified 2 to 7 causes per person.

SOURCE: Field interviews.

There are, however, significant differences in perspective between Maya and non-Maya. The Maya once again take the long view. It is also a more local view, grounded in the exploitation of laborers on the henequen plantations, the long-term regional dominance of Yucatán, and the specific omissions of the state government, which is seen as less interested than the federal agencies in the condition of the campesino. It also reflects a certain amount of jealousy of the non-Maya migrants, including re-located Guatemalan refugees as well as colonists from other parts of Mexico, who are seen to be favored by both levels of government:

> It's not just giving them the best land, all the machinery they need, unlimited credit, while they leave us to scratch in the rocks. They are millionaires there in Bonfil because of the government. And they know how to make even more money. You have to admit that. Who is going to oppose those tall fellows with cowboy hats? And you had better get out of the way when they are drinking! (I-59, ejidatario, Nilchi January 1990)

> The Guatemalans seem like nice boys, and they work hard, but they don't know what is going on here. They are not really in Campeche in their heads, just in their bodies, so why should they get all that assistance? (I-27, ejidatario, Tinún, March 1990)[5]

Of particular concern to the Maya is the declining interest in milpa cultivation. This is seen as both the cause and the consequence of the agricultural crisis; increasing population pressure has reduced the viability of the system, compelling participation in agricultural modern-ization programs that have further diminished the potential for and appeal of making milpa. Out-migration is also a cause as well as a result of this situation:

> Making milpa is real farming, coaxing maize out of the earth without harming it. Mechanized [agriculture] is raping the soil, tearing it up so that there's nothing left for tomorrow. When we abandoned the milpa, that caused the crisis. So in this sense, the crisis was our fault. We should not have been greedy and shared their [the government's] greed. Those who left were smart. They saw that nothing good would come of it. A Maya without a milpa is not a Maya. (I-53, ejidatario, Nilchi, December 1989)

These circular patterns of cause and consequence are apparent also in views of the effects of the crises. Thus, although agrarian policy and state intervention are seen as the root of the agricultural crisis, the abrupt reduction of government resources allocated to rural development pro-grams after 1982 is perceived to be the main hardship resulting from it. Combined with high credit interest rates, low official prices for staples, and the escalating cost of production inputs (particularly of gasoline and fertilizer) this reduction means that the subsidy to ejidatarios built into the industry of disasters is rapidly eroding. Since 1980, the real price of maize has declined 45 percent. A farmer needed half a kilo of maize to buy a liter of diesel fuel in 1985. By the end of 1988 he needed twice as much, as the guaranteed price remained below average national production costs but far above international prices because of continuing inefficiencies, market distortions, and consumer subsidies.

During this period, BANRURAL interest rates exceeded by a significant margin average postcrisis borrowing charges in Mexico and were lowered only in 1990 (from 43 percent to 28 percent). At the same time, credit costs comprised 30–40 percent of total production costs, depending on the crop and the extent of mechanization and use of agrochemicals. This has been the greatest disincentive, in the short term at least, for campesinos under the debt crisis. In the course of two decades of modernization efforts, many campesinos have become accustomed to depending on credit to finance agricultural inputs, and these now tend to be regarded as essential for both mechanized and milpa cultivation to offset declining production resulting from increased population pressure or the introduction of inappropriate crops and farming technology. For example, in Yucatán, the Dinámica de la Milpa (Milpa Dynamics) program demonstrated that chemical fertilizer application resulted in a yield increase of over 100 percent in both first-year and second-year milpa over a two-year period from 1980 to 1982 (Arias Reyes, 1984).[6] Since that time, however, input costs and interest rates have become so high that, except in the most favored zones, deficit production is virtually inevitable at current crop prices for all ejidatarios relying on credit (Tables 6.3 and 6.4). Thus a hectare of mechanized maize costed on the basis of an average yield for Campeche of 1.5 tons per hectare will not cover credit liability and interest charges unless, in fact, at least 2 tons per hectare are produced. Milperos operating with credit for improved seed, fertilizer, and pesticide have to obtain almost 1.5 tons per hectare to clear their debt obligations, though average yields under this regime are 1 ton per hectare. Since good maize soil is very limited and production is highly vulnerable to climatic vicissitudes, this means that the majority of ejidatarios are likely to default on their loans.

More significant, from the campesinos' perspective, is that at this level of production most of the crop must be sold to pay the debt, and therefore they will have to buy maize to sustain their households throughout the year. A family composed of three adults and three children consumes at least 3 kilograms of shelled maize a day and feeds an additional 1.5 kilograms or more to domestic livestock, meaning that 1,642 kilograms are required for subsistence annually.[7] To obtain this level of surplus from

TABLE 6.3   Net Value of Maize Production, Campeche, 1989

| | | Net Value by Credit Category (1,000 pesos)[c] | | |
| | | | Digging-stick Maize | |
Yield (tons/ ha)	Market Value[a] (1,000 pesos)	Mechanized Maize (731,880 pesos/ha credit liability)	With Fertilizer and Pesticide (487,806 pesos/ha credit liability)	With Pesticide Only (343,003 pesos/ha credit liability)
4.0	1,480	748	–	–
3.0	1,110	378	–	–
2.0	740	8	–	–
1.75	648	(84)	160	–
1.5	580	(152)[b]	92	237
1.25	462	(270)	(25)	119
1.0	370	(362)	(118)[b]	27
0.75	278	(453)	(210)	(65)
0.5	185	(547)	(303)	(158)[b]

[a]At 370,000 pesos/ton.
[b]Average for state of Campeche; negative values indicated by parentheses.
[c]Market value minus credit liability, including interest charges.
SOURCE: SARH, 1989.

mechanized maize grown with credit, 2.8 tons per hectare must be produced from two hectares or 2.5 tons from three hectares (the average plot
size per capita in ejidal projects in Campeche). Meanwhile, milperos operating with fertilizer and pesticides would have to obtain 2 tons per hectare
from the average three-hectare milpa in order to cover both credit and
subsistence needs. Because this is feasible only on new frontier or prime
land, the BANRURAL credit program for maize sown by digging stick
was canceled late in 1989.

These repercussions have affected Campeche campesinos differentially
according to their degree of integration into the national economic nexus
and the extent of their involvement in government agricultural policies
and programs. Some have become aware of the effects of the two crises
only recently, while others have almost forgotten what life without crisis
was like. Thus, strategies for coping vary considerably.

Coping with the Debt Crisis

Back to the Milpa in Nilchi

We have gone backwards in the last ten years. We stopped making milpa
to try the government's mechanization, but they don't understand that

TABLE 6.4   Net Value of Rice Production, Campeche, 1990

Yield (tons/ ha)	Market Value[a] (1,000 pesos)	Net Value by Credit Category (1,000 pesos)[c]			
		Mechanized Seasonal Rice (1,388,098 pesos/ha credit liability)	Mechanized Seasonal Seed Rice (1,729,745 pesos/ha credit liability)	Irrigated Mechanized Rice (1,595,669 pesos/ha credit liability)	Digging-stick Rice without Fertilizer (548,697 pesos/ha credit liability)
4.5	2,115	727	385	519	–
3.88	1,824	436	94	228[b]	–
3.5	1,645	257	(185)	49	–
3.25	1,528	140	(202)	(68)	–
3.0	1,410	22	(320)	(186)	–
2.58	1,213	(175)	(517)[b]	(383)	664
2.38	1,119	(269)[b]	(611)	(477)	570
2.0	940	(448)	(790)	(656)	391
1.75	823	(565)	(907)	(773)	274
1.5	705	(683)	(1,025)	(891)	156
1.25	588	(800)	(1,142)	(1,008)	39
1.07	503	(885)	(1,227)	(1,093)	(46)[b]
0.75	353	(1,035)	(1,377)	(1,243)	(196)
0.50	235	(1,153)	(1,495)	(1,361)	(314)

[a]At 470,000 pesos/ton.
[b]Average for state of Campeche; negative values indicated by parentheses.
[c]Market value minus credit liability, including interest charges.
SOURCE: SARH, 1990.

you can't grow maize on ak'alche, so it's back to the milpa in Nilchi. (I-47, ejidatario, Nilchi, January 1990)

Nilchi is a small Maya community thirty-seven kilometers east of Campeche and is the southernmost settlement on the Camino Real. Founded in 1947 by landless laborers who occupied an abandoned henequen hacienda and received a small ejidal grant ten years later, it had some 700 inhabitants in 1990 of whom 140 were ejidatarios working a thousand hectares: from one to four hundred hectares devoted to mechanized maize throughout the 1980s (50 members), forty-nine hectares occupied by an irrigated mango plantation (28 members), and a further forty hectares planted with vegetables on occasion (10 members). The remaining 52 ejidatarios were full- or part-time milperos cum casual laborers.

Despite this diversified (by Campeche standards) economic base, Nilchi appears to sleep in the sun most of the time, with the only visible activity being the scratching of mangy dogs in the overgrown central plaza. Until seven years ago, this section of the Camino Real was bustling with vehicular life as the main artery from the city of Campeche to the densely populated northern Maya zone, in addition to being the shortcut to Mérida. Since the construction of an even more direct route to Tenabo through the mangrove swamps northeast of Campeche, only the occasional motor disturbs Nilchi's somnolence.

Nilchi had an early start in the government campaign to modernize ejidal agriculture in Campeche. In the hope of stimulating commercial production of fruits and vegetables for the city of Campeche, a gravity irrigation system was constructed by the Ministry for Water Resources in the early 1960s. Unfortunately, the project was located on the worst soil in the ejido. Furthermore, the system was plagued by technical problems, and the beneficiaries were unwilling to neglect their milpas for a risky new enterprise, particularly one that involved collective cultivation. In 1967, however, Nilchi was selected for a pilot project to test the feasibility of small sprinkler irrigation units for peasants as part of the ministry's small irrigation works program. Twenty young ejidatarios interested in trying a different kind of agriculture volunteered to join the new unit. Once again, the project was located on inappropriate land, poorly drained ak'alche. Within a year, this new unit was barely functioning because of lack of agricultural extension, misunderstandings about credit, inexperience with irrigation technology and the cultivation of the crops involved, and disputes within the collective and between that group and the rest of the ejido. By the mid-1970s, the project was used only for ten to fifteen hectares of chiles and tomatoes whenever enough members agreed to work together under the credit terms. An irrigated mango plantation was initiated in 1974 on better soil under the auspices of the same plan, but by this time many ejidatarios were unwilling to consider membership because of the previous problems. In the 1980s much of the former sprinkler irrigation project area was incorporated into a larger area devoted to mechanized cultivation of maize and beans with bank credit. The fifty members involved stopped making milpa to devoted all their attention to this activity.

When the debt crisis surfaced in 1982, no one in Nilchi noticed. For the first time agriculture was yielding cash income beyond immediate subsistence needs. The mango growers felt that they were making good dividends with a minimum of effort; little attention was paid to weeding, and inspection for plagues was generally cursory. A brief burst of activity at harvest time, when all the members' families worked in the orchard and in the small packing plant in the village, yielded, together with small supplementary milpas, sufficient money to live on all year and perhaps enough for a small television set or stereo player. The vegetable producers' wives sold tomatoes and chiles in the Campeche market, making enough for cash necessities, while the milpa covered basic subsistence. The mechanized maize growers were able to cover their credit and clear enough in cash and in kind to sustain their households with a few extras from average yields in the early 1980s of 1.5 tons per hectare. Life looked good to Nilchi ejidatarios accustomed to the never-ending struggle in the milpa, where production had fallen to 0.75 ton or less per hectare because of population pressure on the best maize land. Children began to be educated beyond the primary level with the expectation that this would prove useful to modern farmers or even lead to a different career altogether:

> It was at this time that we began to feel that we counted, that what we did mattered outside [Nilchi], that we could participate in society, that our children had possibilities. We were coming out of the closed world of the milpa. The door was opening, because the government was making a lot of movement here, giving a lot of support to the countryside. (I-37, ejidatario, Nilchi, January 1990)

Little by little, this new confidence faded as profits were eroded and debts accumulated. The most severely affected were the mechanized maize growers who had abandoned the milpa for dependence on credit production. Between 1985 and 1990, yields exceeded 1 ton per hectare only once and dropped to a little over 0.5 ton in two seasons (1985 and 1987), because the poor drainage of ak'alche delayed planting and compounded the crop damage from summer storms (Table 6.5). Hurricane Gilbert brought extensive flooding in 1988, and rains during the summer of 1989 caused even worse crop damage, fully justifying the "total losses" declared by the insurance company for both agricultural cycles. Yields of

TABLE 6.5   Credit Production, Nilchi, Campeche, 1984–1989

Crop	Year	Sown (ha)	Harvested (ha)	Production (tons)	Yield (tons/ha)	Value (1,000 pesos)
Mechanized	1984	123	123	186	1.50	6,215
maize	1985	400	375	232	0.58	12,490
	1986	315	245	392	1.24	37,632
	1987	270	167	182	0.67	43,316
	1988	93	0	0	0	Total loss
	1989	297	0	0	0	Total loss
Digging-stick	1984	50	35	28	0.56	625
maize	1987	8	8	6	0.80	1,568
	1989	37	N.A.	N.A.	N.A.	N.A.
Beans	1984	30	30	6	0.20	625

NOTE: N.A. = Not Available.
SOURCE: SARH, 1990.

2 tons per hectare were required to cover credit costs and interest charges at the official guaranteed maize price. The mechanized group had never been able to achieve this level of production on its poor soils and had been in default since 1987. With three successive years of crop failure, it became ineligible for further BANRURAL credit. During this period of deficit production members got by on what they could gather from the maize crop before it was officially delivered to CONASUPO, supplemented by wage labor for neighboring landowners and ejidos (Fig. 6.1):

> Our default was the bank's fault. We told them we shouldn't plant so early, because you have to wait for this soil to drain, for the oak to bloom, but they didn't listen. Then they sent the pesticide too late, so that we had to apply it while the weeds were big. Now they say we won't get any more credit because we are bad boys. But we need the credit to live now. It's our job. What will we do without the bank? (I-38, ejidatario, Nilchi, January 1990)

Some will qualify for PRONASOL credit, but with a credit maximum of 300,000 pesos per hectare it barely covers the estimated cost of digging-stick milpa production, factoring in pesticides and improved seed but not fertilizer (SARH, 1990). In 1990 most members of the mechanized group planned to return to milpa on the hillsides or to cultivate the formerly mechanized lands with digging sticks instead of tractors. They will have to make fertilizer a priority if they are to repay the PRONASOL credit and feed their families, even without interest charges on the loans:

> You can cultivate without machines, but not without fertilizer, not now. There are too many of us now for the milpa to rest enough, and the mechanized field is bad land for maize. None of this land will produce without chemicals any more. We will have to manage to pay for them somehow. We should have joined the mango growers when we had the chance. (I-42, ejidatario, Nilchi, January 1990)

The ten members of the vegetable group are much better off; chiles brought 1,600 pesos per kilogram in 1989. Tomato prices were considerably lower, with an average rural price of 700 pesos per kilogram over the production season (substantially below the Mexico City and Mérida market rates for prime-quality produce). With average yields of 4 tons per hectare for the former and 3 tons for the latter on ten hectares, the ten members could clear almost 1 million pesos each after credit repayment in a good year. These crops are highly prone to disease in this zone, however, and merchant middlemen often pay significantly less than the market value. (In 1989, a 25-kilogram case of tomatoes worth an average of 22,500 pesos in Mexico City's central supply depot brought as little as 5,000

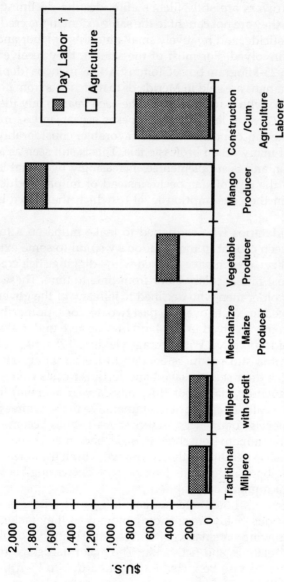

† Day Labor includes credit diarios (cash advances for cultivation labor days) and supplementary income from working family members.

FIGURE 6.1 Average cash income estimates by producer, Nilchi, Campeche, 1989 (SOURCE: field interviews).

pesos in Nilchi). Thus members may barely break even after credit repayment. The only hope for substantial improvement would be participation in the state government's new intensive tomato program, but this would require rehabilitation and expansion of the irrigation system.

The mango growers are still Nilchi's elite, despite declining profit margins, because they are not caught to the same extent in the credit trap; only fertilizer, pesticide, and relatively small amounts of labor and cultivation costs are involved. For most of the season, they receive 8,000–15,000 pesos for a 25-kilogram box of Tommy Atkins mangos (depending on whether the mangos are sold in Mérida or to merchants from northern and central Mexico who travel to Campeche each year to buy the crop). They expect to receive at least 3 million pesos a year and as much as 6 million if marketing opportunities are favorable, considerably more than the salary of many urban professionals. This is still seen as a "tight budget," however, and is supplemented increasingly by casual labor in agriculture or in the city of Campeche instead of milpa production in order to maintain the consumption level to which they have become accustomed.

The twelve ejidatarios who continued to make milpa on a full-time basis have also been caught in the inflationary spiral to some extent; all of them use fertilizer, eleven have worked with "digging stick credit" on occasion, and most hire ancillary labor from time to time. These individuals are mainly older men who declined to join any of the government schemes introduced in Nilchi over the past two decades, primarily out of reluctance to become involved in any kind of collective undertaking and suspicion of outside initiative. With average yields of 0.75 tons per hectare with fertilizer, milpa still produces enough to feed a family. However, there is no surplus after seed is saved and fertilizer costs covered, and therefore supplementary day labor (fifty days a year average) for local landowners and wealthier ejidatarios is imperative in the winter months before the milpa cycle commences. In recent years it has become noticeably harder for the milpero household to make ends meet, even with the very restricted cash expenditures that have always been the norm for such families, and numbers of domestic livestock are decreasing because the feed is needed for human consumption.

Increasing stress on household budgets affects all Nilchi producers (Fig. 6.2). Many households are spending more than they make despite retrenchment, drawing on small capital reserves, selling valuables, and borrowing from relatives and fictive kin. The major hardships resulting from the crisis are seen to be increased isolation due to high transport costs and the prohibitive price of clothing, which prevents many parents from educating their children beyond the primary level. A less discussed but strongly felt deprivation is the shortage of funds for liquor and beer.

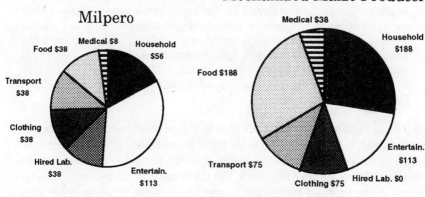

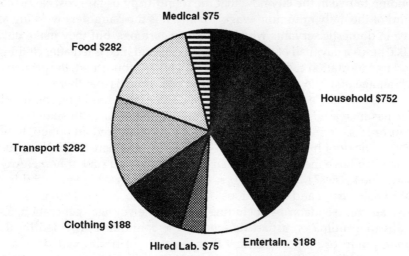

Note: Household Items include appliances, e.g. television, stereo, refrigerator.

FIGURE 6.2   Average household expenditure estimates by producer, Nilchi, Campeche, 1989 (SOURCE: field interviews)

Covering food costs is a real problem only if the household has to rely on purchased maize for extended periods:

> Everybody has a turkey in their yard for Christmas, and we don't worry about the price of beef because we never buy it. We only eat pork when we go to Campeche and deer if we get lucky in the hunt. We don't have the habit of eating fish, and by the time it gets here you wouldn't want it anyway. Basically, we are accustomed to eat only tortillas, eggs, and rice with lots of chile, with chicken from time to time, and there are natural waters [fruit beverages] and maize [gruel] to drink, so we don't suffer in this respect because of our self-sufficiency. (I-40, ejidatario, Nilchi, December 1989)

The agricultural production that is the primary source of income as well as the main food source for most households is supplemented by small revenues generated by the sale of fruits and vegetables from the *solar* (yard), honey, and livestock, but these are of diminishing importance because the costs of travel to Campeche to market the produce almost cancel out the profit. Virtually every household has a member working in Campeche, but these relatives contribute little to the family budget, tending to live in the city now that the round-trip bus fare costs almost a third of the daily minimum wage. Mainly, it is the daughters working as live-in domestic servants who bring home earnings, but they make only 5,000 pesos a day (half of the minimum wage), and little is left after clothing and transportation costs. As far as the parents are concerned, the principal advantage of urban employment for their offspring is that there are fewer mouths to feed. Casual agricultural wage labor in surrounding communities has increased, but opportunities are limited to forty to sixty days a year or less. Permanent out-migration is not considered an option, however: "The door has closed again. Now there is nowhere to go. You leave when you have the bus fare. When you are poor you stay at home. Anyway, who knows? Maybe it's worse elsewhere. At least here your children don't have drugs and distractions" (I-37, ejidatario, Nilchi, January 1990). Instead, more ejidatarios, including some of the younger generation, are cultivating milpa on a part-time basis; the continuity provided by the small group of milperos means that the store of traditional skills and native seed has not been lost as it has in many other Maya communities.

In Nilchi "the crisis" means the agricultural crisis. If life is getting harder, it is because of the failure of agriculture, the blindness of the bank to variability in local conditions, the negligence of the government in failing to guarantee crop prices and interest rates that will provide a decent living for the producer. Some also admit that the crisis is partly their own fault—a result of the ejidatarios' lack of cohesion and motivation to increase production and their failure to realize that unless they make the effort to find out about new agricultural programs and demand assistance they are likely to be left out. (For example, Nilchi ejidatarios had not heard of PRONASOL at a time when this was the prime topic of conversation throughout most of the Camino Real). Community leaders maintain that they intend to change this, among other things improving Nilchi's appearance by whitewashing houses and walls, paving the streets, and relocating the ruined hacienda stack in the main plaza, where refreshment kiosks will be opened to attract tourists. Some of this may be feasible if PRONASOL becomes operative on a significant scale in Nilchi, because repaid credits are to be allocated to social projects in the community. Most Nilchi ejidatarios are, however, more preoccupied with feeding their families. For the majority the debt crisis means a contraction of options wherein return to the milpa appears to be the only feasible solution: "We were deceived into believing that there was a better life for the Maya away from the milpa. We won't be deceived again" (I-39, ejidatario, Nilchi, December 1989).

Hedging Bets in Pomuch

> No matter what they say, life hasn't treated people here too badly. One person has a masonry house, another has a color television, the younger ones have their motorbikes. How did they get that? From agriculture. Yes, it costs more to live, and the crops earn less, but you can produce more and try different things to diversify your income and make sure that something will have results. The main problem is that some still lack ambition. They want the government to give us everything on a plate, even if it is broken. (I-8, ejidatario, Pomuch, March 1990)

Pomuch, the "place of the frog," is one of the larger settlements in the Camino Real. Located sixty-eight kilometers north of the city of Campeche on both the shortcut and the railway to Mérida, the town is a bustling community, swarming with children and teenagers due to a baby boom since improved access to medical care. Thus the population has doubled over the last twenty years to approximately eight thousand inhabitants in 1990. A full range of urban services has been developed to accommodate this increment, including secondary and preparatory schools, a health center, a public market, a post office, telephone, electrification, and piped water, recently extended to the barrios. As in most rural towns in Campeche, however, sewage systems are restricted to the urban core, and the majority of the inhabitants defecate in the yards of their homes, in many cases not even constructing a latrine. Consequently, gastrointestinal and respiratory infections are widespread.

Despite its size and urban characteristics, Pomuch is basically a community of farmers who leave their one-room huts before dawn to walk, bicycle, or ride in an ejidal truck to their fields, located as far as twenty to thirty kilometers from town wherever reasonable agricultural soil can be found. Traditionally, Pomuch depended on making milpa and beekeeping, with some small-scale forestry activities, although some of the older inhabitants had been laborers on nearby henequen haciendas. Milpa was always a precarious activity in this zone of limited good soil, however, and by the late 1960s increasing pressure of population on the land, together with a communications system well-developed for Campeche at that time, stimulated out-migration among the younger generation in particular. In 1969, a small irrigation project was initiated for Pomuch ejidatarios as part of an attempt to stem this tide. Initially, twenty-eight ejidatarios worked 120 hectares with three wells, growing mechanized maize and beans. In 1990, there were forty-nine members working 216 hectares with five wells cultivating maize, mango and zapote orchards, vegetables, and watermelons.

At the onset of the debt crisis in 1982, the Pomuch project members were just emerging from a crisis of their own. Early experiments with a variety of fruits, vegetables, forage, and oil seed crops had shown promise but proven impossible to sustain because of a combination of technical problems and planning and implementation errors, such that low-value mechanized maize production, mainly without irrigation, became the norm. Even though the Pomuch project was located on some of the best agricultural soil in Campeche (kan-kab), maize yields rarely exceeded 2 tons per hectare because of the droughts, floods, and plagues common in this region, and profits were modest or nonexistent. A fifty-hectare mango orchard planted in 1975 was regarded by many members as a high-risk undertaking because of problems with the irrigation system and the vulnerability of the young trees to disease. These disappointments compounded the internal dissension that had plagued the project since its inception, with the result that by the late 1970s more time was devoted to feuding than to farming. Friction was reduced by dividing up the project wells and terrain between the dominant families and their followers to form three independent working groups, each with its own agricultural priorities.

As in Nilchi, the first few years of debt crisis appeared to have little impact. One group of twelve utilizing the land around well 1 continued to depend on mechanized maize, and planted a few watermelons and a small zapote orchard. A second group of twenty ejidatarios at wells 2 and 3 cultivated the young mango plantation in addition to maize and raised small livestock. A third group with seventeen members at wells 4 and 5 also had maize and small orchards, but was more interested in diversified vegetable production. With the addition of high-value fruits and vegetables to staple cultivation, profits increased and members began to make plans for expansion despite noticeable increases in the cost of living.

In 1986 "things began to degenerate again" (I-2, ejidatario, Pomuch, December 1989). Members of the well 1 group burned most of their orchard while firing maize stubble in preparation for planting. Their old tractor fell apart when they had just finished paying for it and because of the high cost of a new loan could not be replaced. The ejidal pickup was "held together with wire because of the lack of funds for repairs" (I-5, ejidatario, Pomuch, December 1989). The group at wells 2 and 3 had to put down their livestock, which had been acquired for them by SARH, because of birth defects. All three groups lost more than 50 percent of their maize crop in summer storms. In 1987 yields were normal, but the well 1 group defaulted on its loan because two members refused to pay their share of the debt, and thus the whole group was ineligible for new credit in 1988. The next year brought Hurricane Gilbert, which flattened the maize and greatly reduced orchard yields. Tree crops are not insured against acts of God, but members were covered by insurance for the maize, which was declared a total loss even though more than half was salvaged for sale and household consumption. Additional food supplies were received as part of the federal and state disaster relief program: "At that time, we didn't know whether to blame God or the government for the problems in the countryside. Things were crazy. The total loss of a crop meant some profit for us instead of debt to the bank. A good year meant that we had to pay back all the credit, and we couldn't, so in default again" (I-7, ejidatario, Pomuch, December 1989). The group at well 1 missed the good fortune of a salvageable total loss because it had been ineligible for credit.

Today the Pomuch project members feel that Hurricane Gilbert was the turning point and the worst is over. This was reinforced by the government's "gift" after Gilbert of nursery stock and vegetable seeds to afflicted projects. The ejidatarios are particularly encouraged by the recent emphasis on irrigated vegetable and fruit production by the state government in collaboration with federal agencies such as SARH. The plan is to rehabilitate the more viable projects in the Camino Real and Los Chenes for intensive production of high-value crops, the original intent of the national small irrigation program twenty years ago. This is compatible with the belief of most Pomuch project members that hedging one's bets—diversification—is the only sensible strategy in the modernized agricultural sector: "The way agriculture is structured in Mexico, you get into most trouble if you depend on maize. If you can diversify, grow crops with value, and find reliable markets, then you can make enough to beat the bank. But you have to have confidence in yourself and in each other, because we have to work in groups to a certain extent" (I-3, ejidatario, Pomuch, March 1990).

The lack of shared purpose within the working groups continues to be the main problem. Membership has remained unusually stable, in part because the wells have continued to function (although far below capacity) and in part because members have been reluctant to admit newcomers who might disturb their fragile unity. Nevertheless, significant disagreement continues to disrupt cultivation. The group at well 1 continues to be led in spirit by an eighty-six-year-old former hacienda laborer and political activist who believes strongly in social justice. His visions of a future for Pomuch ejidatarios as professional horticulturalists and fruit exporters tend to intimidate other members, who still see themselves as simple milperos. His son is following the same path of treating agriculture as both business and politics, believing that only the strong can use the system to their advantage. The family lives simply, allocating its resources to investments that will expedite agriculture such as paid labor and the purchase of key inputs, and this inspires envy among members who spend all that they make on household needs. For example, in the harvest season of 1989, the leader's son bought the requisite sacks for the family's shelled maize. Others in the group were unable to proceed with processing the crop because CONASUPO had refused to supply new sacks to ejidatarios still in debt for those provided two years previously. In the interim, the unit sack cost had increased from 1,000 pesos to 5,000 pesos. Such intragroup disparities tend to be translated into acts such as the firing of maize stubble without warning the ejidatario working the adjacent parcel or the leveling of irrigation channels and borders overnight.

Resentment has been compounded by the credit system, under which, until recently, the entire group has been held liable for the default of individual members. Under the new system operative in 1990, the tomato group working five irrigated hectares at well 1 was composed only of the eight members who had paid all their previous debts. This group had hopes of dividends of 2.5 million pesos each at the beginning of that season, but a pest had discolored the fruit and reduced its market value. The members would prefer to plant the sauce tomato, which does well in the changeable spring climate of the peninsula, but the SARH agronomists insist on the salad tomato, which brings prices in the export and major national markets of up to 110,000 pesos for a twenty-five kilogram box:

> If it weren't for the greed of the government to produce more tons, to have the prettiest fruits and vegetables, our lives would have more security here. But the Americans won't eat spotty Mexican fruits. They want perfect, poisoned fruits, like with Alar, so the mangos have to be treated in the

hydrothermic plant in Cayal, the tomatoes have to be sprayed and dusted. We like taste over beauty, just as we like *criollo* maize and not the hybrid, but it doesn't matter to the government what we want. We are just stupid farmers. What do we know? (I-12, ejidatario, Pomuch, March 1990)

When credit is available, the members can make more than 1 million pesos each from tomato production if official sales contracts have been arranged so that they are not at the mercy of the middlemen and if they do not have to give away too many free cases to government field personnel. Most years, however, the members rely on mechanized maize, which barely covers household subsistence in a normal production year after credit repayment. Thus the only reliable cash income is 200,000–300,000 pesos obtained from the sale of squash seeds to oil extraction industries in Campeche or Mérida (Fig. 6.3).

The group at wells 2 and 3 has also suffered from dissension, particularly in connection with a subgroup that grows only maize. Those with income from the now-mature mango plantation, with an average yield of 5 tons a hectare, can earn up to 9 million pesos a year from sales to merchants from Guadalajara and Monterrey. Future prospects are even better, as the state has recently signed contracts for the export of 80,000 boxes to the United States and an additional 320,000 to the state of Jalisco at premium prices. Thus, the fourteen Pomuch "mango millionaires" have little in common with the six other members who share their well, who are struggling to avoid default and subsist on the 0.5 ton per hectare of maize that remains after credit repayment in a normal year. Because this amounts to less than a ton per capita, most members without a share in the mango plantation are compelled to seek supplementary wage labor in order to cover household subsistence needs.

The third group, at wells 4 and 5, works in greater harmony most of the time, largely because of the more secure productive base created by a relatively efficient irrigation system. It is able to plant both irrigated and seasonal maize, and squash, tomatoes, chiles, watermelons, mangos, and zapotes; "this way, if nature castigates us in one crop, she will provide bounty in another" (I-14, ejidatario, Pomuch, March 1990). Members plant over a hundred hectares of maize per year and expect to make some 2 million pesos each after credit repayment and household needs are covered. In addition they receive an average net income of 1.5 million pesos each from fruits and vegetables and expect this to increase with expanded tomato production.

Most Pomuch members feel that life is getting better as a result of the project, which has protected them, to a degree, from the worst repercussions of the debt crisis. Nevertheless, the increased cost of living causes some individual hardships, together with modifications in spending

200

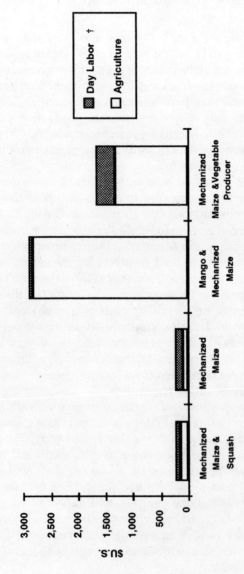

† Day Labor includes credit diarios (cash advances for cultivation labor days) and supplementary income from working family members.

FIGURE 6.3 Average cash income estimates by producer, Pomuch irrigation project, Campeche, 1989 (SOURCE: field interviews)

patterns and life-styles. One member cannot afford specialized medical treatment for his wife, another has had to take his sons out of secondary school, a third has had to sell his motorbike because it needed expensive parts. All members agree that they are not eating as well as a decade ago, consuming less protein and more tortillas, while bottled sodas, which were ubiquitous a decade ago, have become an occasional treat:

> You make the food stretch more. There's a half a kilo of pork instead of a kilo, and you eat pintos instead of black beans, because the merchants charge contraband prices due to the scarcity. But beans are not the beginning and end of Mexico. And if you have to put chicken instead of turkey in your Christmas tamales, who will notice the difference? And they say that Coke is bad for you anyway. (I-5, ejidatario, Pomuch, December 1989)

This apparent resignation to cutbacks is due to changing consumer priorities: "You make your needs simpler, so that you can afford the little luxuries, a new radio, a stereo, or, in other words, things that were luxuries, like a bicycle or a television have become necessities here now. You have to stay in contact with the world" (I-8, ejidatario, Pomuch, March 1990). The high cost of clothing is also a major concern, particularly for those dependent on maize production. Rising transportation prices are accepted with relative equanimity; the round-trip train ticket to Campeche is still only 2,000 pesos, the same as passage on top of the freight in a truck. Furthermore, for the majority these expenses have been offset by the extension of social security medical services to ejidatarios working with credit, a great boon to household budgets (Fig. 6.4).

Project members agree that the ejidatarios who have suffered most from the crisis in Pomuch are those without access to good maize land or accumulated capital such as livestock and the younger generation, who have to go to work in Campeche or Cancún in construction or the tourist trade. While it is considered desirable for youths to leave Pomuch to pursue professional careers, casual urban labor is not considered prestigious, particularly since the higher cost of city living consumes most of the wages. For example, a small room without kitchen facilities in Cancún may cost 400,000 pesos a month, with the result that with full employment at minimum wage a construction worker would only have 160,000 pesos to live on. This makes a second job necessary for most and means that little if any money can be sent back to the family. In Pomuch as in much of the modern world, "the only thing our sons bring home is their appetites and their laundry" (I-12, ejidatario, Pomuch, January 1990). The few with children in the professions do, however, expect financial support in times of trouble or at least a turkey or a substantial present at Christmas.

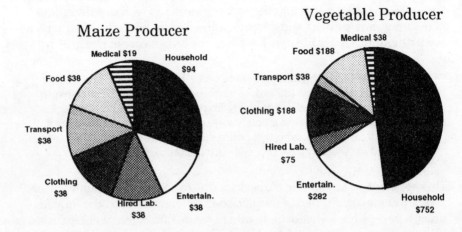

Maize Producer

Medical $19
Household $94
Food $38
Transport $38
Clothing $38
Hired Lab. $38
Entertain. $38

Vegetable Producer

Medical $38
Food $188
Transport $38
Clothing $188
Hired Lab. $75
Entertain. $282
Household $752

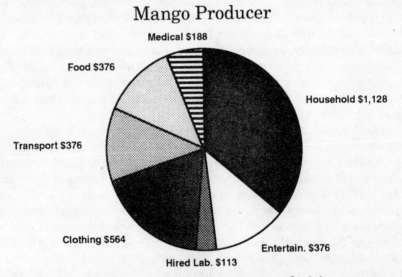

Mango Producer

Medical $188
Food $376
Household $1,128
Transport $376
Clothing $564
Hired Lab. $113
Entertain. $376

Note: Household Items include appliances, e.g. television, stereo, refrigerator.

FIGURE 6.4   Average household expenditure estimates by producer, Pomuch irrigation project, Campeche, 1989 (SOURCE: field interviews)

Migration to Campeche and Mérida, already a fact of life in the Camino Real in the late 1960s, has accelerated under the debt crisis, with the tourist boom area of Quintana Roo as the new magnet. Progress toward lucrative crops in the irrigation units has been too slow to convince many of the project members, let alone their offspring, that a good living can be made from agriculture. For the young, agriculture means maize, toiling in the sun in the face of imminent disaster from droughts, floods, and poisonous snakes for at best a meager living and, more likely in recent years, default to the bank. As horizons broaden, rural aspirations give way to urban dreams, the fruits of the milpa to a daily wage in construction. The state government is attempting once again to turn the migration tide by means of the new intensive fruit and vegetable program on rehabilitated irrigation projects. It remains to be seen whether sufficient visible progress can be made quickly enough to make agriculture an attractive option for young campesinos rather than the debt bondage it appears to be today.

Pomuch project members feel fortunate to have been insulated from the worst effects of the debt crisis by belonging to a unit whose irrigation system has continued to function despite problems, with sufficient land per capita and soil good enough to produce yields above the cost of inputs for the most part. Even more significant than these objective factors have been the initiative and adaptability of the project members themselves. These individuals have been able to make a dent in the government agencies' absolute control of project crops and marketing strategies through their awareness of potential options and alternative ejidal support services and their willingness to take risks and seek a viable formula for hedging through diversification. As a result of these efforts, often involving almost daily meetings between the ejidatarios and the agrarian bureaucracy, together with the renewed state interest in irrigation project rehabilitation, the members hope for a better future. It is significant, however, that few members have brought their sons into the project. Unless agriculture improves rapidly and dramatically to become a demonstrably remunerative proposition, members wish for a different life for the next generation away from the sweat, dirt, and disappointments of the farmer's existence—one with security and respect:

If all agriculture were mechanized, irrigated, and devoted to export crops worth money, and the bank were the place you stored your profits instead of your losses, then that might be a good life for your son. We'll believe it when we see it. Until then, let them study to become teachers, technicians, anything but construction workers. Changing the mud of the country for the dust of the city as a laborer is not a step up. It is just a different kind of bondage. (I-3, ejidatario, Pomuch, February 1990)

Minding Their Own Business: The Mennonite Solution

> How did they make their colonies produce so much so soon after their arrival? How do they manage to make money from maize? They even make money from the milpa. What's the secret of the Mennonites' success? (I-117, ejidatario, Poc-Boc, January 1990)

Less than fifty kilometers west of Pomuch in the sparsely settled frontier zone between the Camino Real and the Los Chenes district, Mennonite colonists began to establish a new home in 1983. Their parents had settled in Durango in 1928, having left "somewhere in the old country to find land to work in peace" in the New World, where they hoped to be free from religious persecution and cultural incursion (I-91, Mennonite colonist, campo 3, Hecelchakán, January 1990). Many such Mennonite groups had left Europe after World War I, with Canada and Mexico favored as initial destinations, from whence communities often moved on once more when frontier in-filling threatened their freedom to maintain their traditional agrarian way of life.[8] Over fifty years after their arrival in Durango, after an unsuccessful attempt to find additional land in that state to accommodate a new generation, the Mennonites learned that there was room for new colonists in Campeche. They had sent elders to explore the possibilities and purchased approximately two thousand hectares of unused national lands as private property in the municipio of Hecelchakán, an hour or more by truck from the municipal seat via a rough unpaved road. Other colonies were established thirty kilometers to the south in the municipio of Tenabo and near Iturbide in the municipio of Hopelchén, close to the Quintana Roo border.

By 1990, tall blond Mennonite men in heavyweight blue dungarees and straw hats, followed by women "dressed plain" in long, dark dresses, kerchiefs, and stockings, had become a familiar sight in the market towns of northern Campeche. Just seven years after the initial settlement, the Hecelchakán Mennonites had firmly established seven adjacent colonies (known locally as campo [camp] 1, campo 2, and so on, although each has a more attractive community name, such as Colonia Las Flores). The colonies are located in a relatively large basin with good soil (kan-kab), and most of the brush was cleared for agriculture within the first two years. Each colony is composed of about a dozen compact farms with houses spaced along the access roads. Neat one- and two-story concrete block houses, washed white, are reminiscent of East European farmhouses. The houses are surrounded by tidy barnyards, outbuildings, small orchards, vegetable patches, and flower gardens, separated from the neighbors by carefully fenced fields. This ordered universe appears to be a different world from the clustered Maya village, which looks like an integral part of the surrounding brush, with palm-thatched huts and lush yards where chickens and children run wild in noisy confusion.

This sharp contrast in settlement form reflects a significant difference in purpose and function. While both Maya and Mennonite communities are clearly peasant in terms of the importance of the individual household as a multidimensional socioeconomic unit and dependence on traditional farming technology and subsistence production, for the Mennonites the community transcends the family. Thus the driving force behind Mennonite colonization is the need to safeguard community integrity and guarantee survival as the next generation in turn requires new lands to accommodate its progeny. The Mennonites need a milieu where they will be left alone to pursue these goals in enclaves where their traditions, religious beliefs, and life-style can be protected via self-sufficiency and deliberate self-segregation up to an expedient point.

In Durango not enough good land was available to sustain the generational "hiving-off" cycle. Campeche offered a relatively isolated frontier with room for expansion, and both the government authorities and the Maya inhabitants were prepared to live and let colonists live as long as they did not disturb the tranquil pace of local life:

> In Durango now there are too many people—too many transients and murderers because of the unemployment. And it became too noisy, too commercialized. It's much better here in Campeche where it's quiet, a better environment for the children. The Maya are peaceful people and let us alone, while the authorities are helpful, but don't interfere. (I-91, Mennonite colonist, campo 3, Hecelchakán, January 1990)

The Campechano authorities and the Maya are, however, intensely curious about the Mennonites' way of life and their ability to establish an apparently secure productive base in a short time. It is agreed that they work very hard and have learned how to farm in Campeche as well as or better than the locals, but at the same time they are viewed as crazy to work so hard in the tropical heat, to choose to live in isolation without electricity, refrigeration, and other modern conveniences, to keep women and children in seclusion, and to eschew vanities such as mirrors and bright garments. Furthermore, the Maya are scrupulously clean and wear light cotton clothing adapted to the humid tropical climate, and they think that the Mennonites, with their heavy workclothes, are dirty and smell bad.

Hard work and honest sweat are the dominant motifs in the Mennonite colonies. Only a few farms have drilled wells, so most families haul water from neighbors in horse-drawn carts. This scarcity, together with the prescribed lack of preoccupation with appearance that "living plain" demands, means that water is not to be wasted on unnecessary bathing. (They prefer rain water to drink as the ground water is highly calcareous and tends to cause kidney problems in the older generation.)

The Mennonites work from dawn to dusk at agricultural and household tasks, with well-defined division of labor by age and sex. Households are large and multigenerational, married sons living and working with their fathers until they have the financial and labor resources to establish homes and farms of their own. The head of the family and the older sons spend most of their time in the cleared fields where maize is produced for sale. Younger sons care for the four or five head of double-purpose livestock—Indo-Brazil and Holstein crosses bred for both dairy products and meat. Milk is sold to local Maya communities and to three Mennonite farmers who make cheese to sell within the community, in Mérida and Campeche, and for limited export. Young men have also learned to make milpa on the rocky slopes ringing the valley. Meanwhile, the women perform domestic chores, care for barnyard animals, and work in the fields as needed, for example, in collective work parties at harvest time. Generally, they stay close to home, except for visits to neighbors and the small community shops, and rarely accompany their menfolk on weekly shopping trips to Hecelchakán.

Jacobo Muller has three married sons, all living in his house, and eighteen grandchildren so far. On a warm January day, the whole extended family is engaged in processing a pig which was butchered at dawn, as they do perhaps three times a year. The men mix and stuff sausages which will be smoked for a couple of hours. The women are cutting meat into chunks for canning. A sister in Saskatchewan once sent some special lids for preserving jars. "Are these safer than mayonnaise lids?" (I-91, Mennonite colonist, campo 3, Hecelchakán, January 1990). The pork has been sitting on the porch table in the heat for hours under constant attack from flies, so that the potential problem with botulism due to use of jars and lids not intended for canning is likely to be compounded by other health hazards.

Jacobo talks easily in Spanish to the visitor about agriculture, life in Durango, Campeche and his household, but is vague about social and religious practices in the community. He proudly displays a receipt for 256,000 pesos for the week's milk sales in Hecelchakán. The sons smile occasionally and make surreptitious comments in Low German dialect: "How could anyone marry that woman? She never stops talking!" The women avoid eye contact with the outsider and converse among themselves in low voices. Dirty blond children play in the dust with homemade wooden toys, such as a cart and a top. Older children are fascinated by the driver's mirror on the visitor's car. There will be pickled pig's feet for dinner and wheat bread. The Mennonites grow maize, but they rarely eat it.

The children attend one of four schools (eventually each colony will have one). The schoolmaster in campo 3 has over forty children in his care. He is the permanent teacher as he is good at it; some other schools rotate the position among qualified community members. He teaches reading, writing, and arithmetic—"which even girls should know if they are to be useful wives" (I-92, Mennonite colonist, campo 3, Hecelchakán, January 1990). Spanish is taught, but generally boys do not acquire much until they start to accompany their fathers to town on errands; girls pick up only a few words and phrases, being discouraged from interacting with outsiders. Girls and boys play separately in the schoolyard at skipping games or tag under the schoolmaster's watchful eye. The master does not know where the community's ancestors came from in Europe: "We look forward rather than back, inside rather than out. That's our way. We mind our own business" (I-92, Mennonite colonist, campo 3, Hecelchakán, January 1990).

By minding their own business, the Hecelchakán Mennonite communities appear to have profited rather than suffered from the debt crisis. When asked about its effects, Mennonite farmers first reply that "the crisis is a Mexican affair" or "the crisis is Mexican politics," where "Mexican" means both Mexico City and "non-Mennonite" just as to many of their neighbors it connotes "non-Yucatec" or "non-Maya" (I-91, Mennonite colonist, campo 3; I-95, Mennonite colonist, campo 1, Hecelchakán, January 1990). However, they frequently refer to themselves as Mexicans in general terms and even on occasion as Campechanos, despite their brief residence in the state. Further questioning about the impact of the crisis produces more specific comments, such as "It affects the Maya more because they don't want to work hard," "The Campechanos have a problem because they have lost their self-sufficiency," and "The crisis is actually very selective in its effects in the countryside, so we are selective in how we participate in the economy" (I-95, I-96, Mennonite colonists, campo 1, and I-91, campo 3, Hecelchakán, January 1990).

Selectivity, expediency, and minding the community's business appear to be the keys to the Mennonites' survival. While they are essentially self-sufficient in dairy produce, eggs, poultry, meat, honey, fruits, and vegetables and make their own clothing, they need cash for farm implement parts, tools, rope, carpentry and building supplies, cloth, shoes, wheat flour, and other domestic items. The men also require spending money for meals on their weekly trips to Hecelchakán or occasional visits to Campeche and for cigarettes and beer (the latter consumed only in town). Money is also spent in the colonies on soft drinks, consumed warm because of the lack of refrigeration, popsicles sold by vendors from Hecelchakán, and small household and food items such as batteries, crackers, cheese, steak sauce, and dried seasonings. Most important, the Mennonites need to continue to build their savings to set up the next generation in new colonies. In order to be able to do this in a restricted local economy, a shrewd eye for diversification possibilities is vital. Pragmatism is also essential, particularly because the Mennonites do not believe in the unrestricted use of modern technology. Since Mennonite agriculture is geared often to outside commerce as well as to self-sufficiency, a degree of expediency is required in compromising beliefs with production and marketing imperatives. For example, a market may be lost if the traditional horse and buggy is used to transport the produce instead of trucks, or valuable land may remain unsown if only tractors with the permitted iron-wheeled tires are employed (Everitt, 1969). The Hecelchakán Mennonites are somewhat more liberal than other branches in that their buggies may have rubber tires and they will ride to town by bus or truck to save time. Even more important, they were quick to rationalize the use of modern equipment for mechanized maize cultivation and transport of the crop, "because it comes as part of the credit package, and we don't have to do the driving because they send the operators too. Then, too, they take the maize by truck to CONASUPO, but that doesn't concern us because we are not the ones who are going to receive it or consume it" (I-91, Mennonite colonist, campo 1, Hecelchakán, February 1990). They also use the services of the local SARH veterinarian to a much greater degree than do neighboring ejidos and private property owners.

In 1989, the Hecelchakán Mennonites planted 1,595 hectares of mech-anized maize in the seven colonies with BANRURAL credit involving 121 farmers, together with a further 919 hectares grown by 128 free producers (Table 6.6). Yields per hectare on the lands harvested "in good condition" ranged from 3.2 tons to 3.7 tons for maize grown with credit and from 3 tons to 3.2 tons on the free producers' land. Half of the maize planted was declared a partial or total loss as a result of heavy rains and floods that encouraged insect pests. Overall yields per hectare were considerably higher than the regional average, however, as Mennonite cropland desig-nated a loss was almost 50 percent less than the norm for ejidal projects. The SARH agronomists supervising cultivation felt that this was because of the care that the Mennonites give to cultivation: "When they weed, they really weed, and their fields are fenced so that they can graze the cattle on the stubble before they burn" (I-148, civil servant, Tenabo, February 1990). Even more important to the relative success of the Mennonites is their ethos of community solidarity, economic achievement, and accumulation of a capital cushion, such that: "They don't have to make a career out

TABLE 6.6   Credit and Free Production, Maize, Hecelchakán Mennonite Colonies, Campeche, 1990

Colony	Number of Cultivators	Sown (ha)	Harvested in Good Condition[a] (ha)	Harvested Partial Losses (ha)	Declared Total Loss (ha)
Campo 1	33	662	177	297	187
Campo 2	21	238	127	23	88
Campo 3	9	147	51	35	61
Campo 4	15	130	53	47	29
Campo 5	10	75	51	14	10
Campo 6	19	227	185	25	20
Campo 7	14	116	102	8	6
Total with credit	121	1,595	746	449	401
Free producers	128	919	450	300	169
Total	249	2,514	1,196	749	570

[a]Average yield, 3 to 3.75 tons/ha.
SOURCE: SARH, 1990.

of disaster, they don't need to collect the insurance just to break even. So they always pay, they are never in default" (I-149, civil servant, Hecelchakán, March 1990).

Almost all of the maize produced from the milpa as well as from the mechanized land is sold to CONASUPO in Hecelchakán at the regulated market price. At this yield level, the Mennonites could make a net profit of 1.5 tons per hectare after credit repayment, earning some 3 million pesos per member or up to 6 to 9 million pesos per household, depending on the number of adult sons still living at home. Other cash income is derived from the sale of milk, cheese, peanuts, eggs, poultry, and other small livestock. Shortly before Christmas of 1989, plump Mennonite turkeys were on sale in Hecelchakán market for 40,000 pesos, half the going rate in the city of Campeche. An increasingly important source of income is house construction; the Maya like to hire the Mennonites instead of local builders because they work faster, charge less, and do a better job. The Mennonites are also in great demand as mechanics and welders.

All in all, the Mennonites are clearly very comfortably off by rural Mexican standards, with average annual household incomes (with two or more families per household) of around 20 million pesos a year.[9] Since they produce most of what they consume, the bulk of this income can be saved for investment or emergency capital. Thus the Mennonites' response to the debt crisis is to carry on with their normal strategy for both economic and social survival—hard work, a large household and community labor pool, self-sufficiency, and self-imposed isolation except where they see realistic opportunities for making a profit in the local economy. The fact that they are able to prosper under the debt crisis shows the distinct advantage of being able to use the Mexican agricultural system without, ultimately, being dependent on it:

> The trouble with agriculture around here is that the ejido lacks resources, both financial and human. The Maya know agriculture. They know the land. We have learned from them how to read the soil, to clear the brush, to make milpa. But they don't want to work because they lack motivation. They just don't know how to make money. The whole system stifles initiative. I don't think that they will ever produce until they can set themselves free to farm in their own way. (I-91, Mennonite colonist, campo 3, Hecelchakán, January 1989)

From Rice to Ranching in Bonfil

> In reality, the majority in Bonfil have profited from the debt crisis, since it gave the last blow to rice cultivation here, so the government lost interest and left us free to find our own way. Those who have failed to prosper are those who would have been poor anyway, even if rice had continued to give [good yields], since they lack the initiative to make sound investments such as in cattle or a business of their own. If you don't look out for yourself, someone will trample on you. That's why collective agriculture is doomed in Mexico, because everybody has to take care of his own interests first. (I-61, ejidatario, Bonfil, February 1990)

As we have seen, the Bonfil ejidatarios had once earned large dividends from mechanized rice cultivation and achieved an unprecedented degree of ejidal participation in agricultural decision making. In the long run, however, their unique collective experiment had failed. At the onset of the debt crisis in 1982, Bonfil was in default to BANRURAL for 114 million pesos in rice credit, including interests accrued from previous debts, and owed millions more for agricultural equipment. Collective cattle production was flourishing, but this success did not offset declining morale. In 1983 the ejidatarios sold half the herd to clear the bank debt and divided up the remainder. Shortly thereafter, they divided up half the ejido's land. Thus, in the early years of the debt crisis, the attention of the Bonfil ejidatarios was devoted to attempting to salvage something tangible at the individual level from a failing collective project.

Two-thirds of Bonfil's five hundred ejidatarios are now essentially individual cattle ranchers. Most do not engage in any crop farming at all, making a comfortable living from average herds of fifteen head of double-purpose cattle per capita, together with smaller-scale livestock rearing activities including sheep and goats. Some 4,000 liters of raw milk is sold locally or in the city of Campeche at 1,200 pesos a liter. Production could be higher, but the herds are undermilked because of the lack of a processing plant. Six households are engaged in cheese production on an irregular basis. Most of the yearling bull calves are sold, bringing 1 million pesos each in 1990.

Incomes of Bonfil households dedicated primarily to cattle average 17 million pesos from sales of milk and young livestock. Operating expenses are low because few maintain improved pasture, veterinary supplies are still relatively cheap, and the limited amounts of labor required, mainly for herding and fencing, can be supplied by family members (Fig. 6.5). Ranchers are free to devote much of their time to ancillary income sources such as nonagricultural wage labor or small businesses such as trucking, retailing, and auto and appliance repair. Most Bonfil ranchers agree that "the crisis has worked to our benefit, because it got us out of high-risk agriculture, freed us from government interference, and sent up the price of beef and milk" (I-62, ejidatario, Bonfil, February 1990).

A sharp contrast exists between the Bonfil ejidatarios involved in cattle ranching and the remaining one hundred and seventy individuals who opted out of the livestock business when the collective herds were redistributed. Over half of these have abandoned agriculture altogether and make a reasonably secure living from business endeavors established with capital from project dividends or as full-time construction laborers living most of the time in the city of Campeche. In addition, ten Bonfil project members work as heavy-equipment operators for private contractors or parastatal enterprises, earning more than twice the daily minimum wage.

Approximately sixty ejidatarios depend for subsistence on two to three hundred hectares of mechanized maize, cultivated with credit on the limited areas of better soil on the edges of the poorly drained valley bottom. They have been in default each agricultural cycle since 1985, except when insurance covered the total loss occasioned by Hurricane Gilbert in 1988. Average yields of less than 0.75 ton over this period have been insufficient to support a household and have therefore been supplemented by independent cultivation of two to three hectares of milpa on the valley slopes, where yields of 1.5–2 tons per hectare can be obtained in the first year of cultivation under normal rainfall conditions. Even with this supplement, subsistence is very precarious, and maize growers are forced to seek as many days of casual agricultural wage labor as possible

212

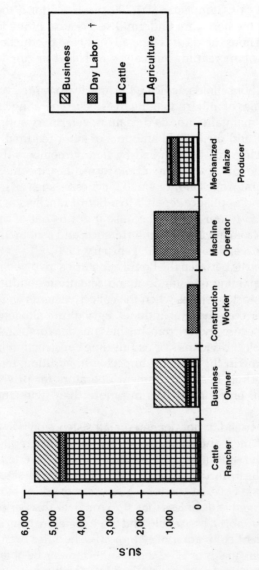

† Day Labor includes credit diarios (cash advances for cultivation labor days) and supplementary income from working family members.

FIGURE 6.5   Average cash income estimates by producer, Bonfil, Campeche, 1989 (SOURCE: field interviews)

to support their households. Unfortunately, they are competing in the local labor market with Guatemalan refugees from the neighboring camp at Quetzal-Edzná. Since the arrival of the refugees in Campeche in 1984, they have come to be the preferred hired labor pool in the region by virtue of their reputation for hard work, their pacific disposition, and their willingness to work for less than the minimum wage; even the Bonfil ejidatarios choose to hire them rather than their compatriots:

> If you hire a Guatemalan you get value for your money. He works hard, doesn't fight, and takes orders. Now, in contrast, the little Maya have a rest whenever you turn your back and are always going home. The worst are those from here [Bonfil]. They fight, demand more money, and won't obey orders, and they are either going off to the cantina or are hung over. The problem here is that people think that they are too good to be laborers (I-63, ejidatario, Bonfil, March 1990).[10]

Virtually all households in Bonfil receive some supplementary income from offspring working in Campeche or as agricultural laborers in the United States. Financial assistance on a regular basis is not expected from married professional children, who comprise perhaps 10 percent of the younger generation as secondary and preparatory schooling has been available in Bonfil for a decade and higher education is valued by the majority. Nevertheless, education does not necessarily improve the chance of finding full-time employment locally at what most Bonfil inhabitants consider to be a liveable wage. Thus young men from both affluent and poor households often spend up to three years at a time in the United States, usually as migrant farmworkers, followed by a year back home, mainly doing nothing until family fortunes compel them to go north again. Working "on the other side" to sustain one's family had been common among these colonists even before they came to Campeche, but the numbers of youths *buscando el gordo* (looking for the prize) in the United States has increased considerably since the contraction of the rice program and the privatization of the herds. These northern excursions are becoming more difficult as a result of the crack-down on illegal workers in the United States, and it is not uncommon for deportees to return to Bonfil with empty pockets just a few weeks after their departure. Even for those with legal papers, however, permanent residence in the United States is not seen as a desirable option, since: "You live well on the other side. But despite all the screw-ups here—the failure of rice, the lack of work, the fights, the corruption—Bonfil is home. It's where we belong. We would rather live here all the time, if the economic base could support us" (I-70, ejidatario, Bonfil, February 1990).

In view of the relatively high incomes and living standards of the majority of Bonfil's ejidatarios, it is not surprising that complaints about the impact of the debt crisis on household budgets tend to be similar to those of middle-class urbanites (Fig. 6.6). Young men bemoan the high price of gasoline, the cost of repairs for motorbikes, the price of beer and liquor, and the restrictions on increments in the minimum wage under the official wage and price control pact. Older men complain about the price of saddles (280,000 pesos for a good quality item from northern Mexico), and pickup trucks (perhaps 35 million pesos for a new vehicle). Women are distressed over the high cost of clothing and refrigerators. Most households have cut back on the acquisition of major consumer items, although spending fads continue to be gratified by and large.

The sixty households dependent solely on agriculture and casual wage labor for subsistence are in much more difficult circumstances under the debt crisis. For these families, crop failure means worry about where tomorrow's tortillas are going to come from, while even a good harvest does not allow for "the little luxuries we had become accustomed to—a beer, a Coke, a cup of coffee, some cigarettes, a trip to town just to look around" (I-77, ejidatario, Bonfil, February 1990). In these circumstances, even primary education for their children is difficult for most families to achieve, and full-time employment outside Bonfil for as many offspring as possible is the main goal. These families tend to blame the agricultural crisis in general and the failure of the rice project in particular for their afflictions, while the immediate cause of their poverty is seen to be their wealthier neighbors, "who got ahead through [ejidal] politics and fraud" (I-77, ejidatario,Bonfil, March 1990).

The debt crisis and the failure of rice have freed many Bonfil ejidatarios from the curbs on independent initiative imposed by government intervention so that they can make their own way as relatively wealthy ranchers or entrepreneurs. At the same time, these conditions have severely contracted opportunities for those still dependent on project agriculture and for the younger generation, who are compelled to range throughout Mexico or the United States in search of casual labor to sustain their families. Thus, the situation has both promoted entrepreneurship and stimulated proletarianization, depending on individual household circumstances. Increasing income differentiation has eroded the community as a unified social group sharing interests and goals to an agglomeration of individuals, each preoccupied, first and foremost, with their own diverging destinies:

The really sad thing is the death of the collective, which weakened little by little with each agricultural failure. That made some people happy, because they saw the chance to get rich from the government's fiasco by trampling on their neighbors. But when the individual realizes his ambitions at the expense of the group, well, that does not make Bonfil a pleasant place to live. (I-63, ejidatario, Bonfil, February 1990)

Mechanized Maize Producer

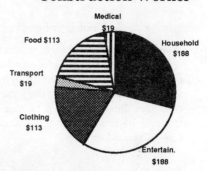

Construction Worker

Business Owner

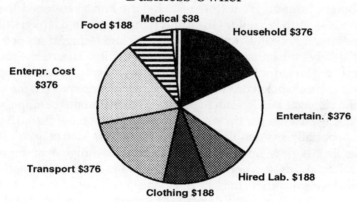

Cattle Rancher

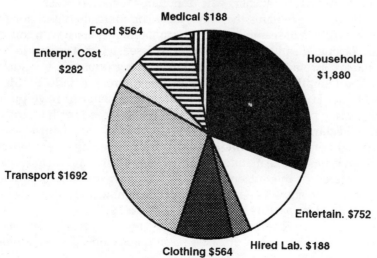

FIGURE 6.6 Average household expenditure estimates by producer, Bonfil, Campeche, 1989 (SOURCE: field interviews)

Subsisting on the Candelaria Frontier

> It seems to me that the government is still preoccupied with the frontier, with the forest. It looks green and fertile, therefore it will produce wonderful crops. Then when reality proves otherwise, the forest makes a convenient grave in which to bury the failure. Campeche is full of this kind of cemetery. But now there is no more forest, no more frontier. Will this mean the end of illusions and the beginning of reality? (I-151, civil servant, Candelaria, March 1990)

Forgotten in the forests, the Candelaria colonists appear to be almost anesthetized to formal economic aspects of the debt and agricultural crises. For them, the crisis began almost thirty years ago, when the government brought them to the Candelaria and abandoned them to survive as best they could. Given the limited commercial agricultural activities in the zone, the contraction of credit and technical support have had relatively little impact. Only a few hundred of the fourteen thousand hectares considered initially to have commercial crop potential are now devoted to mechanized production with credit. Consequently, the majority of the colonists are dependent on two or three hectares of milpa, which yield at most 0.9 ton per hectare of maize and little more than 0.3 ton of beans (especially susceptible to the high humidity). Two crops a year are feasible in this zone, and yields tend to be a little higher in the winter cycle, when less destruction is caused by pests and storms. Nevertheless, at these levels of production, most colonists run out of maize within a few months of harvest and depend for subsistence on cattle and other domestic animals, small backyard gardens, and limited amounts of casual labor for the private ranchers who dominate the local economy.

Cattle rearing remains the only viable commercial activity for those colonists with a little capital or the determination to persist with collective credit societies despite the deception and dissension that appear to be the inevitable concomitants of participation in such groups in the Candelaria. Herds are small, however, except in the colonies Estado de México and Miguel Hidalgo; here almost half of the ejidatarios have pursued cattle rearing on a serious basis, averaging fifteen head per household on twenty-hectare individual parcels supplemented by pasture "leased" from neighbors. Estado de México is also the only colony where concerted attention is paid to the maintenance of sown pasture, and there is considerable interest in the outcome of a FIRA experiment on a local demonstration plot to show the benefits of supplemental feeding of sugarcane and rice flour for pasture extension. This colony sells milk in the town of Candelaria when road conditions permit as well as locally. Despite this initiative, any expansion of cattle rearing activities in the Candelaria colonies will be an uphill struggle. Since the frontier was first opened up, the cattle business has been controlled regionally by a powerful association of local ranchers and merchant middlemen. The colonies are severely disadvantaged in this context by the small scale of their operations, their continuing isolation, and their economic marginality. Often, animals must be killed because of the lack of veterinary care, or sold too young, underfed, and at a loss to the middlemen rather than directly to the Escárcega freezer plant because the household requires money immediately. Most families sell three or four animals a year, receiving 3,200 pesos a kilogram for a prime young bull and 2,500 pesos for a cow if they can afford to sell to the plant and wait several weeks for payment. Even if sales to the middlemen can be avoided, the colonists still tend to loose in transactions with the plant, as differential rates are paid according to the grade of the meat, and the ejidatarios often are either unable to gauge the quality accurately or to argue with the judgement of the assessors. The only other sources of cash income are from petty sales of domestic livestock, eggs, and garden produce or of basic groceries and soft drinks in the converted front rooms or porches of houses. In addition, a few artisans, such as furniture makers, manufacture rustic items for the colonists on order.

The wealthiest households in the two colonies with regular income from cattle and milk sales—fewer than 10 percent—are lucky if they make 2 million pesos a year, and of this amount at least 20 percent must be used to purchase supplementary maize for family consumption and feed (Fig. 6.7). The remainder subsist from milpa that rarely covers household maize needs, surviving on a day-to-day basis from the very limited amount of occasional agricultural labor available, mainly in fencing and pasture maintenance. These households estimate average annual cash income at less than 300,000 pesos a year. This is extreme poverty by Campeche standards, resulting in part from the fact that even almost thirty years after the colonization of the Candelaria, the migrants' knowledge of local conditions and expertise in tropical agriculture does not compare with that of natives. The maguey and nopal cactus seen frequently in the settlement gardens testify to the colonists' yearning for the familiar landscapes of their arid northern homeland, and many still attempt to grow temperate zone crops in their parcels, despite repeated failures. For these poor families, the debt crisis has exacerbated their physical isolation. There is no bus service to the colonies, and the round-trip fare to Candelaria on top of the freight in merchants' trucks has risen to 4,000 pesos. The expense of travel has cut marketing trips from weekly to once monthly, and some colonists have not gone "outside" for several years. Ejidal leaders are unable to travel to Campeche on behalf of the

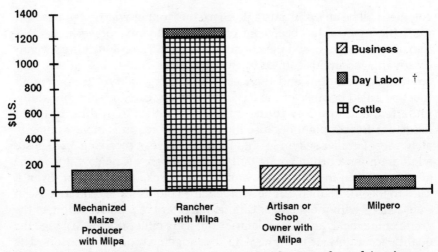

† Day Labor includes credit diarios (cash advances for cultivation labor days) and supplementary income from working family members.

FIGURE 6.7   Average cash income estimates by producer, Candelaria colonies, Campeche, 1989 (SOURCE: field interviews)

members as often as they feel is necessary because it costs $10,000 pesos each way (Fig. 6.8).

The debt crisis also means that the cost of clothing keeps many children out of primary school and, together with the increasing expense of room and board in town, has reduced the number of students pursuing secondary education. Nutrition levels are very poor, reflecting the meager harvests and the reduction of food purchases to essentials such as salt, rice, and pasta. The colonists subsist on a steady diet of these items, tortillas, and chiles, supplemented by an occasional egg and fish if they live close enough to the river. Intestinal diseases and respiratory infections are widespread, but there is little money for medicines and health care beyond the most basic level. A heart attack, a stroke, or an accident in the fields is likely to prove fatal in the absence of transportation to the hospital. The fortunate survivor of a snake bite in the eye or a serious machete wound in the leg will have to live with an scarred socket, an empty trouser leg, or a crude prosthesis. In this context, it is not surprising that consumption of alcohol represents the only recreation for many:

> Life here is not exactly gay. You can walk to the square or the river, have a
> Coke if there are some coins in your pocket, watch the road to see if a truck

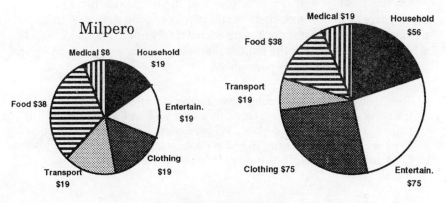

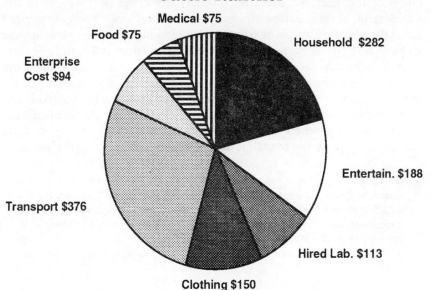

FIGURE 6.8   Average household expenditure estimates by producer, Candelaria colonies, Campeche, 1989 (SOURCE: field interviews)

will pass by, and get drunk on weekends if you can get your hands on some liquor. We meant to have a big party last year for the twenty-fifth anniversary [of the foundation of the colonies], but everybody forgot, I suppose because for us it is nothing to celebrate, being buried here in the forest. (I-107, ejidatario, Estado de México, March 1990)

On the positive side, because many of the original settlers left in the early years of the project, there is still plenty of land available to accommodate the next generation. Youths increasingly opt for casual labor elsewhere in Mexico and in the United States or join the army, however, and these departures are often permanent:

They'll do anything to get out of here. Twelve boys from this colony joined the army last year, because at least they feed you, and ten more got their papers to go to the United States. My sons are in Cancún in construction. They say there is no life here. They don't even want to come home for a visit. They don't help at all. They want to forget us. (I-104, ejidatario, Monclova, March 1990)

The debt crisis has underscored the futility of the whole Candelaria colonization exercise. For the colonists the crisis is their life in the Candelaria, their constant struggle for survival since the government lured them to the Campeche frontier with glowing promises. Most appear to have lost any hope of improving their condition and simply endure from day to day, though some sparks of ambition remain. Even if the debt and agricultural crises should soon come to an end, it seems likely that the colonists will remain stuck in the mud at the end of the road. The Candelaria scheme was the model for two decades of state-planned agricultural development in Campeche's ejidal sector, and its history, in many senses, epitomizes the overall record of achievement of that endeavor:

It all began with the vision of the Candelaria. The reality was far from the vision, but when the government gets an idea that doesn't matter. It's the idea that counts, and convincing people that this idea is the correct way, that it can be done. So really it was only an illusion that there could be agriculture in Campeche. It never really happened. The [debt] crisis made us aware of that. (I-147, professional and former civil servant, Campeche, January 1990)

Notes

1. The Calakmul Biosphere Reserve adjoins the even larger Maya Biosphere Reserve in the Guatemalan Petén (1.32 million hectares), forming part of an international plan for cooperation in the conservation of the natural areas of the border

zone and an ambitious regional project to preserve and enhance the natural, historical, and tourist resources of areas along the "Maya route."

2. The Centro de Investigaciones Históricas y Sociales of the Universidad Autónoma de Campeche played a major role in the creation of the Calakmul Biosphere Reserve and continues to conduct research on environmental and social factors critical to the selection of reserve management strategies. In 1989, an interdisciplinary team from the University of California at Riverside initiated a program of investigation into options for sustainable agriculture and forestry in the Maya realm funded by the MacArthur Foundation.

3. Recent innovative approaches to environmental problems include the *un día sin auto* (a day without a car) program introduced in Mexico City in late 1989 as part of an attempt to clean up the world's most polluted city, and a "debt for trees" swap aiming at reforesting the denuded mountains rimming the Valley of Mexico.

4. La Malinche was the daughter of a Tabascan chief. She was given to Cortés as a concubine shortly after his first landing in Mexico. By letting herself be taken, La Malinche came to symbolize Mexico's own compliance in the conquest—its rape by foreigners, both yesterday and today.

5. Assistance is provided to Guatemalan refugees by the Comisión Mexicana de Ayuda a los Refugiados (the Mexican Commission for Assistance to Refugees—COMAR), funded by the United Nations High Commission for Refugees. There are two resettlement camps in Campeche and a third is under construction. Approximately eleven thousand Guatemalans are accommodated.

6. Yields in first-year milpa rose from 405 kilograms per hectare to 857 kilograms per hectare from 1980 to 1982, while returns to second-year milpa increased from 338 kilograms per hectare to 1068 kilograms per hectare with application of chemical fertilizer by two-thirds of the sample group. Over this period, use of pesticides doubled, being applied by almost half of the milperos in the study. This suggests a relationship between use of pesticide as well as fertilizer and the dramatic increase in yields of second-year milpa, reminiscent of the Carnegie Institution's 1930s experiment near Chichén Itzá, where fifth-year milpa weeded under the ancient method of pulling weeds up completely produced yields exceeding that of the first year (Morley, 1956 [1946]). That is, weed and weed seed eradication may be even more important than soil fertility per se in milpa production.

7. Maize consumption figures for Campeche are based on calculations for a family of six, rather than the average of five members conventional in the earlier literature on the Yucatán Peninsula (Benedict and Steggerda, 1937; Emerson and Kempton, 1935; Morley, 1956 [1946]), but they are proportionally consistent with these early estimates and those of FIRA (1972) and Vogeler (1976) for Campeche. Families in the Maya region of northern Campeche are generally considerably larger, often with six to eight children. It is also common for a married son and his wife to live with his parents and for other adult relatives to live with a nuclear family, making a total of six to twelve members per household. In such cases, half a kilogram per capita of maize a day per member, generated by two or three producers, can be used as a rule of thumb to estimate household needs, including domestic livestock feed.

222 Campesinos and the Debt Crisis

8. Mennonites are a religious sect which originated in the Anabaptist wing of the Protestant Reformation in Switzerland in the first half of the 16th century and spread widely through Central and Eastern Europe, and the Low Countries. They rejected infant baptism and the concept of a state church, believed in nonresistance, and refused to take oaths. As a consequence of this dissidence, persecution by the state has been common. Thus the Mennonites have a history of repeated migrations to remote frontiers in an effort to protect their beliefs and the integrity of their agrarian lifestyle. The ancestors of many of the Mennonites in Mexico today had migrated first to Canada in the 1870s or after World War I. The forefathers of the Campeche Mennonites, however, went directly to Durango from Eastern Europe.

9. Although the Mennonite colonists interviewed were quite open about economic activities in general and specific agricultural enterprises, it was impossible to obtain detailed estimates of household incomes and expenditures.

10. Guatemalans are also employed in excavating the archaeological site at Edzná under a special program of COMAR, with financial support from the United Nations' High Commission for Refugees and Spain. Many Bonfil youths are jealous of the Guatemalans for this reason, since they would like employment close to home at what they consider to be "easy work", with some potential for acquiring a degree of professional skill. The Guatemalans, on the other hand, find the excavations boring.

7

A Way Out

The government has already caught us in its own debt trap. What new snares are they setting now? (I-83, ejidatario, Yohaltún, March 1990)

I don't like to go out in the countryside and see the ruin we caused. We have to do something about it. The government planned this crisis. Can it plan its way out of it? (I-131, civil servant, Campeche, January 1990)

The term ejido is derived from the Latin word for "exit." In feudal Spain, the ejido was a small, unoccupied area of common land located just outside the town gate. In colonial Mexico, the application was broadened to include a wider range of Indian communal lands as part of the Spanish policy of preserving the indigenous land tenure system to a degree (Simpson, 1937; Zaragoza and Macías, 1980). It is not clear, however, whether the colonial ejido embraced all of the communal agricultural lands of the indigenous community (Simpson, 1937) or was devoted to a wide range of public activities excluding crop cultivation (de Ibarrola, 1975) or was intended primarily for pasture (Mendieta y Nuñez, 1977). In any event, it appears to have derived from the pre-Columbian Aztec *altepetlalli*, the people's land, and therefore it could be argued that the idea of the ejido was highly appropriate for application to the unique form of peasant land tenure resulting from the nation's revolutionary struggle.

The modern Mexican ejido connotes restitution of lands and liberties lost—an "exit" or way out of continuing poverty for peasants through state-directed planned agricultural modernization, after land redistribution per se proved to be insufficient to stimulate economic dynamism and fulfil the revolutionary promise of social justice in the countryside. This dual image of the ejido as the ongoing instrument of salvation for the peasant and the state as rural liberator, disseminating the bounty of modern farming technology, has been tarnished by more than two decades of crisis. Even the most ardent agrarian populist has difficulty defending the ejido of today as the instrument of the campesinos' deliverance. The question is whether it is the ejido itself that is at fault or the mistaken policies of the government toward the peasantry or both—and whether, indeed, the two can be divorced. One thing is clear—much will have to change in the countryside before the ejido can guarantee the campesinos an escape from marginality.

Campesinos, the Crises, and the State

In Campeche the ejido was little more than a geographic location for more than fifty years after the revolution. Commercial agriculture was limited to small-scale cultivation of relict plantation crops, the legacy of the export economy established early in the colonial era, as Campeche continued to depend on the exploitation of one or two natural resources right up to the present in a smooth, almost seamless progression of boom-and-bust cycles, while the domestic economy stagnated. Agriculture had until recently a low priority, and the Maya campesinos were left to make milpa in the forests as their ancestors had before them except when summoned by the state to pay political dues to their benefactor for receipt of ejidal lands.

This tranquility (or economic inertia depending on one's perspective) ceased abruptly after 1970, when peasants became the beneficiaries of a barrage of rural development projects. No longer just a place on a map or a block of votes, the ejido was a convenient framework for the modernization of peasant agriculture, as the rural development business became the dominant boom at the local level for bureaucrats, brokers, and beneficiaries. The movement toward collective production units in all ejidal undertakings funded by official bank credit made for more efficient planning, mechanization, and provision and management of other key development inputs, at least on paper. Collective organization also made it easier to manipulate the ejidatarios and to assign blame for failures to the "human element." Even those agricultural development agents who admit to significant government errors tend to maintain that the "backwardness" of the peasantry has been a major obstacle to planned agricultural change. In their eyes, the Candelaria colonies failed because the colonists lacked initiative and neglected the physical infrastructure; the Camino Real and Los Chenes small irrigation units achieved disappointing results because of dissension and because the members opted for hand labor over mechanization in order to get credit for more labor days; Nilchi's maize project lacked dynamism because the ejidatarios were unable to organize efficiently; the Bonfil agribusiness enterprise collapsed because of "bad politics" and the expectation that "the government should give them everything on a plate" (I-131, civil servant, Campeche,

October 1985); and the demise of rice production in Yohaltún owed much to the peasants' apathy.

Thus, from the perspective of the bureaucracy, the default of two-thirds of Campeche's ejidatarios in 1989 was a function of laziness, obstreperousness, irresponsibility, or reluctance to modernize. For many civil servants the success of the Mennonites confirms the validity of this interpretation: they made a profit from mechanized maize when neighboring ejidos were failing, because of hard work, good husbandry, and not making a career of the industry of disasters. It is ironic that the ejidatarios' unwillingness to accept responsibility for their debts is seen as the major obstacle to success when one of the most obvious effects of two decades of government intervention has been the progressive erosion of the ejido's decision-making autonomy.

From the campesinos' viewpoint, the projects initiated by the government over the past two decades have failed because of the usual empty official promises, unrealistic goals, failure to provide the necessary agricultural inputs in sufficient quantities and on a timely basis, concentration on low-value staples on marginal land, and lack of understanding of the actual agricultural possibilities and constraints compared with the peasant in the field. Campesinos recognize that the Mennonites' success owes much to sheer hard work, but they argue that even more than this it is attributable to their ability to make their own decisions—to take advantage of credit and other state-provided inputs when and as they wish—rather than depending on "the system" for their daily tortillas:

> The Mennonites have the luck of not being an ejido. Thus, as owners they have the freedom to farm as they want, while the ejido is the creature of the government, the instrument of its will. Belonging to the social sector means powerlessness and poverty, until the government realizes at last that you can't dictate to nature or to the farmers who must make it bloom. (I-7, ejidatario, Pomuch, December 1989)

If the keys to successful peasant agriculture are production autonomy, local flexibility, and independent initiative, then diminishing state interventionism under national austerity should have enabled at least some peasants to benefit from the demise of the industry of disasters if not from the enterprise itself.

The Bottom Line of the Industry of Disasters: Benefits and Costs

In immediate financial terms, some Campeche ejidatarios evidently have profited substantially from the modernization initiative. These gains have been derived either directly from specific state ventures or, more often, from increased opportunities on a local or regional scale stimulated by planned change of this magnitude. Thus, the Pomuch small irrigation project members, despite continuing vulnerability to erratic weather patterns as a result of well-system malfunctions, find that in general their lives are getting better: "Now, we know more or less where tomorrow's tortillas are coming from" (I-4, ejidatario, Pomuch, December 1989). At the same time, many Bonfil ejidatarios have benefited both from the initial large rice dividends that provided capital for personal business enterprises and, indirectly, from the subsequent failure of agribusiness to provide sufficient income and labor to support all the members, which prompted the majority to seek more lucrative alternative income possibilities. Thus, despite the inefficiencies of the industry of disasters and the inflationary pressures of the debt crisis, for the majority life in Bonfil and Pomuch is more secure than before.

For the ejidatarios in the Yohaltún rice zone and the Candelaria colonists, however, the outcome of planned agricultural development has been planned poverty. In Yohaltún, the beneficiaries were by design merely an accessory to the state farming enterprise. As the government retreated from rice cultivation, the ejidatarios were left with an exhausted wasteland suitable only for cattle or cane. Lacking experience with both, the majority have abandoned all hope of viable agriculture and have joined the exodus to Campeche. Similarly, the Candelaria colonists never had a chance to realize their dreams of a mechanized garden in the jungle; funding was cut almost immediately after both the state and the settlers recognized the obstacles to transforming the tropical forests.

With respect to the environmental context, it is clear that the effort to convert Campeche into a mechanized granary has seriously and sometimes irreversibly depleted the state's ecological capital. Environmental degradation has resulted from the use of heavy machinery that strips and compacts the thin topsoil, lack of crop rotation, attempts to grow inappropriate crops, increasing use of agrochemicals, and, above all, extensive clearing, which triggers microclimatic changes, accelerates soil erosion, and hastens fertility decline while eliminating the natural habitats of the previously diverse flora and fauna. The creation of the Calakmul Biosphere Reserve was an important step in recognizing the extent to which Mexico's forests have been endangered by indiscriminate cutting and clearing, but the reserve is far from virgin land, and the area surrounding it is Campeche's last frontier. Given these circumstances, together with the relative lack of respect for the natural order exhibited by the immigrant colonists predominant in this zone, it is debatable whether an effective management plan for sustainable land use can be enforced.

In terms of social justice, the extent to which the ejidatarios have bene-fited from state-directed agricultural modernization is questionable. The agrarian bureaucracy argues that even where planned development has resulted in severe depletion of the agricultural base, the ejidatarios have profited not only from the few years of good harvest dividends but also from the learning experience with respect to the use of modern farm-ing technology and the mechanics of agricultural credit. It is true that Campeche campesinos have come a long way from the simple Maya milperos or modest frontier colonists of the 1960s. Both the level of formal education and functional literacy have increased dramatically, partly as a result of the increased necessity for paper work in the modernized ejido. The bureaucratization of agriculture means that many ejidatarios have become familiar with situations that used to intimidate them. The peasant who listened with incomprehension to the agronomist in the project field twenty years ago now joins the numerous delegations of ejidatarios demanding action in government offices. However, this apparent change in the peasant role in the agricultural development business tends to be costly in time, and the discourse of such encounters is still largely one-way—transmission of already formulated plans and programs or charges and countercharges about omissions and failures—rather than free exchange of viewpoint. Most harmful, in the long run, to peasant agriculture in Campeche has been the inculcation in ejidatarios of an ethos of failure and fraud as a result of the industry of disasters.

This syndrome owes much to the government's virtual neglect of the ejido for more than half a century as well as to the shortcomings of the agricultural modernization effort. Consequently, many ejidatarios feel that credit and other agricultural supports are their due, irrespective of the harvest outcome:

> Agriculture with credit is our job. In fact, credit is our pay for being ejidatarios, a subsidy that is our right because the government failed to help us before and because the program is failing now. Now, if they want to suspend these payments, they will have to find another way to give us the funds. Really, we don't care whether agriculture succeeds or fails as long as we get the money. In fact, failure is less work for everybody. (I-82, ejidatario, Yohaltún, March 1990)

> Even though rice is failing, we can't just abandon the ejidatarios. We have to find some way to guarantee them a certain income. We will have to find some other program. I don't think PRONASOL will do the job, because there is not enough money involved. The ejidatarios expect more, and they won't pay back the money because they won't agree that it is only a loan, not a wage. (I-131, civil servant, Campeche, March 1990)

Thus, for many Campeche campesinos the agricultural crisis is the direct result of increased state intervention in the ejido and its failure to fulfil the revolutionary promises of land and liberty. Planned development projects have brought at best minimal increases in production, achieved in limited areas at high cost. The greater the scale and scope of operations, the more government decision making has displaced local initiative. Thus, at one end of the spectrum, small-irrigation-project members obtained some leeway to determine the organization if not the content of production after the government's initial enthusiasm for the scheme evaporated, while the Yohaltún ejidatarios were acknowledged laborers in rice cultivation on their own lands from the scheme's inception. At the same time, compulsory collectivization of production has proved divisive, and the failure of the projects to generate full-time employment has advanced the proletarianization they were intended to curb. The majority of ejidatarios have become more vulnerable to economic and political forces beyond their control as a result of increasing dependence on government initiative, particularly since the debt crisis translated marginal agricultural operations into outright deficit production. The Campeche case studies indicate that the ability of ejidatarios to transcend this institutionalized dependency in an era of transition to a free market economy depends on the specific historical, local, and household circumstances and, in particular, on the type and degree of ejidal participation in government agricultural programs.

The Debt Crisis in the Countryside:
Winners and Losers

Given the recency of state intervention in peasant farming in Campeche and the almost immediate recognition of it as an industry of disasters, it is logical that peasants by and large see the debt crisis as merely the latest phase in the government's continuing strategy of sacrificing rural to urban interests. While they are firmly integrated into the national economy, agrarian policy has driven them to its fringes. The net result of two decades of state-planned ejidal development in Campeche has been the creation of a quasi-modernized subsistence sector of marginal peasants, accustomed to large subsidies and dependent on ill-conceived government initiatives. This sector is far from homogeneous, however, and the debt crisis has further accelerated processes of socioeconomic differentiation.

In Bonfil, the regional prototype of the large-scale, capital- and technology-intensive model of state agricultural development, the onset of the debt crisis and the concomitant failure of the rice project have freed many ejidatarios from the restraints on independent initiative imposed by government intervention so that they can make their own way as relatively affluent ranchers, semiskilled laborers, and entrepreneurs. At the same time, for members lacking the capacity to recognize or pursue remunerative individual opportunities the demise of the ejidal rice enterprise and the debt crisis have meant increasing insecurity and poverty as partial proletarians dependent on both infrasubsistence staple cultivation and precarious wage labor. Thus in many senses the relative success of individuals in Bonfil has been attained at the expense of their peers—consequent on the demise of the collective ideal (Table 7.1).

In Pomuch, a project format predicated on small-scale technology transfer has served by and large to shield its participants from the worst effects of the debt crisis. The majority of members have been able to make an increasingly secure living from agriculture because they have good soil, sufficient land per capita, and functioning (if inefficient) wells, and, more important, because they have reorganized to reduce dissension and diversified to minimize their vulnerability to the vicissitudes of the market and the weather.

The Hecelchakán Mennonites have flourished under the debt crisis. Newcomers to Campeche, they quickly learned how to farm to maximum effect in their new environment by dint of hard work, a large labor pool, and by the combination of the best Maya milpa practices with their own proven technologies. They were also quick to see how they could fill in the gaps as the local economy contracted. By "minding their own business," they make a comfortable income from the sale of maize, dairy products, and skills while producing the bulk of their consumption needs. Aloof from contextual crisis and free of the ideological and institutional baggage of the ejido, they have been able to use the Mexican agricultural system to their advantage.

For the Candelaria colonists, abandoned by the government on the frontier, the main impact of the debt crisis has been increasingly extreme poverty, deepening isolation, and permanent out-migration by the younger generation.

Although all sectors of Nilchi's producers have felt the stress of the debt crisis, the lives of mango or vegetable growers at one end of the economic spectrum and of traditional milperos at the other have been affected the least—the former because of the relatively high value of their products even under inflation and without reliable markets and the latter because of their self-sufficiency and the availability of opportunities for supplementary casual labor. The main casualties of the crisis have been the members of the mechanized maize project, for whom the only alternative seems to be to go back to making milpa.

In Yohaltún, the transition from state farming to ejidal responsibility for rice production envisioned by the project's planners coincided with the

TABLE 7.1 Peasants, Proletarians, and the Debt Crisis in Campeche

Category	Type Case	Characteristics	Crisis Impact	Dissolution Trend
1. *Milperos*	Nilchi	Traditional slash-and-burn maize cultivators on individual *ejido*.	Retreat to self-sufficiency. Excluded from bank credit programs. Increased use of fertilizer. Greatly decreased consumer spending. Increasing numbers.	*Reinforcement of peasant status.*
2. Frontier colonists	Candelaria	Planned resettlement of landless laborers from the north-central Mexican uplands in 1963. Development goal: balanced commercial production of foods, cattle, and lumber.	Continued decrease in government support, minimal since 1970. Increased dependence on slash-and-burn agriculture after credit cutbacks. Incipient cattle raising. Intensified isolation as a result of escalating travel costs. Growing outmigration by younger generation.	*Reinforcement of peasant status*, partially offset by second-generation outmigration and a regional "cattle-ization" trend.
3. Mennonite "classic peasants"	Hecelchakán Colonies	Frontier colonies established as "small private properties" after 1982 as part of the generational "hiving" cycle of traditional Mennonite communities.	Insulated from crisis by self-sufficiency and self-segregation strategy. Profited from crisis via commercial maize production, filling vacuum created by retreat to subsistence production of other peasant groups. Increasingly provide semi-skilled labor and services to surrounding communities.	Deliberate *maintenance of classic* communitarian *peasant life-style* focused on amassing capital for the next generation of colonies.

4. Bank peasants	Camino Real small irrigation projects	Intermediate-technology-transfers for Maya peasants since 1970. Development goal: to reduce outmigration via capital-intensive production of high-value crops.	Marginal scale, concentration on low-value staples, malfunctioning infrastructure, and escalating production costs promoted bank loan default and increased partial proletarianization. Recent government emphasis on fruit and vegetable culture on rehabilitated irrigation units may reduce proletarianization and second-generation outmigration to Campeche city and Cancun, Q.R.	Increased partial *proletarianization* and long-term second generation outmigration. Probable *repeasantization* of those currently in default via transfer to new PRONASOL program for marginal staple cultivators.
5. *Ejidal* agri-business peasants	Bonfil	Large-scale agricultural resettlement project for landless laborers from central and northern Mexico, initiated in 1973. Development goal: balanced, heavily mechanized, diversified agriculture and cattle ranching, transformed to rice concentration in the late 1970s.	Rice failure prompted new emphasis on individual cattle ranching, and/or initiation of small business, or intermediate-term outmigration and non-agricultural employment in Campeche city.	*Depeasantization* via formation of incipient commercial rancher, entrepreneurial, and proletarian classes.
6. State agri-business peasants	Yohaltún	Large-scale state-directed rice cultivation on collective *ejidos*. Development goal: to transform Campeche into Mexico's new 'rice bowl' in the late 1970s.	Rice failure resulted in 70% permanent outmigration to Campeche city, while remainder retreat to subsistence cultivation. Incipient cattle ranching.	Complete *proletarianization* of outmigrants and *repeasantization* of the remainder.

first impact of the debt crisis, and this, combined with Campeche's fixation on becoming Mexico's rice bowl, resulted in a further seven years of deficit production. As a result, the ejidatarios have been left with exhausted lands and no firm plans for alternatives, and the majority have abandoned agriculture altogether. The calculated concentration on short-term profit in Yohaltún became an exercise in deliberate environmental destruction and a premeditated sacrifice of social welfare to production quotas.

Campeche peasants who have emerged from the crises with both optimism and options intact include those who operate virtually outside the institutionalized agricultural system, using it to their advantage rather than being used (the Mennonites, Nilchi's milperos), those who have learned to hedge and diversify without relying solely on government initiatives (Pomuch), participants in a few small but relatively high-value orchard or vegetable operations (Nilchi, Pomuch), those with sufficient experience of modern agricultural alternatives, marketable skills, self-confidence, and the entrepreneurship to follow their own inclinations (Bonfil), and individual peasants throughout the state who have seized a variety of opportunities to profit at the expense of their peers through fraud, usury or brokerage. The losers are those who had all their eggs in the government basket and perceive no viable agricultural options now that they have been virtually orphaned by the state (Nilchi's mechanized maize growers, Yohaltún rice project members). Neither winners nor losers under the debt crisis but long-term victims of the state's strategy of experimenting with human lives in the guise of agricultural development are the Candelaria colonists, landless laborers made subsistence agriculturalists a quarter of a century ago and still scratching in the dwindling forests simply to survive.

Strategies for Survival

In addition to stress on agricultural operations as producers, Campeche campesinos have suffered under debt crisis inflation and austerity as consumers. Peasant life has been affected by rising public transportation fares, the 70 percent decline in the real value of the minimum wage since 1983, and increased prices for basic consumer goods—always substantially higher in the country than in the city. Even the very few campesinos whose annual incomes are equivalent to full employment at minimum wage are unable to purchase half of the items in the officially regulated basic food basket, which does not factor in necessities such as transportation, clothing, and educational expenses. Campesinos have cut down drastically on meat and other animal protein consumption, restricted their intake of junk food and soft drinks, curtailed shopping, recreational, and agriculture-related excursions, and stopped buying clothes and shoes except when absolutely essential. In some areas school enrollments have dropped, particularly at the secondary level, because families are unable to afford the uniforms and school supplies and the transportation or room and board. Purchase of major consumer items continues on a somewhat reduced level, however, as items formerly considered to be luxuries such as televisions, stereos, or bicycles increasingly are regarded as necessities. Alcohol consumption appears to have increased, perhaps partly in response to the constriction of other modern-sector purchases and diversions.

One of the most alarming trends in rural Campeche over the past decade is the noticeable deterioration in rural nutrition. The debt crisis should not receive all the blame for this decline, however, because rural diets have been worsening steadily over the past two decades as a result of the growing preference for soft drinks, canned foods, white bread, and packaged snacks and the increasing tendency to give priority to purchases of major consumer items over foodstuffs. In addition, the repercussions of deteriorating diets for general rural health conditions have been offset to some extent by the expansion of social security medical coverage to ejidatarios working in the modernized agricultural sector.

Campeche campesinos seem to accept the current stress on household budgets with relative equanimity, as one of the temporary downswings to which they are well accustomed. Instead of collective political mobilization in protest, the crisis has triggered a series of adaptations at the household level that tend to involve manipulation of long-standing strategies for economic survival rather than the invention of new ways of dealing with adversity (Grindle, 1989). Thus campesinos are tightening their belts, growing more crops using traditional technology without credit, seeking additional casual labor if it is available, and revising their priorities.

Political protest about these hardships is not considered beyond traditional institutionalized response. For the majority of Campeche campesinos, "politics" means first and foremost the PRI, which is still believed to be at least cognizant of its debt to the countryside. In this sense, the PRI is seen almost as a separate entity, over and above the specific members of the current government, and thus somewhat divorced from its failures: "The party has the finest minds, the most powerful men in Mexico, but they are not good at selecting the best men for the government—only jackasses and thieves get the jobs" (I-4, ejidatario, Pomuch, December 1989). At the local level, however, the party and its official peasant organs tend to be ignored or viewed as merely mouthpieces for empty political rhetoric. A few of the more politicized campesinos have joined the Partido del Frente Cardenista de Reconstrucción Nacional (the Cardenist Front for National Reconstruction), an activist party oriented to protest marches and land invasions. Others sympathize with the national aspirations of the Partido de la Revolución Democratica (the Democratic Revolutionary Party), which represents a coalition of the reform wing of the PRI and a variety of opposition factions created to challenge the ruling party's 1988 presidential candidate under the leadership of Cauhtémoc Cárdenas, the son of the former president. Most Campeche campesinos see this alternative as "more of the same," however, despite the leader's illustrious name, and tend to regard any kind of organized politics as a waste of time.

At a more immediate level, "politics" means ejidal leadership and the competition with other ejidos for a share of the shrinking agrarian spoils. Until recently, ejidal leaders tended to be either old guard, favored by local party minions and often deeply involved in the co-optation and corruption inherent in these networks, or political innocents vulnerable to manipulation. Modernized ejidal agriculture requires literacy, knowledge of accounting, experience with the agricultural development business, and the ability to represent the membership's interest with clarity and force in the interminable meetings with government agencies. A talent for fraud, however, is still seen by many ejidatarios as a leadership advantage in view of the perceived necessity for negotiating failure. This kind of maneuver can easily backfire; a leader who cheats on behalf of his ejido may well cheat the membership for his own benefit. Inevitably, this type of climate fosters disruptive factionalism, with the result that many ejidatarios prefer to steer clear of involvement in ejidal business altogether.

Regional associations of ejidal producers offer another potential avenue for political action, but generally protests are sporadic, short-lived, and related to specific issues. For example, in December 1989 a group representing the association of maize growers of the Camino Real and Los Chenes marched on the governor's palace to protest BANRURAL's refusal to renegotiate the ejidos' defaults. The police were called, and several ejidatarios were injured slightly in the ensuing melée. Despite widespread publicity, few campesinos were aware of this incident, and those who were showed little sympathy for the protesters, whom they considered stupid to have wasted their time on a fruitless exercise. Evidently, the adversities brought by the agricultural crisis and the debt crisis have done little to stimulate widespread rural mobilization in Campeche, as each household continues to cope with hardship in its own way:

A family's problems are private. You don't want your neighbors to know. And you certainly don't want the authorities to find out your name, to have something to use against you. That's why it's better to mind your own business, to stay at home and keep your mouth shut. That's the best way to defend yourself and your family. (I-23, ejidatario, Tinún, March 1990)

By and large, most Campeche campesinos have managed to "defend themselves" reasonably well up to this point, but there is a strong sense that this state of affairs cannot continue much longer. Furthermore, the debt crisis, together with increasing exposure to the mass media and the forays of family members in search of work, have heightened campesinos' awareness of their vulnerability to forces beyond their control. The government at least is a known entity, predictable in its very arbitrariness. Thus, while many campesinos welcome the retreat of the state from the farmer's field, others fear being abandoned to those external forces.

Depeasantization and Repeasantization

The history of state-planned intervention in ejidal agriculture in Campeche is relatively short, but the processes initiated or accelerated during this period will long outlast the specific policies and programs that fostered them. Before state intervention, rural-urban migration was only incipient, mainly confined to the more densely settled northern Maya zone. By 1990, it had spread to many regions of Campeche, particularly where the failure of large-scale planned agricultural developments has been most spectacular. Twenty years ago, only a small percentage of campesinos were accustomed to supplementing their milpa with a few days of casual agricultural labor in the vicinity of their homes. Today the majority of Maya campesino households have at least one family member resident in Cancún or the city of Campeche. Native Campechanos still rarely leave the peninsula in search of employment, while ejidatarios from the failed rice projects of Yohaltún and Bonfil or from stagnant frontier settlements such as in the Candelaria range more widely throughout Mexico or the United States as migrant agricultural laborers as they did before coming to Campeche as colonists.

The failure of planned ejidal modernization to create viable agricultural enterprises and provide full employment, together with the depression of the staple crop sector, has been directly responsible in many cases for the movement toward the cities. Changing aspirations among the peasantry are also important in this exodus. With increasing access to higher education, the spread of the mass media, and decreasing physical isolation because of improved transportation systems, the sons and daughters of Campeche campesinos no longer automatically expect to spend their lives in the countryside simply because they were born there. The debt crisis was an additional spur in many regions: "Why stay there and go hungry when you can come to the city and go hungry but see something of life?" (I-126, laborer, Campeche, November 1989).

Depeasantization has clearly been accelerated by the social and economic changes in the countryside over the last two decades. For the majority of campesinos, however, the process falls short of proletarianization; it is only in areas of absolute agricultural failure that permanent out-migration and total dependence on wage labor have become the norm for the full range of the economically active population. Furthermore, it is solely in the most depressed and remote areas such as the Candelaria where significant numbers of the younger generation leave home for good and discard any future prospects of working ejidal land. In the rest of the state, proletarianization remains partial and cyclical, as family members leave to work elsewhere for a while, then return to share the normal life of the rural household.

Depeasantization in Campeche differs substantially from that in many other regions of rural Mexico. In contrast to the situation in the center and north of the country, Campeche still has still sufficient land for its current population (although not necessarily in the immediate vicinity of existing settlements), and the limited development of the local economy restricts opportunities for wage labor available relatively close to home. Furthermore, distance from the main markets for casual labor in Mexico and the United States and regional separatism combine to make migrant labor an option only for colonists from areas with a tradition of such excursions. Campeche also differs from areas of rural Mexico where labor migration has become a fact of life in that remittance income is generally not an important element in the survival of peasant households. Campesino families do not expect to receive significant support from adult children employed locally or elsewhere in the peninsula as wage laborers or even as professionals if they live away from home. In fact, it is quite common for campesino households to continue to support adult unmarried children indirectly by raising their offspring. The few households with members working in distant regions of Mexico or in the United States for extended periods or on a permanent basis may receive regular financial contributions, but these are likely to diminish or cease altogether within a few years of the migrants' departure.

In recent years, depeasantization is beginning to be offset to a certain extent by repeasantization. For example, in many parts of the Camino Real and Los Chenes, ejidatarios who a decade ago cultivated maize with tractors and credit in large clear-cuts made by heavy machinery now work smaller areas within these tracts without loans and by hand, relying on digging sticks, machetes, and burning to sow the crop and control the brush. In Nilchi, the mechanized maize group, defeated by poor soil and inevitable loan default each year, plan to abandon the project land altogether and go back to making milpa in the pockets of more fertile land on the hillsides, as in this community the store of traditional skills and native seed has not been lost, as has been the case in many neighboring ejidos. Meanwhile, milperos who had remained aloof from the mechanization movement but had taken advantage of credit for digging-stick cultivation with fertilizer and pesticides now work without official support, discontinuing use of pesticides and herbicides but considering fertilizer essential.

These adaptations may prove to be only a short-term response to crisis, readily reversible if profit margins for peasant crops improve substantially. Even so, the new agricultural policies of the Salinas administration exhibit a clear bias toward the most economically viable ejidos. The severely decapitalized and often demoralized casualties of the industry of disasters in regions such as Campeche, where agricultural modernization has been more fiction than reality, are unlikely to be able to join the ranks of market-competitive peasants in the foreseeable future. This disadvantaged position is likely to be reinforced by interim incentive programs such as PRONASOL, because the majority will have no alternative but to apply their interest-free loans to staple crop cultivation. In essence, contrary to the government's proclaimed intent, this strategy implies the de facto repeasantization, at least in the short term, of those who have failed to perform satisfactorily in state agricultural modernization programs. In other words, the only assistance that the majority of Campeche peasants can expect from the government in the immediate future is likely to recreate subsistence household units relying on low-value staples cultivated in the traditional way.

Campeche campesinos clearly have good reason to be concerned about the legacy of the crises of agriculture and debt. In particular, there is uncertainty whether the state, which in large measure created these crises, will or can do anything to improve prospects for less-favored farmers, given its failures. There is, however, a general sense that some gains have been made—that a better future is still possible as long as the government allows peasants the freedom to farm as best they can without discontinuing all supports for marginal producers:

> You can see that for most people the quality of life in the countryside is better than before. We are less isolated, more in touch, with greater access to services and, in your house, an asbestos roof, a cement floor. We may complain, but who would want to go back to the old days? What concerns us is what the government is going to do next. Up until now, they have made chaos out of agriculture. We can't afford for them to screw up again. There isn't much left to ruin! Now they owe us at least the chance to try ourselves. (I-21, Tinún, March 1990)

The Future of Peasant Agriculture

Campesinos have a very practical and immediate view of the production process, the constraints on their operations, and their realistic options. Asked what might be done to improve peasant agriculture, they reply that credit should be more flexible, interest rates lower, crop prices higher, inputs reasonably priced and readily available at the appropriate time in the agricultural cycle, government agencies more efficient and less corrupt, marketing, transportation, and storage made a priority, infrastructure maintained, appropriate new technologies sought and delivered with adequate support, and new, more remunerative agriculture complexes, adapted to the state's tropical ecological niches, identified. Most important, the agrarian bureaucracy should not only acknowledge but learn from the local experience of farmers.

These goals are substantially compatible with the spirit of the agricultural reforms initiated by the Salinas administration, although the development agencies assign them different priorities according to their various mandates. In particular, agencies at the state level seem confident that significant progress can be made in several of these areas in short order; decentralization of agricultural decision making may allow state agencies to learn from and correct past mistakes, incorporating recent agricultural research on a Campeche-specific basis. Despite the magnitude of the undertaking, many state agrarian officials seem enthusiastic about their new role. Their task tends to be restricted, however, to a technical level and to target sectors rather than being an attempt to transform the peasant condition:

> When we worked for the ministry [of agriculture] in the 1960s we really felt that we were doing something worthwhile, out in the country every day, teaching the campesinos everything, how to progress. There is nothing like that now, just a little bit of technical advice. The bureaucracy today lacks humanity and understanding of campesino culture. They don't realize the importance of what the campesinos know about agriculture here. (I-147, professional, Campeche, January 1990)

Current enthusiasm is due in part to the optimism generated by the Salinas reforms—some bureaucrats being inspired to quote the president's latest "sayings"—but perhaps largely to the recency of state agency entry into the agricultural development business. At the state level, the illusions of the neophyte agrarian bureaucrats remain relatively untarnished, aided by the fact that they tend to be much better paid than their federal counterparts.

In the state agricultural development strategy for Campeche, in conformity with national policy, intensification and rationalization of production now take precedence over indiscriminate expansion of the cultivated area. For rice this means contraction of the crop area to the river zone and probable concentration on irrigated cultivation, which would increase profit margins substantially by improving both yields and reliability of production. For maize the emphasis is on new varieties of hybrid seed. The Centro de Investigaciones Agrícolas de la Península de Yucatán (the Center of Agricultural Research for the Yucatán Peninsula) recently announced two new drought-resistant hybrids, one intended for mechanized production and one for milpa cultivation. These varieties are expected to provide yields of 3 tons per hectare, triple the current average production in the area (*Diario de Yucatán*, 23 September 1990). Under ideal conditions, field experiments have achieved as much as 5–6 tons per hectare—impressive results given the minimal budgets that government agricultural research agencies have been allocated over the past decade. Because Campeche has relatively little soil suitable for mechanized cultivation of maize and other staples, considerably lower yields can be expected from the new varieties in much of the state. There is also some concern that the intensification drive will fall into the same trap as previous productivity efforts, with the objective of obtaining the highest possible yields per hectare overriding prudent soil conservation practices.

In addition to intensification, state plans for future agricultural development include a new emphasis on regional specialization, again in keeping with changing national policy. Thus, in addition to the belated recognition that rice should be confined to the river zone, mechanized maize production with credit is to be restricted to the most appropriate soils in the northern Camino Real and Los Chenes districts, and cultivation of beans as a commercial proposition has been abandoned. A particular effort is being made to determine the best agricultural options for each region of the state. The former rice zones in the center of Campeche are to be converted to cattle rearing, raised-bed maize cultivation, and possibly sugarcane. In the south, inland from the rice zone, expansion of cattle is being fostered on former frontier lands, to be backed up by increased emphasis on breed optimization and pasture management research if funds permit. In the north, fruit and vegetable production is being expanded under the Programa de Producción Intensivo en Unidades de Riego (the Intensive Production in Irrigation Units Program). In this area, export-grade production of tomatoes, mangos, and citrus in particular is being encouraged in ejidos, since these high-value crops could earn significant dividends for peasants currently dependent on marginal maize cultivation. This effort requires a large investment in rehabilitation of irrigation facilities and maintenance of the functioning units. Extensive technical support for vegetable growers will also be essential, in view of the vulnerability of tomatoes in the humid tropics to pests and diseases. Numerous producers in Yucatán have already been forced out of production, temporarily at least, by the white fly. A further concern is that if the fruit and vegetable program is successful it may reinforce the tendency toward dependence on one or two exports that has characterized Campeche's economy since the colonial era. Thus, rather than stimulating regional agricultural dynamism, fruit and tomato exports may become the only viable sector while the rest of the agricultural economy continues to stagnate.

The dangers of an export-skewed economy are widely recognized in Campeche, at least in theory. In particular, one would expect that the vulnerability resulting from single-crop reliance had been underscored by the recent failure of rice, but the glint in the eyes of agronomists in the new fruit and vegetable program suggests this lesson still has not been internalized institutionally. As long as the agrarian bureaucracy is more concerned with becoming Mexico's premier producer of some crop or other than with improving the vitality of the agricultural base, continued failure is likely on both counts:

> A real problem in agricultural planning in Campeche is this yearning to be number one in some crop, when it is safer to be number ten in a range of products. Perhaps this is because we still lack confidence where Mexico [City] is concerned. We want to be the good boys and come up with our tons, and we want to do better than Yucatán. Or maybe we just want Mexico to know that Campeche exists, that we are good at something. But we have a long way to go before can achieve this position, because really we have to start agriculture from scratch all over again after the disasters. (I-136, businessman and former civil servant, Campeche, January, 1990)

Senior staff and rank-and-file agronomists employed locally by the federal agricultural agencies seem considerably less optimistic than their state-level peers about Campeche's future prospects and, indeed, about the outlook for Mexican agriculture in general. In the main seasoned veterans of the government's campaign to modernize ejidal farming, these civil servants have become habituated to unanticipated obstacles and other frustrations arising from the vast gap between plans designed in the office and the reality in the field, as well as the complexity of structural impediments to comprehensive reform: "It's no use targeting one or two key reforms. For example, raising the guaranteed prices [for staples] won't help the ejido. It's much more complicated than that. There are a million historical and structural factors involved" (I-139, civil servant, Campeche, March, 1990). Inured to malfeasance by both politicians and agrarian institutions, these veterans tend to be somewhat cynical about any official pronouncements of sweeping change in the government's modus operandi in the countryside: "Words won't increase production" (I-139, civil servant, Campeche, March 1990).

In this context, although the abolition of ANAGSA, the restructuring of BANRURAL, and the elimination of field inspectors are perceived to

be essential reforms that are long overdue, they are not regarded as necessarily a harbinger of a corruption-free, dynamic future for agriculture:
"These measures aren't going to solve anything, because corruption will
just find new channels as long as agriculture fails to pay a living wage to
all depending on it" (I-140, civil servant, Campeche, January 1990). Rather,
they are seen to be the product of economic pragmatism and political
expediency—part of the drive to stimulate production and impress the
international financial community in general and the United States in particular with Mexico's determination to clean house. Furthermore, even
those bureaucrats who admit the probable sincerity of recent reforms
doubt that enough can be done quickly enough to produce basic structural
change that will endure beyond the current presidency:

> The problems run too deep, through every aspect of the agrarian structure,
> and too many interests are involved. The president is surrounded by these
> dinosaurs at the highest levels, so he can't do too much too quickly. An
> attack on one or two bad elements in the system won't achieve much at this
> point. It is only symbolic of the desire to change. But you have to start some-
> time, somewhere. (I-136, businessman and former civil servant, Campeche,
> March 1991)

Two controversial issues in particular are seen by the federal agrarian
bureaucracy as requiring resolution before fundamental change in agrarian structure can be achieved: the extent to which the nation should
attempt to feed itself and the future of the ejido. Opinions are divided
with respect to the economic rationality of the government's continuing
preoccupation, albeit less fanatical than in some previous administra-
tions, with regaining self-sufficiency in basic foods. Some bureaucrats are
converts to international comparative advantage, others favor changing
the nation's dietary patterns to conform to new production realities, and
still others remain convinced that self-sufficiency is both essential and
attainable. With respect to the ejido, the majority appear to be convinced
that, for more than strictly economic reasons, it has to be privatized before
peasant production can become efficient. They see the problems of the
ejido as resulting from the innate insecurity and contradictions of a corporate usufruct land-tenure category for the social sector within a capitalist
framework:

> It is not the ejido itself that prevents efficient agriculture but ejidalism, the
> very attitude of the government toward the social sector, which encourages
> other predators such as the coyotes as well. As long as the social sector
> exists in the countryside as a formal, separate category—the ejido—the
> mentality of patronage and exploitation cannot be eliminated, no matter

how much the state withdraws from direct intervention in agriculture. (I-136, businessman and former civil servant, Campeche, February 1990)

In these times of uncertainty, many campesinos feel that the ejido is their sole defense, if not always a very effective one, against extinction. Furthermore, there is still some confidence that the ejido could offer the best way out of poverty if only the government could provide effective and affordable inputs and incentives without assuming complete control over the productive process, or permitting other interests to do so. Consequently, the new policy promoting associations between ejidos and agribusiness tends raise the specter of outright privatization of the ejido, which would erase the state's debt to the countryside before restitution had been made in full. Thus, campesinos are apprehensive about current and future government reforms but are even more concerned about the prospect of being abandoned by the state altogether:

It's only a matter of time before the idea of the ejidatario looses any vestige of the drama and the debt lingering from the revolutionary struggle. You can see this here in our case, where the ruins of the our ancestors are romantic, but not the Maya of today. In the eyes of the government we have no more charm, the man in the milpa with sweat in his armpits. I'm afraid that there will not be a place for this man in the government's vision of the agricultural future after the account is settled. (I-2, ejidatario, Pomuch, March 1990)

Although it is still too soon to assess the full implications of the Salinas agricultural reforms, it is clear that pivotal reorientations in agrarian policy and practice are already having repercussions on the peasantry. In many respects, the impetus for sweeping change in the countryside derives directly from the debt crisis. The drastic cutbacks in public-sector budgets associated with the structural adjustment required by the international financial agencies compelled a long-overdue evaluation of both the dimensions of the agricultural crisis and specific priorities and programs. In particular, debt-crisis austerity prompted the streamlining of the inflated agrarian bureaucracy, the initiation of an attack on visible corruption, and a degree of decentralization of agricultural decision making that has encouraged a search for more viable regional and local options and increased emphasis on the intensification and diversification of production. At the same time, critical assessment of past agricultural development strategies has fostered a concern for environmental protection. This climate of economic rationalization has been conducive to the government's enthusiastic endorsement of the new economic liberalism as the way out of crisis for both city and countryside. In the peasant sector, this reorientation is focused on the drive to transform ejidal agriculture from an industry of disasters to a paying proposition by promoting capital reinvestment. If this restructuring succeeds in stimulating the recovery of Mexican agriculture, it is likely to be emulated by other Latin American countries in similar straits.

For the peasantry, perhaps the most significant aspect of the current agricultural reorientation is not so much the opening-up of the ejido to free market forces as the state's resolve to distance itself from peasant production. The move toward privatization of the ejido appears to signal the end of the revolutionary project, wherein the state assumed responsibility for the achievement of social justice for peasants. The Salinas reforms constitute a major step toward the dismantling of old agrarian ideologies that have constrained the capital accumulation process in the countryside. The majority of peasants, however, have seen little evidence that market forces will operate to improve social conditions.

Nevertheless, the Campeche case studies indicate that coping with the crises has strengthened the capacity of at least some segments of the peasantry to cast off the ideological baggage of institutionalized dependency on the state and take small steps toward assuming some control over their condition. Associations between ejidos and agribusiness are likely only on the remaining rice lands and in new citrus ventures. The majority of campesinos will probably go on making a living much as before, but perhaps with greater opportunities to profit simply from the increased farming flexibility permitted by the fading state presence. The main threat to this relatively optimistic scenario will likely come from the traditional predators on the peasantry—the merchant middlemen, petty bureaucrats, cattle ranchers, and other large landowners—and from new categories of exploiters, such as land speculators. At the same time, campesinos seem better able to defend themselves against exploitation than in the past, even though facing a future which involves very different players and rules from those operative over much of the postrevolutionary era.

Campeche is just one of the "many Mexicos," and the state-modernized ejidal sector emphasized in this book is only one segment of the highly differentiated Mexican peasantry. The experiences of these Campeche campesinos do, however, have significant implications for the Mexican peasantry as a whole. In particular, they provide evidence for the resurgence of independent initiative and a belief in the possibility of a better future despite the legacy of the industry of disasters, underscoring the resilience that has brought the peasantry through centuries of crises.

The prospect of a brighter future may not be as remote as it might appear. At a recent conference on Latin America's futures, a Mexican colleague remarked to me that my peasants "sounded like Trotskyites," while another asserted that they had been brainwashed by an empty revolution. After years of listening closely to my informants, however, I have become convinced that most Campeche peasants are not parroting empty rhetoric. Rather, they have internalized the ideals of the Mexican Revolution and translated them in very pragmatic terms to contemporary reality. They are the true heirs of Zapata, of Cárdenas, with increased determination to obtain social justice whether defined by the state or by the free market. Consequently, while peasants today may not represent a revolutionary force, they cannot be discounted as potential agents for radical change by virtue of their determination, the clarity of their vision, and their refusal to disappear. Furthermore, in spite of the current confusion generated by rapid and radical agrarian restructuring and reform, the direction of evolution of agrarian policy may be increasingly congruent with the grass roots aspirations of many peasants—to enjoy the liberty to farm according to their vision of opportunities—albeit on a very modest scale. If so, the social justice debt that peasants consider their revolutionary legacy may indeed best be settled by the simple fact of freedom from state tutelage.

Twenty years ago, an old Maya campesino, a member of a new government-sponsored irrigation project, gave me his prescription for a way out of the agricultural crisis:

> We could grow pineapples here, too, but it is too difficult the way we work now, all together. The engineers have said that we may be able to divide the land up so that everybody has his own parcel. Each campesino could, I think, have a hundred mecates—more or less four hectares—and sow pineapples, maize, tomatoes, anything he wanted . . . We could make our own arrangements for credit with the bank and everybody would be responsible for what he sowed and reap all the profits. I would have a little plot of pineapples. It would be better if everybody had the same; then we could sell them together for a better price. When all this comes about we will be more emancipated. From my parcel, I will sell tomatoes, chiles, papayas, and watermelons in addition, and with the pineapples I will make quite a lot of money. We will also have chickens, turkeys, pigs, all that, and by this time we will have been cultivating a while and the bank will be disposed to give us good credit. That will be good—a good life. (I-2, ejidatario, July 1970)

Alfredo is now eighty-seven years old. He still walks eight kilometers several days a week to his project where he grows maize without irrigation. He still hopes that his dreams will be realized some day. Perhaps that day has come a little closer.

Bibliography

Aguirre Beltrán, Mario, and Hubert Cartón de Grammont. 1982. *Los jornaleros agrícolas en México*. Mexico City: Macehual.

Alcantara Ferrer, Sergio. 1986. "Selected Effects of Petroleum Development on Social and Economic Change in Tabasco," in Ina Rosenthal-Urey (ed.), *Regional Impacts of U.S.-Mexican Relations*. University of California, San Diego, Center for U.S.-Mexican Studies Monograph 16.

Arias Reyes, Luis Manuel. 1984. "Analisis de los cambios en la produccion milpera de Yaxcaba, Yucatán, 1980–1982," Thesis, Maestro en Ciencias, Centro de Investigación Científica y Tecnológica, Universidad Autónoma de Chapingo.

Arizpe, Lourdes. 1979. "Migración y marginalidad," in Hector Diaz-Polanco et al., *Indigenismo, modernización y marginalidad: Una revisión crítica*. Mexico City: Juan Pablos.

——. 1981. "The Rural Exodus in Mexico and Mexican Migration to the United States," in P. Brown and H. Shue (eds.), *The Border that Joins*. Totowa: Rowman and Littlefield.

——. 1985. *Campesinos y migración*. Mexico City: SEP.

Astorga Lira, Enrique. 1985. *Mercado de trabajo rural en México: La mercancía humana*. Mexico City: Era.

Austin, James, and Gustavo Esteva (eds.). 1987. *Food Policy in Mexico*. Ithaca: Cornell University Press.

Bailey, John J. 1981. "Agrarian Reform in Mexico," *Current History*, vol. 80, pp. 357–360.

Baklanoff, Eric N. 1980. "The Diversification Quest: A Monocrop Export Economy in Transition," in Edward H. Moseley and Edward D. Terry (eds.), *Yucatan: A World Apart*. Tuscaloosa: University of Alabama Press.

Barabas, A., and M. Bartolomé. 1973. *Hydraulic Development and Ethnocide: The Mazatec and Chinantec People of Oaxaca, Mexico*. International Work Group for Indigenous Affairs Document 15.

Barkin, David. 1978. *Desarrollo regional y reorganización campesina: La Chontalpa como reflejo del problema agropecuario Mexicana*. Mexico City: Nueva Imagen.

245

———. 1986. "Mexico's Albatross: The United States' Economy," in Nora Hamilton and Tim Harding (eds.), *Modern Mexico: State, Economy, and Social Conflict*. Beverly Hills: Sage.

———. 1990. *Distorted Development: Mexico in the World Economy*. Boulder: Westview Press.

Barkin, David, and Billie DeWalt. 1989. "Sorghum and the Mexican Food Crisis," *Latin American Research Review*, vol. 23, no. 3, pp. 30–59.

Barkin, David, and Timothy King. 1970. *Regional Economic Development: The River Basin Approach in Mexico*. Cambridge: Cambridge University Press.

Barkin, David, and Blanca Suárez. 1982. *El fin de la autosuficiencia alimentaria*. Mexico City: Centro de Ecodesarrollo and Nueva Imagen.

Bartra, Roger. 1974. *Estructura agraria y clases sociales en México*. Mexico City: Era.

———. 1982. *Campesinado y poder político en México*. Mexico City: Era.

Bartra, Roger, and Gerardo Otero. 1987. "Agrarian Crisis and Social Differentiation in Mexico," *Journal of Peasant Studies*, vol. 14, no. 3, pp. 334–362.

Beaucage, Pierre. 1991. "Mexican Peasants at the Crossroads: Once Again?" in Michael Howard and Douglas Ross (eds.), *Mexico's Second Revolution?* Burnaby: Simon Fraser University Centre for International Studies.

Becker, David, Jeff Frieden, Sayre P. Schatz, and Richard L. Sklar. 1987. *Postimperialism: International Capitalism and Development in the Twentieth Century*. Boulder: Lynne Rienner.

Benedict, F. G., and M. Steggerda. 1937. *Food of the Present-Day Maya Indians of Yucatan*. Washington, D.C.: Carnegie Institution Publication 456.

Bizarro, Salvatore. 1981 "Mexico's Poor," *Current History*, vol. 80, pp. 370–374, 393.

Bojórquez Urzaiz, Carlos E. 1985. "La casa de Josué en Campeche: Milenarismo y crisis," in Carlos Bojorquez Urzaiz et al., *Cuatro ensayos de historia Yucateca*. Mérida: Universidad Autónoma de Yucatán, Escuela de Ciencias Antropológicas.

Brannon, Jeffrey, and Eric N. Baklanoff. 1987. *Agrarian Reform and Public Enterprise in Mexico: The Political Economy of Yucatan's Henequen Industry*. Tuscaloosa: University of Alabama Press.

Bray, Marjorie Woodford. 1989. "Latin America's Debt and the World Economic Crisis," *Latin American Perspectives*, vol. 16, no. 1, pp. 3–12.

Calva, José Luis. 1988. *Crisis agrícola y alimentaria en México 1982–1988*. Mexico City: Fontamara.

Canak, William (ed.). 1989. *Lost Promises: Debt, Austerity and Development in Latin America*. Boulder: Westview Press.

Carr, Barry. 1986. "The Mexican Left, the Popular Movements and the Politics of Austerity," in Barry Carr and Ricardo Anzaldría Montoya (eds.), *The Mexican Left, the Popular Movements, and the Politics of Austerity*. University of California, San Diego, Center for U.S.-Mexican Studies Monograph 18.

Cartón de Grammont, Hubert (ed.). 1986. *Asalariados agrícolas y sindicalismo en el campo Mexicano*. Mexico City: Juan Pablos.

Centro de Estudios Económicos del Sector Privado. 1987. *La economía subterránea en México*. Mexico City: Diana.

Centro de Investigaciones Agrarias. 1980. *El cultivo del maíz en México*. Mexico City: Centro de Investigaciones Agrarias.

Chardon, Roland E. 1963. "Hacienda and Ejido in Yucatán: The Example of Santa Ana Cuca," *Annals of the Association of American Geographers,* vol. 53, pp. 172–185.

Chayanov, A. V. 1966. "Peasant Farm Organization," in D. Thorner, B. Kerblay and R. Smith (eds.), *A. V. Chayanov and the Theory of Peasant Economy.* Homewood, Ill.: American Economic Association. (Originally published in 1925.)

Cockcroft, James D. 1974. "Mexico" in Ronald H. Chilcote and Joel C. Edelstein (eds.), *Latin America: The Struggle with Dependency and Beyond.* Cambridge, Mass: Schenkman.

———. 1983. *Mexico: Class Formation, Capital Accumulation and the State.* New York: Monthly Review Press.

Comisión del Grijalva. 1966. *Proyecto de la Chontalpa.* H, Cárdenas, Tabasco: La Comisión del Grijalva.

Cook, Scott. 1988. "Inflation and Rural Livelihood in a Mexican Province: An Exploratory Analysis," *Mexican Studies,* vol. 4, no. 1, pp. 55–77.

Cordero, Rolando, and Carlos Tello. 1983. *México: La disputa por la nación.* Mexico City: Siglo XXI.

Crummett, María de los Angeles. 1985. *Rural Class Structure in Mexico: New Developments, New Perspectives.* Notre Dame: University of Notre Dame, Helen Kellogg Institute for International Studies.

Cumby, Robert, and Richard Levich. 1987. "On the Definition and Magnitude of Recent Capital Flight," in Donald Lessard and John Williamson (eds.), *Capital Flight and Third World Debt.* Washington, D.C.: Institute for International Economics.

de Ibarrola, Antonio. 1975. *Derecho agrario: El campo base de la patria.* Mexico City: Porrua.

de Janvry, Alain. 1981. *The Agrarian Question and Reformism in Latin America.* Baltimore: Johns Hopkins University Press.

de Janvry, Alain, and Carlos Garramon. 1977. "The Dynamics of Rural Poverty in Latin America," *Journal of Peasant Studies,* vol. 4, pp. 206–216.

Díaz del Castillo, Bernal. 1958. *The True History of the Conquest of New Spain 1517–1521.* J. M. Cohen, trans. and ed., London: Penguin. (Originally published in 1527.)

Dietz, James L. 1989. "Debt, International Corporations, and Economic Change in Latin America and the Caribbean," *Latin American Perspectives,* vol. 16, no. 1, pp. 13–30.

Dinnerman, Ina R. 1982. *Migrants and Stay-at-Homes: A Comparative Study of Rural Migration from Michoacan, Mexico.* University of California, San Diego, Center for U.S.-Mexican Studies Monograph 5.

Echeverría Zuno, Alvaro. 1984. *Problema alimentaria y cuestión rural.* Mexico City: Nueva Imagen.

Eckstein, Salomon. 1966. *El ejido colectivo en México.* Mexico City: Fondo de Cultura Económica.

Edelman, Marc. 1980. "Agricultural Modernization in Smallholding Areas of Mexico: A Case Study in the Sierra Norte de Puebla," *Latin American Perspectives,* vol. 7, no. 4, pp. 29–49.

Emerson, R. A., and J. H. Kempton. 1935. "Agronomic Investigations in Yucatan," *Carnegie Institution of Washington Yearbook,* vol. 34, pp. 138–142.

Esteva, Gustavo. 1978. "¿Y si los campesinos existen?", *Comercio Exterior* (Mexico City), vol. 28, pp. 1436–1439.

———. 1980. *La batailla en el México rural*. Mexico City: Siglo XXI.

Everitt, John. 1969. "Terra Incognita: An Analysis of a Geographical Anachronism and an Historical Accident, or, Aspects of the Cultural Geography of British Honduras, C.A," M.A. thesis, Simon Fraser University.

Ewell, Peter, and Thomas T. Poleman. 1980. *Uxpanapa: Agricultural Development in the Mexican Tropics*. New York: Pergamon Press.

Fariss, Nancy M. 1984. *Maya Society Under Colonial Rule: The Collective Enterprise of Survival*. Princeton: Princeton University Press.

Faust, Betty. 1988. "Cosmology and Changing Technologies of the Campeche Maya," Ph.D. thesis, Syracuse University.

Feder, Ernst. 1977. *Strawberry Imperialism: An Inquiry into the Mechanism of Dependency in Mexico*. The Hague: Institute of Social Studies.

FIRA (Fondo de Garantía y Fomento para la Agricultura, Ganadería y Avicultura, later Fondo Instituido en Relación a la Agricultura). 1972. *Estudio agropecuario del estado de Campeche y algunos consideraciones para su desarrollo*. Campeche.

Folan, William J. 1984. "El parque ecoarcheológico Calakmul," *Centro de Investigaciones Históricas y Sociales, Información*, 8, Universidad Autónoma de Campeche, pp. 161–185.

———. 1988. "Calakmul, Campeche: El nacimiento de la tradición clasica en la gran Mesoamerica," *Centro de Investigaciones Históricas y Sociales, Información*, 13, Universidad Autónoma de Campeche, pp. 122–190.

Fox, Jonathon. 1987. "Popular Participation and Access to Food: Mexico's Community Supply Councils, 1979–1985," in Scott Whiteford and Ann Ferguson (eds.), *Food Security and Hunger in Central America and Mexico*. Boulder: Westview Press.

Frank, Andre Gunder. 1967. *Capitalism and Underdevelopment in Latin America: Historical Studies of Chile and Brazil*. New York: Monthly Review Press.

———. 1969. *Latin America: Underdevelopment or Revolution*. New York: Monthly Review Press.

Frobel, Folker, et al. 1985. *The New International Division of Labour: Structural Unemployment in Industrialised Countries and Industrialisation in Developing Countries*. Cambridge: Cambridge University Press.

Gates, Gary R., and Marilyn Gates. 1972. "Uncertainty and Developmental Risk in Pequeña Irrigación Decisions for Peasants in Campeche, Mexico," *Economic Geography*, vol. 48, no.2, pp. 135–152.

Gates, Marilyn. 1972. "A Photographic Test for Attitude Measurement: A Cultural Examination of Peasant Attitudes to Agricultural Change in Campeche, Mexico," Ph.D. thesis, University of British Columbia.

———. 1976. "Measuring Peasant Attitudes to Modernization: A Projective Method," *Current Anthropology*, vol. 17. no. 4, pp. 641–665.

———. 1981. "Partial Proletarianization and Reinforcement of Peasantry in the Mexican Ejido," *North South*, vol. 6, no. 12, pp. 72–82.

———. 1988a. "Institutionalizing Dependency: The Impact of Two Decades of Planned Agricultural Modernization on Peasants in the Mexican State of Campeche," *Journal of Developing Areas*, vol. 22, pp. 293–230.

——. 1988b. "Codifying Marginality: The Evolution of Mexican Agrarian Policy and its Impact on the Peasantry," *Journal of Latin American Studies*, vol. 20, pp. 277–311.

Gates, Marilyn, and Gary R. Gates. 1976. "Proyectismo: The Ethics of Organized Change," *Antipode*, vol. 8, no. 3, pp. 72–82.

Gliessman, S.R., R. García and M. Amador, 1981. "The Ecological Basis for the Application of Traditional Agricultural Technology in the Management of Tropical Agro-Ecosystems," *Agriculture, Ecosystems, and Environment*, vol. 7, pp. 173–185.

Gobierno Constitucional del Estado de Campeche. 1986. *Plan Campeche 1986–1991.* Campeche: Gobierno del Estado de Campeche.

——. 1989. *Prontuario estadístico 1989.* Campeche: Gobierno del Estado de Campeche.

——. 1990. "Programa nacional de solidaridad." MS.

Gómez Pompa, Arturo. 1976. *Regeneración de selvas.* Xalapa: INIREB.

González Casanova, Pablo, and Hector Aguilar Camín (eds.). 1985. *México ante la crisis.* 2 vols. Mexico City: Siglo XXI.

Goodman, L.W., et al. 1985. *Mexican Agriculture: Rural Crisis and Policy Response.* Washington, D.C.: The Wilson Center, Latin American Program, Working Paper 168.

Gordillo de Anda, Gustavo. 1990. "Policies for Modernizing the Agricultural Sector: Financial and Technical Support," in *The Development of Agriculture in Mexico: Current Prospects and Policies.* Austin: University of Texas, Institute of Latin American Studies, The Mexican Center, Conference Publications Series, 90–02.

Gradwohl, Judith and Russell Greenberg. 1988. *Saving the Tropical Forests.* Washington D.C.: Island Press and the Smithsonian Institution.

Grayson, George. 1981. "Oil and Politics in Mexico," *Current History*, vol. 80, pp. 379–383, 393.

Griffith-Jones, Stephany, and Osvaldo Sunkel. 1986. *Debt and Development Crises in Latin America: The End of an Illusion.* Oxford: Oxford University Press.

Grindle, Merilee S. 1977. *Bureaucrats, Peasants and Politicians in Mexico: A Case Study in Public Policy.* Berkeley: University of California Press.

——. 1985. "Rhetoric, Reality and Self-Sufficiency: Recent Initiatives in Mexican Rural Development," *Journal of Developing Areas*, vol. 19, pp. 171–184.

——. 1986. *State and Countryside: Development Policy and Agrarian Politics in Latin America.* Baltimore: Johns Hopkins University Press.

——. 1988. *Searching for Rural Development: Labor Migration and Employment in Mexico.* Ithaca: Cornell University Press.

——. 1989. "The Response to Austerity: Political and Economic Strategies of Mexico's Rural Poor," in William Canak (ed.), *Lost Promises: Debt, Austerity, and Development in Latin America.* Boulder: Westview Press.

Guillén, Arturo R. 1989. "Crisis, the Burden of Foreign Debt, and Structural Dependence," *Latin American Perspectives,* vol. 16, no. 1, pp. 31–51.

Guillén, Hector. 1984. *Origines de la crisis en México.* Mexico City: Era.

Hamilton, Nora. 1975. "Mexico: The Limits of State Autonomy," *Latin American Perspectives,* vol.2, no. 2, pp. 81–108.

———. 1982. *Mexico: The Limits of State Autonomy: Post-Revolutionary Mexico*. Princeton: Princeton University Press.

———. 1984. "State-Class Alliances and Conflicts. Issues and Actors in the Mexican Economic Crisis," *Latin American Perspectives*, vol. 11, no. 4, pp. 6–32.

Hamilton, Nora, and Tim Harding. 1986. *Modern Mexico: State, Economy and Social Conflict*. Beverly Hills: Sage.

Hank González, Carlos. 1990. "La modernización y el desarrollo del campo Mexicano." Paper presented to the second Coloquio Binacional sobre el Desarrollo Agropecuario Mexicano y la Modernización del Sector, Austin, Texas.

Hardy, Clarisa. 1984. *El estado y los campesinos: La Confederación Nacional Campesina (CNC)*. Mexico City: Nueva Imagen.

Harris, Richard L. 1978. "Marxism and the Agrarian Question in Latin America," *Latin American Perspectives*, vol. 5, no. 4, pp. 2–26.

Hartlyn, Jonathon, and Samuel Morley (eds.). 1986. *Latin American Political Economy: Financial Crisis and Political Change*. Boulder: Westview Press.

Heath, John Richard. 1989. "The Dynamics of Mexican Agricultural Development: A Comment on Bartra and Otero," *Journal of Peasant Studies*, vol. 16, no. 2, pp. 276–285.

Henderson, John S. 1981. *The World of the Ancient Maya*. Ithaca: Cornell University Press.

Instituto Nacional de Estadística, Geografía e Informática. 1990. *Gaceta Informativa*, vol. 2, no. 2.

Inter-American Development Bank. 1984. *External Debt and Economic Development in Latin America*. Washington, D.C.: IADB.

Johnson, Bruce, Cassio Luiselli, Celso Cartas Contras, and Roger D. Newton. 1987. *U.S.-Mexico Relations: Agriculture and Rural Development*. Stanford: Stanford University Press.

Joseph, Gilbert M. 1980. "Revolution from Without: The Mexican Revolution in Yucatan, 1910–1940," in Edward H. Moseley and Edward D. Terry (eds.), *Yucatan: A World Apart*. Tuscaloosa: University of Alabama Press.

Kearney, Michael. 1980. "Agribusiness and the Demise or the Rise of the Peasantry," *Latin American Perspectives*, vol. 7, no. 4, pp. 115–124.

Landa, Diego de. 1978. *Yucatan Before and After the Conquest*. Trans. and ed. William Gates. New York: Dover. (Originally published in 1566.)

Lanz, Joaquin. 1937. *Ensayos históricos*. Mérida.

Ley Federal de Reforma Agraria, 1971. 1981. Mexico City: Porrua.

Lomelli, Arturo. 1991. "Perspectives and Needs of the Mexican Consumer in the Current Socio-Economic Crisis," in Michael Howard and Douglas Ross (eds.), *Mexico's Second Revolution?*. Burnaby: Simon Fraser University, Centre for International Studies.

Looney, Robert. 1985. *Economic Policymaking in Mexico: Factors Underlying the 1982 Debt Crisis*. Durham: Duke University Press.

Lundell, C. L. 1937. *The Vegetation of the Peten*. Washington D.C.: Carnegie Institution Publication 478.

Magana Toledano, J. Carlos. 1985. "Historia demográfica de las ciudades de Mérida y Campeche. 1809–1810," in Carlos Bojórquez Urzaiz, et al., *Cuatro ensayos de historia Yucateca*. Mérida: Universidad Autónoma de Yucatán, Escuela de Ciencias Antropológicas.

Marcusson, Henrik Secher, and Jans Eric Thorp. 1982. *The Internationalization of Capital: the Prospects for the Third World*. London: Zed.

Matheny, Ray T., Deanne L. Gurr, Donald W. Forsyth, and F. Richard Hauck. 1983. *Investigations at Edzná, Campeche, Mexico*. Vol.1. Papers of the New World Archaeological Foundation, no.46. Provo: Brigham Young University Press.

Mendieta y Núñez, Lucio. 1977. *El problema agrario de México y ley federal de reforma agraria*. Mexico City: Porrua.

Menéndez, Ivan. 1981. *Lucha social y sistema político en Yucatán*. Mexico City: Grijalbo.

Messmacher, Miguel. 1967. *Campeche: Análisis económico-social*. Campeche.

Mines, Richard. 1981. *Developing a Community Tradition of Migration: A Field Study in Rural Zacatecas, Mexico*. University of California, San Diego, Center for U.S.-Mexican Studies Monograph 3.

Moguel, Julio (coordinator) al. 1989. *Historia de la cuestión agraria Mexicana: Los tiempos de la crisis*. Mexico City: Siglo XXI.

Moreno Toscano, Alejandro. 1968. *Geografía económica de México (Siglo XVI)*. Centro de Estudios Históricos, Nueva Serie 2, El Colegio de México, Mexico City.

Morley, Sylvanus. 1956. *The Ancient Maya*. Stanford: Stanford University Press, 1946, 3rd. edition. (Originally published in 1946.)

Moseley, Edward H. 1980. "From Conquest to Independence: Yucatan Under Spanish Rule," in Edward H. Moseley and Edward D. Terry (eds.), *Yucatan: A World Apart*. Tuscaloosa: University of Alabama Press.

Nations, James D., and Robert B. Nigh, 1978. "Cattle, Cash, Food, and Forest," *Culture and Agriculture*, vol. 6, pp. 1–5.

Nesbitt, Paul H. 1980. "The Maya of Yucatan," in Edward H. Moseley and Edward D. Terry (eds.), *Yucatan: A World Apart*. Tuscaloosa: University of Alabama Press.

Ostler, Patrick. 1989. *The Mexicans. A Personal Portrait of a People*. New York: Harper and Row.

Otañez Toxqui, Gervacio, and Beatriz Equihua Enríquez. 1981. *Comercialización del chicle en México*. Mexico City: Instituto Nacional de Investigaciones Forestales.

Otero, Gerardo. 1989. "The New Agrarian Movement: Self-Managed Democratic Production," *Latin American Perspectives*, vol. 16, no. 4, pp. 28–59.

Paré, Luisa (ed.). 1987. *El estado, los cañeros y la industria azucarera*. Mexico City: UAM-UNAM.

———. 1988. *El proletariado agrícola en México: ¿Campesinos sin tierra o proletariados agricolas?*. Mexico City: Siglo XXI. (Originally published in 1977.)

Partridge, William L., and Antoinette B Brown. 1983. "Desarrollo agrícola entre los mazatecos reacomodados," *América Indígena*, vol. 43, no. 2, pp. 343–362.

Pastor, Manuel, Jr. 1987. *The International Monetary Fund and Latin America: Economic Stabilization and Class Conflict*. Boulder: Westview Press.

———. 1989. "Latin America, the Debt Crisis, and the International Monetary Fund," *Latin American Perspectives*, vol. 16, no. 1, pp. 79–110.

Pastor, Robert A. (ed.). 1987. *Latin America's Debt Crisis: Adjusting to the Past or Planning for the Future*. Boulder: Westview Press.

Peña Castilla, Agustín. 1986. *Campeche histórico: Breve guía*. Mérida: Maldonado-INAH-SEP.

Piña Chan, Roman. 1977. *Campeche Durante el Período Colonial*. Mexico City: INAH.

Plan global de desarrollo 1980–1982. 1980. Mexico City: Estados Unidos Mexicanos, Poder Ejecutivo Federal.

Poleman, Thomas T. 1964. *The Papaloapan Project: Agricultural Development in the Mexican Tropics*. Stanford: Stanford University Press.

Prieto, Ana. 1986. "Mexico's Nacional Coordinadoras in a Context of National economic Crisis," in Barry Carr and Ricardo Anzaldría Montoya (eds.), *The Mexican Left, the Popular Movements and the Politics of Austerity*. University of California, San Diego, Center for Mexican-US Studies Monograph 18.

Rama, Ruth and Fernando Rello. 1982. *Estratégias de las agroindustrias transnacionales y política alimentaria en México*. Mexico City: UNAM.

Rama, Ruth, and Raul Vigorito. 1980. *El complejo de frutas y legumbres en México*. Mexico City: Nueva Imagen.

Redclift, Michael. 1980. "Agrarian Populism in Mexico: The 'Via Campesina'," *Journal of Peasant Studies*, vol. 7, no. 4, pp. 492–502.

Redfield, Robert. 1941. *The Folk Culture of the Yucatan*. Chicago: University of Chicago Press.

Redfield, Robert, and Alfonso Villa Rojas. 1934. *Chan Kom: A Maya Village*. Washington D.C.: Carnegie Institution Publication 448.

Reed, Nelson. 1964. *The Caste War of Yucatan*. Stanford: Stanford University Press.

Rello, Fernando. 1985. "La crisis agroalimentaria," in Pablo González Casanova and Hector Aguilar Camín (eds.), *México ante la crisis*, vol. 1. Mexico City: Siglo XXI.

Restrepo Fernández, Ivan. 1978. "Presentación," in David Barkin, *Desarrollo regional y reorganización campesina: La Chontalpa como reflejo del problema agropecuario Mexicano*. Mexico City: Nueva Imagen.

Rubio, Blanca. 1987. *Resistencia campesina y explotación rural en México*. Mexico City: Era.

Rummerfield, Benjamin. 1984. "Mexican Petroleum Exploration, Development," *Oil and Gas Journal*, July, pp. 77–80.

Salinas de Gortari, Carlos. 1990. *Segundo informe del gobierno. Excelsior*, 2 November, Sección A-4, pp. 1–8.

Sanderson, Steven E. 1981. *Agrarian Populism and the Mexican State*. Berkeley and Los Angeles: University of California Press.

———. 1985. *The Americas in the New International Division of Labor*. New York: Holmes & Meyer.

———. 1986. *The Transformation of Mexican Agriculture: International Structure and the Politics of Rural Change*. Princeton: Princeton University Press.

Sanderson, Susan. 1984. *Land Reform in Mexico: 1910–1980*. Orlando: Academic Press.

Sandoval Palacios, Juan Manuel. 1982. "Development of Capitalism in Mexican Agriculture: Its Impact on the Humid Tropics: The Case of the Yohaltún

Project in the Southeastern State of Campeche," Ph.D. thesis, University of California at Los Angeles.

Santos de Hoyos, Alberto. 1990. "Partnership in Production: An Option for Modernizing the Agricultural Sector," in The Development of Agriculture in Mexico: Current Prospects and Policies. Austin: University of Texas, Institute of Latin American Studies, The Mexican Center, Conference Publications Series 90–02.

SARH (Secretaría de Agricultura y Recursos Hidráulicos). 1979. "Proyecto para el Aprovechamiento Agropecuario. Zona Yohaltún-El Retiro, Valle de Edzná, Estado de Campeche." MS.

———. 1990. "Programa nacional de modernización del campo. Informe general." MS.

Schejtman, Alexander. 1981. *Economia campesina y agricultura empresarial: Tipología de productores del agro Mexicano.* Mexico City: CEPAL and Siglo XXI.

Scherr, Sara, Jeanette. 1985. *The Oil Syndrome and Agricultural Development: Lessons from Tabasco, Mexico.* New York: Praeger.

Scholes, France V., and Ralph L. Roys. 1968. *The Maya-Chontal Indians of Acalán-Tixchel: A Contribution to the History and Ethnography of the Yucatán Peninsula.* Norman: University of Oklahoma Press.

Siemens, Alfred H. 1966. "New Agricultural Settlement along Mexico's Candelaria River," *Inter-American Economic Affairs,* pp. 23–39.

———. 1979. A Decade of Colonization along a Tropical Lowland River in Mexico," *Geo-Journal,* vol 3.1, pp. 41–51.

Simpson, Eyler N. 1937. *The Ejido: Mexico's Way Out.* Chapel Hill: University of North Carolina Press.

Simpson, Lesley Byrd. 1941. *Many Mexicos.* Berkeley and Los Angeles: University of California Press.

Singelmann, Peter. 1978. "Rural Collectivization and Dependent Capitalism," *Latin American Perspectives,* vol. 5, no. 3, pp. 38–61.

Smith, Gordon W., and John Cuddington (eds.). 1985. *International Debt and the Developing Countries.* Washington D.C.: World Bank.

SRH (Secretaria de Recursos Hidraúlicos). 1967. *Plan nacional de pequeña irrigación.* Mexico City.

———. 1974. *Los caminos del Valle de Edzná: El renacimiento del valle.* (Film.) Mexico City.

Spalding, Rose. 1988. "Peasants, Politics and Change in Rural Mexico," *Latin American Research Review,* vol. 23, no. 1, pp. 207–219.

Stallings, Barbara, and Robert Kaufman (eds.). 1989. *Debt and Democracy in Latin America.* Boulder: Westview Press.

Stavenhagen, Rodolfo. 1970. "Social Aspects of Agrarian Structure in Mexico," in Rodolfo Stavenhagen (ed.), *Agrarian Problems and Peasant Movements in Latin America.* New York: Doubleday.

———. 1975. "Collective Agriculture and Capitalism in Mexico: A Way Out or a Dead End?," *Latin American Perspectives,* vol. 2, no. 2, pp. 146–163.

Steggerda, Maurice. 1941. *Maya Indians of Yucatan.* Washington D.C.: Carnegie Institution Publication 531.

Street, James H. 1981. "Mexico's Economic Development Plan," *Current History*, vol. 80, pp. 373–378.

Szekely, Miguel and Ivan Restrepo. 1988. *Frontera agrícola y colonización*. Mexico City: Centro de Ecodesarrollo.

Tellez Kuenzler, Luis. 1990. "The Development of Agriculture in Mexico: Sectoral Modernization," in *The Development of Agriculture in Mexico: Current Prospects and Policies*. Austin: University of Texas, Institute of Latin American Studies, The Mexican Center, Conference Publications Series 90–02.

Terán, Sylvia. 1976. "Formas de conciencia social de los trabajadores del campo," *Cuadernos Agrarios*, vol 1 (October-December), pp. 20–36.

Thorp, Rosemary, and Lawrence Whitehead (eds.). 1987. *Latin American Debt and the Adjustment Crisis*. London: Macmillan.

Vasconselos, José. 1936. *Ulises Criollo*.

Vogeler, Ingolf. 1976. "The Dependency Model Applied to a Tropical Frontier Region," *Journal of Tropical Geography*, vol. 43 (December), pp. 63–68.

Wadell, Hakon. 1937. "Physical-Geological Features of Petén, Guatemala," in Sylvanus G. Morley, *The Inscriptions of Péten*, vol. 4. Washington D.C.: Carnegie Institution.

Walsh, John. 1983. "Mexican Agriculture: Crisis Within Crisis," *Science*, vol. 219, pp. 825–826.

Warman, Arturo. 1978. "Frente a la crisis: Política agraria o política agrícola," *Comercio Exterior*, vol. 28, no.6, pp. 681–687.

——. 1980. *"We Came to Object": The Peasants of Morelos and the National State*. Baltimore: Johns Hopkins University Press.

——. 1983. *Los campesinos: Hijos predilectos de la revolución*. Mexico D.F.: Editorial Nuestro Tiempo. (Originally published in 1972.)

Wauchope, Robert. 1934. *House Mounds of Uaxactun, Guatemala*. Washington D.C.: Carnegie Institution Publication 436.

Wessman, James W. 1984. "The Agrarian Question in Mexico," *Latin American Research Review*, vol. 19, no. 2, pp. 243–259.

Wiarda, Howard. 1987. *Latin America at the Crossroads: Debt, Development and the Future*. Boulder: Westview Press.

Wilson, Eugene M. 1980. "Physical Geography of the Yucatan Peninsula," in Edward H. Moseley and Edward D. Terry (eds.), *Yucatan: A World Apart*. Tuscaloosa: University of Alabama Press.

World Bank. 1986. *Poverty in Latin America: The Impact of Depression*. Washington, D.C.: World Bank.

——. 1991. *World Development Report*. Oxford: Oxford University Press and the World Bank.

Yates, Paul Lamartine. 1981. *Mexico's Agricultural Dilemma*. Tucson: University of Arizona Press.

Yúñez Naude, Arturo. 1988. *Crisis de la agricultura mexicana*. Mexico City: Fondo de Cultura Económica.

Zaragoza, José Luis, and Ruth Macías. 1980. *El desarrollo agrario y su marco jurídico*. Mexico City: Centro Nacional de Investigaciones Agrarias.

Acronyms

ANAGSA	Aseguradora Nacional de Agricultura y Ganadería, National Agency for Agricultural and Livestock Insurance
BANJIDAL	Banco Nacional de Crédito Ejidal, National Ejidal Credit Bank (later BANRURAL)
BANRURAL	Banco Nacional de Crédito Rural, National Rural Credit Bank
BID	Banco Interamericano de Desarrollo, Inter-American Development Bank
COINCE	Comisión Intersecretarial de Nuevos Centros de Población Ejidal, Interministerial Commission for New Centers of Ejidal Population
COMAR	Comisión Mexicana de Ayuda a los Refugiados, the Mexican Commission for Assistance to Refugees
CONASUPO	Compania Nacional de Subsistencias Populares, the National Basic Foods Company
COPLAMAR	Coordinación General del Plan Nacional de Zonas Deprimidas y Grupos Marginados
CNC	Confederación Nacional Campesina, the National Peasant Confederation
DAAC	Departamento de Asuntos Agrarios y Colonización, the Department of Agrarian Affairs and Colonization (later SRA)
FIRA	Fideicomiso Instituido en Relación a la Agricultura, Fiduciary Trust Instituted with Relation to Agriculture
GATT	General Agreement on Tariffs and Trade
GDP	Gross Domestic Product
IMF	International Monetary Fund
LFA	Ley de Fomento Agropecuario, the Law for Promoting Agicultural and Livestock Production
NCPE	Nuevo Centro de Población Ejidal, New Center of Ejidal Population
PECE	Pacto para la Estabilidad y Crecimiento Económico, Pact for Stability and Economic Growth

255

PEMEX	Petróleos Mexicanos, Mexican Petroleum Company
PIDER	Proyecto de Inversiones Públicas para el Desarrollo Rural, Public Investment Project for Rural Development
PRI	Partido Revolucionario Institucional (Institutional Revolutionary Party)
PRONASOL	Programa Nacional de Solidaridad, National Solidarity Program
PSE	Pacto de Solidaridad Económica, Pact for Economic Solidarity
PRONAGRA	Promotora Nacional de Granos Alimentícias, National Food Grain Promotion Company
SAG	Secretaría de Agricultura y Ganadería, the Ministry of Agriculture and Livestock (later SARH)
SAM	Sistema Alimentario Mexicano, the Mexican Food System
SARH	Secretaría de Agricultura y Recursos Hidráulicos, the Ministery of Agriulture and Water Resources
SRA	Secretaría de Reforma Agraria, the Ministry of Agrarian Reform
SRH	Secretaría de Recursos Hidráulicos, Ministry of Water Resources (later SARH)

Glossary

ak'alche   A heavy clay soil (gley vertisol) characteristic of poorly drained bottomlands, considered by the Campeche Maya to be unsuitable for maize cultivation.

barrio   Colonial city quarter, now an established suburb as opposed to *colonia
popular* (recent public housing project or squatter settlement).

cacique   Rural boss, usually a local politican, influential landowner, or merchant.

campesino   Man of the country, peasant—commonly including *ejidatarios, mini-
fundistas, comuneros* (members of indigenous communities), full-time, seasonal,
and occasional laborers (landless or with rights to land).

cartera vencida   Loan default, referring in the ejidal sector to agricultural credit
extended by BANRURAL.

comprador   Merchant middleman.

coyote   Merchant middleman (comprador).

diario   Daily wage, generally conforming to the officially designated minimum
for the region, referring in the ejidal sector to payment advanced for a day's
labor as part of a bank credit package.

ejidatario   An individual with legally recognized individual or collective rights to
farm land belonging to an ejido. The term is often employed interchangeably
with campesino.

ejido   A form of peasant usufruct land tenure combining communal title vested
in the state with individual rights to land worked individually or collectively,
originating in the dissolution of *hacienda* (large private landholdings) during
the postrevolutionary land reform after 1917. Until the January 1992 amend-
ment of the 1917 Constitution, ejidal lands could not be sold, mortgaged,
leased, or otherwise alienated, although in practice such contraventions have
been widespread.

encomienda   An institution used in Spanish America in the sixteenth century,
wherein the Spaniard was granted Indians as an entrustment, to convert to
Christianity and to protect, receiving in return tribute including labor.

h-men   Maya shaman or spiritual leader.

kan-kab   A well-drained, yellow-red soil (rhoeadic luvisol), with high organic matter, that collects at the foot of slopes, considered by the Campeche Maya to be the best soil for maize cultivation.

la industria de siniestros   The industry of disasters—a term commonly applied to state agricultural modernization programs for the ejidal sector, wherein crop failure, chronic indebtedness and institutionalized corruption, particularly involving credit and insurance fraud, became the norm.

mecate   A twenty-by-twenty meter square. Twenty-five mecates equals one hectare.

milpa   Small cornfields, often sown with interplantings of beans and squash, cultivated by *roza-tumba-quema* (slash-and-burn or swidden system).

milpero   A campesino cultivating milpa on a regular basis, primarily by means of traditional agrarian technology and mainly for family consumption.

minifundia   An infrasubsistence private landholding under four hectares in size.

peón   Prior to the 1917 land reform a permanent agricultural laborer on a *hacienda* (large landholding), often under debt bondage to the *patrón* (landowner). Currently, the term can refer to a variety of day, seasonal, or permanent unskilled laborers, both rural and urban.

patrón   A rural landowner who employs peones; any employer or boss, rural or urban.

proyectismo   The "project fever" syndrome, characterized in the state-planned agricultural modernization arena by the proliferation of large-scale, expensive developments emphasizing physical infrastructure.

siniestro total   Crops planted with bank credit officially declared a "total loss"— often a device for insurance fraud.

Index

159(table), 160, 165, 166, 168, 169, 170, 171, 170(table), 175, 184, 185, 186, 187, 188, 189, 190(table), 194, 196, 197, 198, 199, 210, 202, 203, 204, 206, 207, 208, 209, 216, 217, 221, 224, 225, 229, 236, 225, 229, 232, 234, 236, 239, 244
  and Maya identity, 107, 109, 110, 116, 119, 120, 184, 195
  and Mexican identity, 13, 37
  household consumption, 185, 217, 221(n7)
  mechanized yields, 14, 141, 145, 148, 160, 166, 169, 170, 175, 185, 186, 186(table), 189, 196, 197, 199, 208, 209, 211, 239
  milpa yields, 114, 115, 117, 118, 123, 126, 131(n7), 175, 185, 189, 192, 216, 221(n6)
  net value of production, 186(table)
  raised-bed cultivation, 160, 166, 176(n6), 239
  supplementary household purchase, 185, 217
  See also Maya; *Milpa*
Mangos, 25, 99, 123(fig.), 147, 148, 149(table), 150(table), 160, 170, 170(fig.), 187, 188, 190, 191(fig.), 193(fig.), 196, 198, 200(fig.), 202(fig.), 229, 239
Mangrove, 188
Maya, 5, 22, 23, 73, 74, 75, 76, 77, 78, 79, 80, 81, 82, 83, 84, 93, 94, 95, 96, 104(n1), 109, 110, 111, 115, 116, 117, 118, 120, 121, 123, 124, 126, 131, 144, 152, 154, 155, 159, 161, 164, 167, 176(n6), 180, 182, 184, 187, 188, 194, 195, 204, 205, 206, 207, 209, 210,224, 225, 244
  agricultural ritual, 95, 96, 109, 110, 113, 114, 116
  attitudes to agricultural crisis, 182–184
  attitudes to debt crisis, 180–182
  attitudes to nature, 93, 95, 110, 112, 114, 117–119, 180, 184, 225
  beekeeping, 123, 196
  Classic, 73, 77, 78, 104(n1), 115, 117, 152, 176(n6)
  cosmology, 93, 95, 96, 109, 112, 120
  deities, 95, 110, 112, 114
  identity and *milpa*, 107, 109, 110, 116, 117, 119, 120, 184, 195
  modernization, 74, 93, 94
  moral order, 93, 96
  Postclassic, 77, 104(n2)
  pre-Columbian agriculture, 76, 78, 93, 109, 112, 115, 117, 152, 176
  Preclassic, 78
  religion, 78, 79, 82
  resistance to domination, 73, 74, 79, 81, 82, 180
  resistance to Spanish Conquest, 74, 79, 81, 82
  soil typology, 110, 111(table)
  "Speaking Cross," 82, 105(n6)
  syncretism, 74, 79, 95, 116
  War of the Castes (1847–1849), 74, 81, 82
  water management, 77, 78, 95, 110, 112, 114, 152, 176
  weather prognostication, 95, 113

  See also Campeche (state); Maize; *Milpa;* Yucatán Peninsula
Mayapan, 75, 104(n1)
Mecate, 112, 113, 114, 115, 244
Melchor Ocampo (*ejido*), 164
Mennonite colonies (Hecelchakán), 24(map), 204–210
  and agrarian bureaucracy, 205, 208, 225
  capital accumulation, 208, 209
  cattle (double-purpose), 206, 208
  communitarianism, 205, 208, 210
  consumer spending, 207
  credit, 208, 209(table)
  dairy products, 206, 207, 209, 229
  diversification, 208
  division of labor, 206
  in Durango, 205
  economic expediency, 205, 207, 208, 229
  evaluation, 230(table)
  "hiving-off" cycle, 205, 208
  household budgets, 207, 208, 209
  "living plain," 204, 205
  and Maya, 205, 207, 209, 210
  mechanized maize production, 208, 209(table), 225, 229
  milpa, 206, 209
  and modern technology, 208
  as peasants, 205, 230(table)
  religious and cultural freedom, 204, 205
  seclusion of women, 205, 206
  self-segregation, 205, 210, 230(table)
  self-sufficiency, 205, 207, 210, 229, 230(table)
  settlement form, 205
  siniestro total (total loss), 208
  success of, 225, 229
  wage labor, 209
  See also Agriculture (Campeche); Agricultural crisis (Campeche); Camino Real; Campeche (state)
Mennonites, 5, 23, 24, 204–210, 222(n8), 225, 229, 232
Merchant middlemen, 37, 38, 39, 56, 130, 139, 141, 143, 190, 217, 241, 243. *See also Coyotes*
Mérida, 24(map), 76, 80, 81, 82, 84, 87, 91, 95, 98, 105, 126, 188, 190, 192, 195, 199, 203, 206
"Mexican miracle," 34, 35, 40, 66(table), 136
Mexican Revolution (1910), 2, 6, 7, 20, 31, 33, 35, 36, 56, 57, 65(table), 72(table), 83, 105(n7), 177, 178, 224, 244
Mexico City, 73, 95, 190, 207, 221, 240
Migrant labor, 16, 18, 19, 137, 139, 149, 152, 157, 161, 210, 213, 214, 228, 235, 236
  in Mexico, 152, 157, 214, 235, 236
  remittances, 18, 19, 201, 213, 214, 236
  in the United States, 137, 139, 140, 152, 157, 201, 213, 214, 220, 235, 236